What We Have Done

What We Have Failed to Do

Assessing the Liturgical Reforms of Vatican II

KEVIN W. IRWIN

Paulist Press
New York / Mahwah, NJ

Cover image by alteregos / 123rf.com
Cover design by Cynthia Dunne, www.bluefarmdesign.com
Book design by Lynn Else

Library of Congress Cataloging-in-Publication Data

Irwin, Kevin W.
    What we have done, what we have failed to do : assessing the liturgical reforms of Vatican II / Kevin W. Irwin.
        pages cm
    ISBN 978-0-8091-4848-6 (alk. paper) — ISBN 978-1-58768-297-1
    1. Catholic Church—Liturgy—History—20th century. 2. Liturgical movement—Catholic Church—History—20th century. 3. Liturgical reform. 4. Vatican Council (2nd : 1962–1965 : Basilica di San Pietro in Vaticano) I. Title.
    BX1975.I79 2014
    264`.02—dc23

                                                                                    2013021150

ISBN: 978-0-8091-4848-6 (paperback)
ISBN: 978-1-58768-297-1 (e-book)

Published by Paulist Press
997 Macarthur Boulevard
Mahwah, New Jersey 07430

www.paulistpress.com

Printed and bound in the
United States of America

Contents

Dedicated to
Jeremy Driscoll, OSB

Preface

The spring of 2013 turned out to be a momentous time for the Roman Catholic Church. Pope Benedict XVI resigned the See of St. Peter and was succeeded by Pope Francis, the first pope from Latin America and the first Jesuit pope. Those historic events coincided with a different kind of academic semester for me. Instead of teaching at the Catholic University of America in Washington, DC, I was teaching the CUA students on a semester abroad in Rome and, like them, was privileged to witness history in the making with a papal conclave and the inauguration of a new pope. It was an exciting time to be in Rome! I often invited the students to be with me when acting as a commentator for the media. (Thank you, CNN, and many others!) It was also an exciting time to be with the students inside the classroom and on several field trips in Rome to visit churches, monasteries, and architectural monuments—a kind of "show and tell" on the university level.

One of those trips was to my alma mater, the Pontifical Ateneo of Sant'Anselmo. Our host and guide was Fr. Jeremy Driscoll, OSB, to whom I dedicate this book. His presentation on the Rule of St. Benedict was perfect for an audience not trained in things monastic but eager to learn about the breadth of our Catholic tradition. Fr. Jeremy lectured to us in the very *aula*, or hall, in which I had defended my doctoral dissertation many years ago.

When I had been planning this semester in Rome, I spoke with the present prior of Sant'Anselmo, Fr. Elias Lorenzo, OSB, from St. Mary's Abbey in Delbarton, New Jersey, about the possibility of using a guest room at Sant'Anselmo for study, writing, and prayer on the days I was not teaching. He generously agreed.

(Then again, this is not surprising; hospitality is a key Benedictine charism.) So on most of the days on which I did not teach, I walked up the Aventine hill, fired up my laptop, and worked. (I am not certain what the presence of wired Internet in every room says about monastic silence!)

I would join the monks for midday prayer (sung in Latin in Gregorian chant) in the chapter room and follow them to *pranzo* (lunch) in the refectory. Here there is no table reading at *pranzo* but conversation, so that students can catch up on what they are studying (here and at other Roman universities), and the professors can share (and receive uninvited critiques!) about what they are researching and writing. Coffee often follows in the professors' lounge. Given this tranquil and welcoming setting, it is no surprise that I was able to do a lot of thinking and writing and to finish this manuscript.

Especially on those visits to Sant'Anselmo and in many other conversations during that semester (sometimes over meals in favorite restaurants—how Roman!), I enjoyed and was enriched by the company of Fr. Jeremy. He is a true monk-scholar who divides his time between Mt. Angel Abbey in Oregon and Sant'Anselmo. He is sought after by many—myself included—for counsel and advice. We have been friends for over twenty years, a friendship I cherish more than I can say.

Before becoming cardinal archbishop of Westminster in London, Basil Hume served as abbot of Ampleforth Abbey in Yorkshire, England. He once told the monks that they should always want a deeper, more contemplative vocation. This meant that a Benedictine teaching in school should always have the heart of a Carthusian, and an active religious should always have the heart of a monk. Why? The Christian life is *both* prayer and work. Work without prayer is ungrounded and can be self-deceptive. Prayer without work is a fantasy and does not reflect the Christian vocation: to find and serve God in church and in the marketplace. Mary *and* Martha. Even monks and religious, he said, should always seek for a deeper prayer life. *Ora et labora.*

Cardinal Hume also once said to his monks, "Take God very seriously, take your vocations seriously, don't take yourselves too seriously."

Spring 2013 was a semester to do all of that in teaching, commenting on a papal resignation and election, and writing. Throughout those four months it was imperative to try to do all of that with a proper perspective of prayer and work. I thank Fr. Jeremy and his Benedictine confreres at Sant' Anselmo for helping me do that by their example of prayer and academic work. *Ora et labora* indeed.

Works for me, a monk at heart.

Asking the Important Questions

Even though I have lived "inside the Beltway" in Washington, DC, for close to three decades, not a day passes that I do not realize in some way or other that I am a New Yorker in exile. Therefore, it will be no surprise to learn that I am a fan of the novels of Orthodox Judaism written by Chaim Potok and set in New York, specifically in Brooklyn and the Bronx. Toward the end of the novel *In The Beginning*, Potok captures, in my opinion, something of the real genius of education when he depicts a father and his son talking about the process of learning and the teacher's role in that process. Potok writes this poignant dialogue between father and son:

> "David," he said, after a long moment.
>
> "Yes, Papa?"
>
> "You are learning a lot from Mr. Bader."
>
> "Yes."
>
> "He is a good teacher."
>
> "Yes."
>
> "I am glad. Because he is doing my job and I do not like others to do my job unless they can do it better than I can. But I want to tell you something my brother David, may he rest in peace, once said to me. He said it is as important to learn the important questions as it is the important answers. It is especially important to learn the questions to

which there may not be good answers. We have to learn to live with questions, he said. I am glad Mr. Bader is a good teacher and I am glad he tells you truthfully that he does not have answers to all your questions."[1]

The purpose of this modest book is to shed some light on, and to invite discussion about, the experience in which Catholics have been engaged since the Second Vatican Council in implementing and praying the liturgy as reformed after the Council.

A number of questions are on my mind as I begin this book, which is aimed at all of us who worship God today through these revised rituals and who seek to take a second look at the liturgy since Vatican II. At a time of heightened rhetoric about the liturgy (not to say about most things!), the intended tone here is meant to be reverential yet not uncritical of what has been done to implement the reformed rites. Each of us stands on the shoulders of those who have gone before us in the life of the church. That we might see some things differently from the way our forebears did does not mean that we should ever be uncharitable or unkind, even as we might want to deepen and nuance what has been done in the liturgy.

Hence the phrasing of the title: *What We Have Done, What We Have Failed to Do*. We have done many things well. In fact, all the surveys of American Catholics since Vatican II about the liturgical reform indicate high levels of satisfaction with it. At the same time, they are not uncritical, especially regarding preaching, music, and a sense of belonging.[2] (Interesting for me is the fact that none of these factors depend on ritual books; rather, they rely on pastoral liturgical judgments in light of the reformed liturgy. This will also be apparent as this book unfolds.) We also need to think about what has been unfinished and perhaps even unbegun. This book will, I hope, be of particular benefit for all those involved in preparing and leading us in the reformed liturgy: bishops, priests, deacons, readers, servers, cantors, musicians, eucharistic ministers, and the variety of pastoral ministers whose daily efforts shape how and what we celebrate.

Descriptions and definitions of liturgy abound from a variety of sources, authors, and periods of the church's life. Allow me to weigh into this arena and offer the following, working description, containing a number of things that, in my judgment, are intrinsic to understanding the liturgy as officially sanctioned by the Catholic Church, and as celebrated in the variety of places in which Catholics worship:

Working Definition of *Liturgy*

Liturgy is the privileged act through which the Christian people are continually immersed into, and participate in, the reality of the living God through Christ's paschal mystery, by means of the power of the Holy Spirit, in the midst of the engaged communion of the gathered assembly of the church. The church is where Christ continually acts in an ongoing and unique way, as Head of its members, in and through the whole church, as well as in the communion of local assemblies to make present and available his unique act of redemption in acts of worship that are familiar, sacred, good, true, and beautiful. These acts of worship are celebrated in our contemporary world and in our particular cultural contexts in a privileged and yet provisional way through the use of effective words, signs, and symbols, as these words, signs, and symbols are experienced in our human bodies: by means of the things of creation and of human manufacture, but especially through the senses of sight, sound, smell, taste, and touch; through the use of our faculties of mind, heart, will, and imagination; and through the use of human speech, gesture, movement, and silence. We celebrate according to the rhythm of a yearly calendar containing feasts and seasons, in order that the church may be continually shaped and formed by what it experiences in and through this act of worship. In this unique way called liturgy, we offer thanks and praise to God to acknowledge the action and presence of the Trinity in the world and in the lives of the assembly, to enable those in the church to live lives more fully converted to the Gospel in and through what is enacted for our sakes and for our salvation until liturgy and sacraments cease and what we experience here is made full, real, and complete in the world to come.

Throughout what follows, this working definition will be in the back of my mind and will help to shape my observations.

A number of questions are on my mind as I begin this book. Allow me to pose twenty of them as challenges, with a few brief comments about each. You yourselves can likely add several more of your own. (These challenges are numbered only to facilitate discussion about them, not to prioritize them in any way.)

1. How to deepen the advances made in celebrating the reformed liturgy and to adjust things that might not have advanced the reform...

The most complete reform of the liturgy ever undertaken in the history of Western Christianity at one time took place after Vatican II. This enormous undertaking deserves to be nothing less than the best we can offer to God. But in hindsight we may have to look at some well-worn but what may be debatable or even questionable practices. Those in the generation (or two) before us did their very best to implement the changes. But with hindsight, some things that we did might need a second look. The issue here is not novelty or "change for the sake of change." It is to deepen what was begun well. As is stated in the letter to the Philippians 1:6 (and as is used in the church's rites of ordination and some rites of profession): "May the Lord who has begun this good work in us bring it to completion."

2. How to foster both a greater comprehension of the sacred liturgy and a fuller participation in it...

The aim here is to understand what occurs uniquely in the liturgy and to experience it as fully as possible through the liturgical forms the church has given us. Liturgy requires understanding what takes place and the means used in experiencing it. The kind of "understanding" required is more experiential than cognitive, especially given the "event" and "dynamic" character of the liturgy presumed in the definition above. This involves communicating through our bodies, minds, imaginations, and hearts using sight, sound, taste, touch, smell, and so forth.

3. How to respect the liturgy for its own sake in glorifying God and sanctifying those who celebrate it…

The liturgy has and is an end in itself. The purpose of the liturgy—used in magisterial statements since the assertion of Pope Pius X in 1903, through and beyond Vatican II's Constitution on the Sacred Liturgy of Vatican II (*Sacrosanctum Concilium*)—is that it is to glorify God and sanctify us. It is as simple, and as complex, as that.

4. How to recognize how much one liturgy can (or should) be expected to "do"…

Because the liturgy is so central to the church's life and because Sunday is the one time each week that the church gathers, there is a real temptation to add (too many?) things onto the liturgy. Making the liturgy "do" things can be manipulative. Yet the liturgy "does" a number of things, not all of which can be predicted or preprogrammed. My concern here will be to try to balance the shape of the reformed liturgy with the myriad legitimate concerns often brought to it—for example, dismissals of catechumens, candidates, and children; catechesis on a variety of topics; installation of various parish ministers; diocesan stewardship appeals; second collections; and so on. Anyone in pastoral and especially parish ministry knows well what I mean! In my opinion, we often presume and ask the liturgy to do too much.

5. How to understand the key assertion of Vatican II's Constitution on the Sacred Liturgy that "the liturgy is the summit toward which the activity of the Church is directed; at the same time it is the font from which all her power flows"… (n. 10)

If the liturgy is at the very heart of all that the church does and is, then it requires very special care, reverence, and respect. It also needs other things to support how this astounding assertion ("summit…and font") can be a reality. Among these are deepening conversion, engagement in various forms of personal prayer, commitment to others, and service outside the liturgy. The liturgy cannot "do it all" in terms of prayer and (obviously) in living the Christian life. This summit and font needs a grounding in other kinds of prayer and in leading a virtuous life.

6. How to reemphasize particular Catholic characteristics in and from the liturgy that might have been eclipsed in some of the reform...

At the very time when Roman Catholics were revising and implementing the liturgy, so were the non–Roman Catholic "liturgical churches," such as the Anglicans, Episcopalians, Lutherans, Methodists, and Presbyterians. This common enterprise has had significant and long-lasting effects; for example, a (more or less) stable three-year set of scripture readings in the Sunday Lectionary. Yet, while being ecumenical in as honest and constructive a way as possible, I want to raise up some things that we Catholics can and should pridefully bring to the ecumenical situation today both in liturgy and in all of church life. Another way of putting this is that there may have been an unintended osmosis of some aspects of the vernacular style that we Catholics took over from the practice of other churches that we might now want to reevaluate.

7. How to assist church communities with increased liturgical and pastoral demands at a time of decreased numbers of ordained priests...

There are strains on the interrelationship among the presumed triad that marks the priest's life—proclaiming the Word, presiding at the liturgy, and engaging in direct pastoral care (as gleaned from the documents of Vatican II and the repeated assertions of Pope John Paul II). The reality of priests presiding at an increased number of liturgies, with diminished time for immediate and direct pastoral care for those communities needs to be a part of any ongoing conversation about liturgical reform. How we face into this issue may well be the very survival of "a sacramental church."

8. How to offer suggestions on improving the celebration of the sacred liturgy without being perceived as "a liturgical terrorist"...

Unfortunately, in the zeal to implement the reforms of Vatican II, some liturgists have worked using this premise: "You have heard it said, but I say to you" (modifying the post-Beatitudes text from the Sermon on the Mount in Matthew 5).

And then they proceeded to offer definitive answers and techniques about the liturgy without, at times, paying due attention to the totality of the reformed sacred rites themselves (with their various options), the liturgical tradition behind them, and the communities who celebrate them. No one likes to be forced into something. I hope that the suggestions made here (many of which are themselves debatable) might carry their own weight on their intrinsic merits. Nothing argued here will deviate from any of the liturgical rites reformed after Vatican II, from Vatican instructions or directives since then, or from the directives of the United Stated Conference of Catholic Bishops' guidelines or norms.

9. How to assert the normativity of the Roman Rite while also encouraging the legitimate variety allowed in its celebration for a variety of communities...

I am thinking here of the (classic) differences between and among cathedral liturgy, parish liturgy, shrine liturgy, monastic liturgy, liturgy in religious communities, liturgy in schools and on university campuses, as well as liturgy among parishes and in participation based on language and ethnic composition. All of these communities participate in the same Roman Rite. The historical data tells us that a variety of liturgical communities have been served by the Roman Rite but not in exactly the same way. A prime example is the structure and practice of the Liturgy of the Hours or the prayer texts and scripture readings for saints particular to religious communities—for example, monastic books for the Liturgy of the Hours, the *Jesuit Lectionary*, and the *Jesuit Sacramentary*, the rank for particular saints' commemorations in local dioceses, most if not all of which are officially endorsed and sanctioned by the Vatican's Congregation for Divine Worship. The variety in practices within the unity of the Roman Rite will need to be kept in mind throughout.

10. How to maintain the valuable familiarity of the current ritual while instituting new liturgical changes...

My concern here is that, for more than four decades, we have witnessed an astounding amount of ongoing changes to the liturgy, whose reform was and is officially sanctioned by church authorities. Despite this, there should also be a familiarity with the liturgy's rites gained over time so that they are not opaque or difficult to appreciate or to participate in. To change the ritual too often is to invite an instability that is the polar opposite of the kind of familiarity that the liturgy should provide. I would hope that any changes recommended here might be seen as enhancing what has been done, a kind of "midcourse correction" rather than "reinventing the wheel."

11. How to understand the role of liturgy in the "new evangelization"...

The Rite for the Christian Initiation of Adults sets the first two stages of preparation for baptism as pre-evangelization (and inquiry) and the catechumenate. This reflects the classic understanding that evangelization leads to initiation. The challenge today is that we have many baptized nonbelievers and baptized "non-practicers." Hence, what is today called the "new evangelization" is an attempt to approach these Catholics and to invite them back to the regular practice of the faith—especially the liturgy. The issue here is both how to see the liturgy as a *means* of the new evangelization and also how to have a deeper appreciation of and a richer experience of the liturgy as an important *goal* of the new evangelization. In discussions about where liturgy "fits" into the new evangelization, I am concerned that it be viewed not (only) as a place to instruct (specifically through the homily), but also as a means of continuing evangelization and formation. I am concerned that we not *use* the liturgy, but that the entirety of the liturgy shapes and forms us in the divine image and likeness, again and again, as a major goal of the new evangelization.

12. How to raise salient points from conciliar and other church documents as being not just normative but mandatory in making liturgical decisions, when working with those who have little experience with understanding these documents...

In a "blogosphere" culture it is often difficult to differentiate the relative weight we should give to assertions about the church. In what follows, I will indicate what sources I am drawing from and why. As a professor, I need to respect and deal creatively with the background and religious literacy my students bring to the classroom and to invite them to study and savor what the church teaches us in the breadth of our Catholic tradition, at Vatican II, and since. This often means, for example, teaching the footnotes to the Constitution on the Sacred Liturgy as well as the text itself for the breadth of church sources (especially patristic, liturgical, and magisterial sources) on which it is based. These are bedrock sources from church documents of the highest rank and should be respected as such. With regard to the church's liturgy (as well as most things?), just because it is in print does not mean that it is right. This means paying close attention to the genre and rank of the documents at issue.[3]

13. *How to comment on the externals of the liturgy, while always inviting participants to see beyond them to the inner reality of the ways in which God is working through the liturgy...*

Externals in liturgy matter. They matter a great deal because through them God communicates with and acts among us, and we communicate with God and one another. But the heart of the matter in liturgy is how God works through externals in unpredictable and amazing ways. Liturgy has its own finality (as I noted above)—the glorification of God and the sanctification of humans. Liturgy should always be understood to be the church's privileged *means* toward that end. But the very means we use to accomplish this matter is based on the sacramental and incarnational principles.

14. *How to argue that we might well need a "new liturgical movement" (or elements toward one) without succumbing to the temptation that what the church needs is yet one more program...*

In my own study and teaching of the liturgy I have learned a great deal from studying those who are often called the "pioneers" of the late nineteenth- and twentieth-century Liturgical Movement. In point of fact, this was less a codified "movement" than it was a group of people who (especially in hindsight) worked toward many of the goals of the reform of the liturgy after Vatican II. Among others they were monks, pastors, pastoral ministers, members of religious communities, textual scholars, university professors, musicians, catechists, artists, architects, and popes. I will draw on some of their insights in this book, not to create a "new program" for the church but to help to deepen and enliven the one thing that we all have in common in the church— the liturgy. In the end I will not argue for a new program; rather, I will argue for some things that might comprise a part of ongoing liturgical catechesis. (I will need to distinguish what I have just asserted from some Internet sites entitled "New Liturgical Movement" or variations on the phrase).

15. How to understand what is meant by the act and the art of the liturgy...

In the liturgy of Holy Thursday, we hear: "Whenever the memorial of this Sacrifice is celebrated the work of our salvation is accomplished" (from the Prayer over the Gifts; also partially cited in the Constitution on the Sacred Liturgy, n. 2).[4] Therefore, the liturgy is nothing less than Christ's *act* of salvation renewed for our sakes again and again. But the celebration of the liturgy is also an *art* that draws us into an incomprehensible mystery through all of our senses, minds, and hearts. It is a thing of beauty. Liturgy is more than texts and rites. It is art through which the work of our salvation is accomplished.

16. How to talk about the art and craft of liturgy as largely the "work of human hands" and the result of human artistry and creativity, at a time when the use of technology is presumed in a fast-paced, instant communication, Internet, e-mail, and Facebook culture...

I am thinking here of the positive role that technology does play in understanding and learning about the liturgy. Clearly Internet sites and Internet-based research are very positive means for sharing information about the history and the theological meaning of the liturgy. At the same time, I think using technology (such as the iPad®, iPod®, cellphone, and MP3 players) in and during the liturgy (and even before and after it for personal *lectio divina*) needs to be evaluated very, very carefully lest the latest form of handheld device even be considered as a possible substitute for carefully designed and artfully crafted liturgical books, participation aids, and so forth.

17. *How to balance an emphasis on Catholic identity, with liturgy and sacraments at its heart, with the mission dimension of the Christian life...*

Recent discussions of what it means to be a Catholic and what the characteristic elements of Catholicism are serve to help us reemphasize who we are and what our faith tradition means. At times the discussions have served to remind us of how important sacraments are for Catholics and Catholic identity. My only caution here is that identity should always be linked to mission lest concern for things "inside the church" cloud over the always less neat and, therefore, far more challenging agenda of witnessing in the world to what we celebrate and believe. Clarity about Catholic identity must always involve clarity about the church's mission in the world. The church and its worship should always serve our witnessing to the kingdom of God already experienced here on earth, even as we yearn for it to be fully realized in the kingdom of heaven.

18. *How to guide those who preside, preach, and participate in liturgical roles and ministries in ways that will help them do well, and that will also help them appreciate on ever-deeper levels what God does for them and for us in and through the liturgy...*

Among the issues here is how to balance being well prepared for our liturgical roles in each and every celebration of the liturgy and performing those roles well, with experiencing the liturgy always as what God is doing for us that transcends our (hard) work and effort. After these years of implementing the reformed liturgy, I hope and pray that we become less and less self-conscious about what we do in the liturgy and more and more aware and appreciative of what God does uniquely and precisely for us through the liturgy.

19. *How to understand the relationship between the revised liturgical rites after Vatican II and the permission given to celebrate the Mass (and certain other rites) as revised after the sixteenth-*

century Council of Trent and codified in the Missale Romanum *published in 1570—in other words, the Tridentine Mass...*

I take at face value Pope Benedict XVI's clear assertions in the *motu proprio Summorum Pontificum* (2007) about the celebration of the liturgy as promulgated after the Council of Trent and the letter from the pope to bishops accompanying it giving permission for the increased use of the Tridentine Mass. He indicated that the reformed liturgy after Vatican II is the "ordinary" form of the Roman Rite and that the Tridentine form would be regarded as "extraordinary."[5] It should be recalled that according to the documents from the Holy See giving this permission for the Tridentine Mass to be celebrated, the purpose was to invite the followers of Archbishop Lefebvre to reconcile with the Catholic Church. It was to be a source of church unity, not an option due to taste or personal preference. In the letter accompanying *Summorum Pontificum,* the pope said that he judged that the celebration of the extraordinary form would be rare. He also indicated that it would be celebrated at the request of a stable group of the faithful. Only when a priest celebrates Mass "in private" would the extraordinary form be celebrated at his choice.[6] Hence, in what follows I will repeatedly refer to the liturgical rites revised after Vatican II and only by way of exception, for comparison and contrast, will I refer to the rites as revised after Trent.

20. How to understand the relationship between liturgy and personal prayer and spirituality...

These terms are important and they are not always distinguished. This will be dealt with more fully in chapter 10. In the meantime, I simply want to clarify that the liturgy is a privileged means for a number of ends, and these ends include growth in grace and deepened conversion to the Gospel and to service to one another. I am concerned about a certain liturgical "fussiness" in which there is a level of self-consciousness about the *doing* of liturgy that sometimes diminishes the proper emphasis on what the liturgy equips and challenges us to do as we live the faith in the marketplace, in the workplace, at home, and at leisure. The comment made after a liturgy that "it went well" may describe the external details and confirm that the liturgy was conducted smoothly. The real issue of whether "it went well" is to see how we live what we celebrate—indeed, how we live the spiritual life.

Why This Book Now?

The *occasion* for writing this book is the fiftieth anniversary of the promulgation of Vatican II's Constitution on the Sacred Liturgy on December 4, 1963. The book's aim is to address and assess some of the strengths and weaknesses of close to fifty years' experience of the reformed liturgy (understanding that the reforms were published beginning in the mid-1960s in Latin, were subsequently translated into the vernacular, and were then implemented.)

The *presupposition* throughout this book is that the liturgical reforms from Vatican II are understood to be normative and that the understanding of what the rites mean—their pastoral implementation and how they influence how we live the spiritual life—are always "works in progress." My own formation, education, and teaching have been based on the historical evolution and theological meaning of the rites of the sacred liturgy (both East and West) and, in particular, on how best to appreciate the theological meaning of the forms of the liturgy reformed after Vatican II. In the end I strive to appreciate the *lex orandi–lex credendi* relationship intrinsic to and as derived from the liturgy. It is clear to me that there were important theological and liturgical reasons why all the liturgies of the Roman Rite were revised after Vatican II. At the same time, there has been a certain officially sanctioned "ongoing reform"—which should be distinguished from the one phrased as "the reform of the reform" (more on that shortly)—that has occurred in the years after the first publication of the revised rites. This is to say that we are now celebrating the second generation of reformed liturgies; for example, the revised and recently retranslated Roman Missal, the *Lectionary for Mass*, the Order for Christian Funerals, the Rites for Presbyteral Ordination, and so forth. In addition, we are also implementing the second generation of the United States Conference of Catholic Bishops' commentaries on the reformed liturgy on music and architecture: *Sing to the Lord* and *Built of Living Stones.* The comments that follow are based on the latest versions of the post–Vatican II liturgical reforms and USCCB documents on the liturgy.

A presumption throughout this book is that there were important liturgical and theological reasons why the *Novus Ordo Missae* of Paul VI and the other revised liturgical rites were crafted and promulgated after Vatican II. With regard to the Mass, among the liturgical reasons was to facilitate active engagement in the sacred liturgy, especially in the vernacular. Among the theological reasons was to expand the contents of the Missal's prayers (*lex orandi*) and the selection of scripture readings.[7] Also among the theological reasons was the fact that no one prayer can say it all; hence, offering a number of options for liturgical prayers can help to open up a number of ways of understanding what is taking place in the liturgy (for example, the Prefaces and Eucharistic Prayers that were added to the Roman Canon after Vatican II). The vast expansion of the scripture readings at Mass was also done to comply with the wishes of the bishops at the Second Vatican Council, as stated in the Constitution on the Sacred Liturgy: "The treasures of the Bible are to be opened up more lavishly, so that richer fare may be provided for the faithful at the table of God's word. In this way a more representative portion of the holy scriptures will be read to the people in the course of a prescribed number of years" (n. 51).

At present, the phrase "the reform of the reform" is being used by a variety of people to support a variety of liturgical "agendas." Some use this phrase as a platform to reestablish a "sense of transcendence" in the liturgy. Others use the phrase to restore Latin as the customary language for the liturgy and the celebration of Mass *ad orientem.* Still others use it to eliminate many of the options provided in the reformed liturgy for the selection of prayers (for example, the Prefaces and Eucharistic Prayers in favor of the Roman Canon only).

This book is not about "the reform of the reform" in that sense; it is about the ongoing implementation of the liturgy as reformed through the church's wisdom after Vatican II. Nor is it about changing the basic structures and forms of the reformed liturgy; it is about the deepening of these reforms already established and promulgated at the highest level of church authority. For me it is important to note that neither the present cardinal prefect nor the archbishop secretary of the Sacred Congregation for Divine Worship in Rome has ever spoken about "the reform of the reform."

Shape of This Book

This book is divided into ten chapters, each dealing with an aspect of the liturgy. Obviously this list of topics is not exhaustive. Nor does each topic carry what I would regard as equal theological and liturgical "weight." But they are at the forefront of my reflections on the reformed liturgy. In deciding what topics to treat, I realized full well that there are other topics that others may want to explore. Again, fair enough, because this book is meant to invite dialogue and reflection. And in a field like the liturgy there are a number of possibilities. The ten here are meant to be catalysts, not limits. I have become increasingly uncomfortable with listing liturgical topics and issues from "top" to "bottom." By this I mean that every aspect of liturgy affects and is influenced by all the others and that each is intrinsically related to the others.

In the next-to-the-last chapter of his highly influential book *The Liturgy of the Hours in East and West*, Robert Taft writes: "Liturgy...reminds us of the powerful deeds of God in Christ. And being reminded we remember, and remembering we celebrate, and celebrating we become what we do. The dancer dancing is the dance."[8] Liturgy is like a dance. The doing of it is it. Reflecting on it requires that we see it as a united whole. In theological circles, the Greek term for the way the Trinity is often envisioned is *perichoresis* ("interpenetration," an "abiding together"). This is to say that the Trinity is three persons in one God abiding in each other as a "three-personed" God who is manifested in and through the liturgy for our deeper incorporation into them.

As we reflect on the post–Vatican II liturgy, we should do so with the understanding that almost all of its elements can be seen to interrelate with and interpenetrate each other, and that it may be prejudicial to single out one or more elements at the expense of the rest (again, taken together). Rather than viewing all these elements "face on," might I suggest that we take a helicopter ride? That way we see the terrain all together, and from a distance take stock of it all of a piece, not parceled out and divided up into its elements.

This is a modest but intentionally serious book aimed at the informed Catholic participant and minister of the liturgy. It is a theological and pastoral reflection on what we have done well and what we might do better in celebrating and living the reformed liturgy. It is not a "how to" book of hints about what to do in celebrating the liturgy; rather, it is a book inviting reflection, discussion, and possible action in the variety of contexts in which the liturgy occurs. Because it is not a (speculative) treatise I have been decidedly spare in including notes.[9]

While this book can be read (with great interest and profit, I hope!) by individuals at home, I envision its being used mostly in a group setting: study days or renewal programs for pastoral ministers; attendee discussions at convocations; deanery or vicariate meetings; in-service days for parish staffs; classes in seminaries or universities (especially courses in pastoral liturgy); and so on.

Since this book is intended to focus on issues in the implementation of the liturgy, I will not repeat here what I have already written in my other books about the Eucharist: *101 Questions and Answers on the Mass* (revised edition) and *Models of the Eucharist* (both from Paulist Press). In the former, the reader will find the latest available information about a number of issues related to the Mass (terminology, issues about each major part of the Mass, music at Mass, and mission). In the latter, the reader will find ten ways of appreciating and understanding the Eucharist; themes that derive from the church's "rule of prayer," that is, the *lex orandi* of the Roman Eucharist; and more.

The liturgy is a jewel best appreciated with light shining on it from a variety of angles. Those who specialize in other areas of liturgical and theological study could well bring to the fore other topics that need discussion and reflection, such as multicultural liturgies. It is important in life to know what you know and to know what you do not know. I defer to a myriad of others to fill in what is lacking in this book's assessment.

Allow me to conclude by thanking those who have reviewed earlier drafts of each chapter and offered very helpful suggestions, comments, and criticisms. In the writing of this book, I have striven to engage in the kind of dialogue in education envisioned at the start of this chapter—a major component of which is "asking the important questions."

CHAPTER ONE

Church Renewal

"Strengthen in Faith and Love Your Pilgrim Church on Earth"

In 1968, between my first and second years of theological studies in the seminary, I began studies for the summer master's degree in liturgy at the University of Notre Dame. When I returned to the seminary that fall, one of the moral theology professors met me in the hallway and (jokingly) said, "Say something in 'liturgy.'" To which I immediately replied, "Church." That was my spontaneous reply reflecting what had been the first and lasting lesson I learned in liturgical studies. Liturgy is about the church.

My thesis throughout this book is that liturgical reforms are meant to serve nothing less than the renewal of the church. Liturgy is church. Church is liturgy. It is that simple. It is that complex.

It is more than noteworthy that the opening words of Pope John Paul II's 2003 encyclical *Ecclesia de Eucharistia* are these: "The Church draws her life from the Eucharist." In that same encyclical he adapts the ancient axiom that states: "The Eucharist builds the Church and the Church makes the Eucharist."[1] In 1982, then Cardinal Joseph Ratzinger asserted, "The Church is the celebration of the Eucharist; the Eucharist is the Church; they do not simply stand side by side; they are one and the same; it is from there that everything else radiates."[2] For me, the titles of the recent synods are telling for both their ecclesial context and their intrinsic mission emphasis: "The Eucharist in the Life and Mission of the Church" (2005) and "The Word of God in the Life and Mission of the Church" (2008). These titles put the emphasis where it is presumed and needed—liturgy is a major part of the church's very life and mission.

That ecclesiology was at the heart of the concern of our forebears in the Liturgical Movement in the late nineteenth and early twentieth centuries is clear. It is also a major reason why they viewed increased participation in, understanding of, and appropriation of the liturgy as important. Those concerns are also our own. But my sense is that, because of sociology and technology, our forebears in the Liturgical Movement were faced with somewhat different problems even though we share with them the theological problem of relating liturgy and church-belonging. Therefore, our response cannot simply be to repeat what they said or did. The prevailing ecclesiology of that time and place (largely Europe) is not ours in a post–*Lumen Gentium*, post–*Gaudium et Spes,* post–Vatican II world.

In his famous book *Models of the Church*, Cardinal Avery Dulles offered a dozen ways that, when taken together, were ways of appreciating what the church is. While he insisted that we not pick or choose one over another, it is clear that some readers did precisely that. But in the end I have learned a great deal from this book precisely because it asked the reader to look at the church from a number of points of view. That the "models" approach to theology influenced my own writing is clear in the title of my book *Models of the Eucharist.*

But if I were to disobey the cardinal and choose a favorite model for the church today, my current preference would be *the pilgrim church on earth*: The church of not-yet-ness. The still-to-be-perfected church. The Bark of St. Peter, on which there are still barnacles and on which barnacles will ever be affixed. This is the church—always in need of purification, always in need of reform, always in need of renewal. Why else would a phrase such as *ecclesia semper reformanda* ("a church always to be reformed") strike such deep roots and yet offer such clear hope as well? As we pray the Preface for All Saints Day and rejoice in the eschatological hope of final and complete fulfillment:

> For today by your gift we celebrate the festival of your city,
> the heavenly Jerusalem, our mother,

where the great array of our brothers and sisters
already gives you eternal praise.
Towards her, we eagerly hasten
as pilgrims advancing by faith
rejoicing in the glory bestowed upon those exalted
members of the Church
through whom you give us, in our frailty,
both strength and good example...

We know full well that "we are not there yet." Why else would
we need to pray, "Be pleased to strengthen in faith and love your
pilgrim church on earth" (a phrase that was added to Catholic
liturgical prayer in 1968 with the addition of then-three
Eucharistic Prayers to the Missal)?

When this petition was written into our euchology (our for-
mulary of prayers) in 1968, I daresay the authors were unaware
of what "pilgrim church" would come to mean in the decades
that followed. In 1968 itself, there were the anti-Vietnam protests
and riots sparked by racial divides (among other things) that tore
apart cities all over the globe. Post-1968 education faculties (especially European) and, some would say, society itself would never
be the same. In the very city in which I live, the 1968 street riots
continue to be current events for many of that city's native population, despite gentrification and the fixing-up of the U Street cor-
ridor and Columbia Heights in the past decade or so.

Today in America we deal with great losses in this pilgrim
church of ours in terms of self-identification that might, at least
in numbers, diminish the church's influence and vitality. The
Harvard sociologist Robert Putnam has named our contemporary
dilemma in *American Grace: How Religion Divides and Unites
Us*.[3] In the religious culture of American Christianity, we have an
increased number of "believers not belongers," who style themselves as "spiritual, not religious...." While we can say with pride
that Catholicism is for those who are both "spiritual *and* religious," as well as for "believers *and* belongers," we also have to
deal with the reality that for every one person who enters the
Catholic Church in America, three leave. Why? I suspect there are
lots of reasons in this "spiritual, not religious" culture, but cer-

tainly two factors are our culture of excessive individualism and the credibility of the church itself for a variety of reasons (sexual abuse, financial mismanagement, and so forth).

It seems that we live in an iPod, iPad, iMac®, iSleep™, and endless other i-devices world. My point is that a small *i* begins how we name countless technological advances and machines. Isn't this ironically fitting for our "I" and "me" culture? When I glance at the magazine rack, I wonder whether we are a culture that has moved from *People* magazine to *Us* to *Self*. And "self" is where some people seem to be stuck. Take the famous line from the movie *Beaches*: Bette Midler leans over the restaurant table and says to her lunch companion, "But enough about me—let's talk about you. What do *you* think of me?"

Catholics belong to a "we" church. As I often say to my students, when it comes to liturgical prayers, always check the pronouns. Almost all (99.9 percent) of the prayers in the Missal use the first-person plural. "*We* ask this" ends each of our prayers. "*We* offer" is a chief characteristic of the Roman Canon's *lex orandi* from time immemorial.[4] Disciples make memory together in the liturgy to become better disciples.

Living the Catholic faith and engaging in Catholic worship have always been a corporate enterprise. We belong to a covenant religion that started with Noah, his sons, his wife, and his sons' wives (Gen 6:18), along with two of every living thing on earth. Of course, it should have started with Adam and Eve, but a tree and an apple got in the way, after which it all went south (or "East of Eden" if you are a Steinbeck fan), and humanity stood in need of a savior. (And to think now that an apple with a bite taken out of it advertises a machine called a computer! An apple with a bite out of it is the reason why we needed a savior. As we sing at the Easter Vigil, "O happy fault, O necessary sin of Adam." Indeed!)

We belong to a covenant religion that continued with our forebears in biblical faith, covenants we read about every three years in the Sunday *Lectionary for Mass* for Lent (Cycle B): the covenant with Noah (First Sunday, Gen 9:8–15); the covenant with Abraham and Sarah and their beloved Isaac (Second Sunday, Gen 22:1–2, 9, 10–13, 15–18); the Law given through Moses (Third Sunday, Exod 20:1–17); the renewal at the time of Cyrus

(Fourth Sunday, 2 Chr 36:14–17, 19–23); and the new covenant prophesied by Jeremiah (Fifth Sunday, Jer 31:31–34). These are such rich and central texts that they deserve study, prayer, and continual reflection. I fear, however, that they are glossed over by the same weeks' legitimately pivotal Gospels: Jesus' temptation in the desert, his transfiguration, and (especially if the A Cycle Gospels are read to coincide with initiations to be celebrated at the Easter Vigil) the Samaritan woman, the man born blind, and the raising of Lazarus (in John 4, 9, and 11, respectively).

Despite the importance of these Gospels, these Old Testament covenant texts should also be pondered and studied as the bedrock relationship on which our faith is based. We are in this together. We go to God together. It is that simple. And in a culture like ours, it is that complex. That liturgy is intrinsic to this sense of belonging is as ancient as the covenants of our forebears in the (Jewish) faith and as contemporary as the latest celebration of the Eucharist and the Hours in our Catholic communities.

Even while admitting the dangers of excessive individualism, we also need to admit that individual initiative has been a characteristic of the United States (and other Western cultures) from our founders through to today. It is an American trait, and not just a materialistic trait. Hence, I am not really convinced that our culture is so selfish and so self-consumed that it cannot accomplish the upbuilding of the church that the liturgy is meant to do. Check out the local paper and read the numerous ads for support groups. Check online and consider the vast array of chat rooms and online resources with message boards, advice, and help. I think of the countless believers committed to recovery groups of many types, admitting weaknesses and inviting the support of others. And in the end, I am always amazed in parish life about how much is done by the volunteer army called the parishioners.

Liturgy is church. Church is liturgy.

Baptism initiates us into the church, the body of Christ. The Eucharist as the body of Christ nourishes us to be the *less* imperfect pilgrim church on earth.

Initiation

The prescription in the Constitution on the Sacred Liturgy could not have been clearer about the revision of the season of Lent in order to draw out its paschal character. It states:

> The season of Lent has a twofold character: primarily by recalling or preparing for baptism and by penance, it disposes the faithful, who more diligently hear the word of God and devote themselves to prayer, to celebrate the paschal mystery. This twofold character is to be brought into greater prominence both in the liturgy and by liturgical catechesis. (n. 109)

With regard to initiation specifically, it gives the directive that the Order for the Christian Initiation for Adults be revised:

> Both the rites for the baptism of adults are to be revised: not only the simpler rite, but also the more solemn one, which must take into account the restored catechumenate. A special Mass "for the conferring of baptism" is to be inserted into the Roman Missal. (n. 66)

While modest in length and tone, these prescriptions directed the committees charged with all that is included in revising the euchology, scripture readings, and rites for the season of Lent and for adult initiation to work diligently toward fulfilling these directives. If you combine this with the revised liturgies for the Triduum as modified in the mid-1950s and again after Vatican II, I think it can be said that the church's Lent-Easter experience will never be the same. The prescriptions of Vatican II were taken seriously. The revised liturgies are also taken very seriously.

In almost every community that celebrates the liturgy—I am thinking here principally of cathedrals, parishes, and campus ministries—the liturgy of Lent is marked by ancient, yet ever-new rites for the progressive assimilation of catechumens and candidates into the body of Christ. These include the Rite of Election, the Scrutinies, the rites in preparation for the Easter Vigil, and the

Easter Vigil itself. Enormous energies go into the customary weekly sessions with catechumens and candidates as an essential part of the process that they engage in to become Catholic Christians. (The process is often termed the RCIA—the Rite of Christian Initiation of Adults. It might be worth noting that the more precise title is the "Order" of Christian Initiation of Adults, therefore, the OICA).

While some may see it as an empty gesture (in that anyone can now watch the sacred liturgy on television or computer or be present for the whole liturgy at any time), the Rite of Dismissal of the Catechumens from the Sunday assembly—after the homily but before the Liturgy of the Eucharist—can be a powerful sign of the incompleteness of initiation until water baptism is accomplished or a profession of faith is made, followed by chrismation and then sharing in the Eucharist, enacted and received. This also makes the theological statement that the Eucharist is the renewal of the covenant of baptism and that it is an initiation sacrament.

While commentaries on the scripture readings for the Lent and Easter seasons abound, my own sense is that more needs to be done to draw out the catechetical and theological meaning of the revised euchology for these seasons. It is to be hoped that the continued use of the revised translations in the Roman Missal will themselves continue to be formative and educative.

That the process of adult initiation needs a review is something I have heard from several quarters. From my own experience of presiding at Sunday liturgy regularly at the same parish and of participating in some of the catechetical sessions with the candidates, I offer a few elements of the formation process that might well be reexamined:

LECTIONARY-BASED CATECHESIS

Great emphasis has legitimately been placed on a lectionary-based catechesis for catechumens and candidates prior to adult initiation. However, an *exclusive* reliance on discussing the scripture readings assigned for a given Sunday as the key to catechesis has been found wanting. Among the reasons is that the catechumenate envisioned in the OICA is presumed to be three years,

25

coinciding with the three-year Sunday Lectionary, while the preparation for most adult initiations is actually just a year long, or even less. This means exposure to only one series of texts when exposure to three is envisioned.

Another reason is that the importance of understanding the theology of, and rationale for, Catholic teaching and practice can sometimes be lost when such emphasis is placed on processing the scriptures. I do not want the scriptures to be replaced by doctrinal input. I wish for a "both...and" approach whereby there is a laying out of doctrinal and catechetical themes that emerge from the scriptures to be proclaimed and processed by the catechumens, candidates, and their sponsors. To repeat: I do not mean that catechesis or instruction on the *Catechism of the Catholic Church* should replace preaching on the scriptures; after all, we are there to hear the scriptures and through the homily to be drawn into them more fully and effectively. What I do mean is that homilies can and should be doctrinally informed and theologically accurate.

WEEKLY SESSIONS

It is common that, after being dismissed after the homily from the Sunday eucharistic assembly, the catechumens and candidates meet with their sponsors and the parish or campus ministry initiation team. Here again is an opportunity to draw out catechetical and theological themes from the Sunday scriptures and to delve into each more deeply. These weekly sessions are also a time for deep bonding among all those involved—those coming into the church and those already initiated who serve as sponsors, the initiation team, and so on. After the rites of initiation at the Easter Vigil, these sessions—which can now take place after Mass—have a real poignancy as the group discusses what happened on that night to them, to their families, to the whole liturgical community. This period of mystagogy is also an ancient, yet ever-new reality during which the newly initiated are assimilated more fully and deeply into church membership.

But there is an issue that has been raised by those who have gone through OCIA and by those who sponsor them, namely, that there is a high degree of "fall off" after the process, the initiation rites themselves, and the period of mystagogy. Some have commented to me that the kind of church experience they received as catechumens and candidates was not sustained after Pentecost. Many did not feel part of the larger liturgical community and, in fact, found that Sunday Eucharist was not sufficient to sustain the kind of formation and church experience they had grown accustomed to in the OCIA. So whether mystagogy is "working" is one issue.

Another might well be whether meeting twice weekly in small groups seems to promise more intimacy than the parish itself can deliver in terms of the large numbers who attend Sunday Eucharist and in terms of how stretched clergy, parish ministers, and staff feel. In addition, on a college campus with the Easter Vigil toward the middle of the second semester, the students disperse by early May and, hence, can no longer avail themselves of the campus-based sense of belonging. Therefore, it's important to emphasize to OCIA teams that they not promise intimacy through the liturgy the way intimacy occurs in close friendships and life partnerships.

THE "CHURCH CATHOLIC"

Initiation structures function regularly on the parish or campus level. They also function on the diocesan level for the Rite of Election, sometimes for the Easter Vigil, and sometimes also for confirmation. But beyond these examples of the parish or campus (which is the "local church" as expressed and experienced by most people today), or of the diocese (which is the "local church" as envisioned by Vatican II), I want to raise the issue of how well our initiation structures function to receive catechumenates and candidates into the church universal.

The other side of the danger of promising a great deal of personal intimacy in the RCIA formation process is the issue of how the parish or campus does in fact relate to the diocese and to the Catholic Church throughout the world. I sometimes wonder whether our more than two thousand year tradition of prayer, belief, liturgy, teaching, and so on, has been eclipsed by the latest era or by one particular era or by a set of personages. I also wonder whether the communion of saints (the church's "family album") is something of a mystery to those we initiate and whether the emphasis on the local parish assembly is too localized. Especially in an era when stability in one location is no longer the presumed way of living (and here I defer to those with more rural experience of church life, since my own is more suburban and urban), I wonder whether we need to think much more globally and universally about the church and express this in our teaching and in preaching. It seems to me that the more we can rely on all levels of church self-expression and church life, the better off we are in terms of reflecting the breadth, depth, history, and current state of who we are as the Catholic Church.

I am frankly concerned with an unintended but nevertheless real "fundamentalization" of the Catholic Church. Admittedly we share many things in common with members of other non–Roman Catholic Christian churches as well as those of other faiths, especially Judaism. But we sell our birthright if we do not at the same time capitalize on who we are and what we do uniquely and particularly. Among those things are liturgy and theology as celebrated in the church universal. The Catholic theological tradition is the furthest thing from fundamentalism as possible. We are a thinking, inquiring, and teaching church. Repetition of past formulas has always ceded in Catholicism to new ways of expressing what we believe in new terminology and in new ways (for example, the difference between the teachings of the Council of Trent and those of Vatican II). That is the breadth into which we initiate new members and sustain the already initiated.

MYSTAGOGY

In addition to what I noted above about weekly sessions, my sense is that the period of mystagogy (after the Rites of Initiation) is often less emphasized than what was envisioned in the reform and that it is a crucial "make or break" time for the newly initiated. What to do in this period often perplexes RCIA teams. I suggest that the newly initiated be invited into a series of *lectio divina* exercises, using the liturgy instead of scripture. It can begin with the blessing prayer used over the water at the Easter Vigil. In subsequent meetings it can include parts of the Liturgy of Eucharist for which they have been absent since their initiation process started: the Presentation of Gifts, the Preface, the Eucharistic Prayers (especially the texts of these prayers in detail), the Lord's Prayer, the Rite of Communion, and the Rite of Dismissal. Given the not-illegitimate emphasis on the Proclamation of the Word during the pre-initiation period, I think it logical and also crucial that the Liturgy of the Eucharist be explored just as deeply since that is precisely what they have been initiated into.

Eucharist

Some other issues about the presumption of church-belonging today need at least to be noted since they affect membership, among which are occasional participation in the Eucharist and disaffection with church leadership.

PARISH MEMBERSHIP

There are people whose Mass attendance is spotty for a variety of reasons. The aftershocks of the sex abuse crisis that has affected the American Catholic Church since the early 1990s—and (very sadly) the revelations of ongoing clerical misconduct, despite the issuance of the "Dallas Charter" on the abuse of minors in 2001—are very much with us and still affect Mass attendance and church-belonging. Wise pastors and parish leaders know where and when to tread lightly about these issues.

People of course also move because of employment or unemployment or other life changes. But at times, *moving* means that they remain where they live but change where they worship. Other people choose to attend Mass less frequently, becoming "occasional" Mass-goers. Pastoral ministers deal with this regularly, and it's especially problematic in sacramental preparation programs when they encounter baptized "non-practicers."

Many (most?) of us belong to a number of levels of church life that are all articulated in and are presumed in the liturgy: the communion of churches throughout the whole world, the diocesan church, and the local liturgical community (principally the parish, but also including religious communities, campuses, schools, and other institutions). At the same time we hold out the value of belonging to a parish and a diocese even in an age of "destination weddings," practices that can well enable people to avoid the issue of church-belonging. The Catholic Church has chosen to divide territories into parishes geographically. This means that wherever one lives one belongs. One may well choose to "parish shop" or to celebrate sacraments in other settings, but in the end Catholics know that they belong to at least one place on which they can rely for ministry and to which they are invited to belong.

MARRIAGES AND FUNERALS

In pastoral practice, the issues of mobility often surface most poignantly in marriage preparation and in rites surrounding dying and death. A number of priests in sabbatical programs relate how awkward it is explaining to couples and family members that weddings are required to take place in church buildings, when right after Vatican II some dioceses did not require it, especially given that open-air Masses for a variety of occasions are common (for example, World Youth Day Masses). Parents of children who are set on outdoor weddings are heartsick, not to say angry, when they realize the prohibition. In addition, parents and pastors often find themselves in the situation of trying to keep the church door open and offer a wide net for church-belonging for the couple, only to find that not being able to celebrate an outdoor wedding can be a game changer, and religious practice for the couple ends there.

Another real difficulty might arise when a couple planning their wedding Mass is invited to celebrate their wedding at a regularly scheduled weekend Eucharist. I have participated in these in Europe. The rationale is that with fewer priests available they simply cannot add one more liturgy to their already full weekend schedule. Moreover, the theology behind it is that one's marriage ought to take place in the local liturgical assembly where one belongs (at least in theory), and what better time and place than a weekend Eucharist? That there will be a clash with the cultural presumption that "*I* plan *my* wedding" is clear. But liturgy is never about "me" or "my" sacrament. It is always about the ecclesial "we" and the reality of church-belonging.

A related potential is the availability of an ordained priest to preside at funerals and weddings. It is not uncommon that weddings and funerals become the responsibility of a deacon or, in the case of burials, of designated laypersons. An ecumenical wedding is often celebrated at a Liturgy of the Word to help avoid the awkwardness of whole parts of the assembly not invited to communion (more on this follows). In some parishes, funerals take the place of the scheduled daily Eucharist. This often works well in order to provide a stable community for the bereaved to pray with and allows the priest to preside at a single Mass, not two (or more), on a given day.

Another issue that surfaces at weddings and funerals concerns the cultural assumptions that exist alongside the liturgy of the church for these occasions. People need to be invited to trust the rites of the Catholic Church. The funeral rites are among the best revisions of the post–Vatican II liturgy. People are both appropriately challenged as well as consoled by them. It can be less easy to convince those to be married that the marriage rite works well if they study it and work with the pastoral team to prepare it. Poignant issues in both cases concern music. This is a case of people expecting that once someone else has done a thing, not to say televised it, they judge that "their" wedding or loved one's funeral can have the same thing or something very similar. Enormous patience, endless hours of explanation, and immediate pastoral sensitivity all come to bear on these very personal and yet often challenging moments in the lives of Catholic believers today. Coupled with the details is the fact that "non-practicers" often present themselves for these liturgies with demands, or at least high expectations.

RECEPTION OF COMMUNION

In 1998, the Catholic bishops of England, Wales, Ireland, and Scotland issued an important teaching document on the

Eucharist entitled *One Bread, One Body*[5] to deal with the issue of differences in belief about the Eucharist among believing Christians (in particular, differences between Roman Catholics and Anglicans) and thus deal with the thorny issue of intercommunion. In an accompanying document about practices, they officially sanctioned the growing practice that those not of the Catholic faith attending a Catholic Eucharist could join in the communion procession, but then, when standing before the priest or eucharistic minister, place their hands over their chest and receive a blessing instead of the consecrated species. The document also states that the minister give a blessing gesture, but prescribes no words to accompany it. This was offered as a useful pastoral response to the possible sense of exclusion when non-Catholic Christians do not receive communion at Mass.

The practice has taken hold in many parts of the world. However, a pastoral difficulty experienced by those who distribute communion is that sometimes communicants do not indicate whether they are receiving (in the hand or on the tongue) or are asking for a blessing until the moment of reception. I will sometimes remind people during the announcements at the end of Mass, for their information the next time they are at Mass, to please adopt the gesture of placing their hands over their chest while they are processing to communion so that I as the minister can accommodate them carefully and calmly.

Especially when it comes to special occasions (weddings and funerals), my own preference is to publish in worship aids the guidelines from the USCCB.[6] The issue at communion is precisely that—being one with one another. Because we are part of one another we partake together in the Eucharist. When we are divided from one another and belong to different churches, religions, or no religion at all, then we do not partake of the one bread. More often than not, this is a serious, dividing issue that often surfaces in programs for adult initiation. The pain experienced when one is not invited to eucharistic communion is palpable, real, and more often than not, very, very deep. But the reality of not sharing in the same faith cannot be jettisoned or forgotten. It is why the reception of communion is a dividing issue. But sadly sometimes what is perceived is not lack of belonging but a sense of judgment about others: that we Catholics who partake are morally or spiritually superior, or that we are better than they are. Not at all! What is crucial is to admit that even we who partake of communion are ourselves unworthy of it.

POSTURES AND GESTURES

The words of the liturgy and (most of) its gestures are pre-determined. In the act of doing the liturgy they are orchestrated for our benefit as members of each other. It is of the nature of the liturgy that these words and gestures shape us. We do not shape them. An important principle enunciated in the *General Instruction of the Roman Missal* (GIRM) is that "uniformity of posture is a sign of the unity of the body of Christ" (n. 42). My concern is when this principle is implemented by a conference of bishops and then implemented in the variety of places where the liturgy is celebrated in a diocese. While gestures are indicated in all of the revised post–Vatican II rites, there are times when the local bishops' conferences of a country can and do make adjustments in some of them. Yet, there are also occasions when a local, diocesan bishop makes judgments about gestures in his diocese. In all of this, the rule of thumb to follow is "when in Rome, do what the Romans do" (or for me, Washington, Baltimore, Arlington, or Richmond). This means that we follow directives of dioceses and bishops' conferences as we interpret and implement the prescriptions of the revised rites. But there are times when different directives cause an instability when the liturgy ought to foster stability. Dare I offer the example of the holy days of obligation, and when the Solemnity of the Ascension is celebrated in the various regions in the United States?

In addition, it is presumed that everyone in the diocese is employing the same postures, a uniformity that supports the unity of the church. But, admittedly, not all postures are uniform in a diocese, and the intended unity may not be reflected in these postures. In addition, there is some debate as to whether local bishops should have the authority to determine the list of things that are left to their discretion in the GIRM (among others, the posture before the distribution of communion). The counterargument is that the bishops' conference should decide what is in the best interests of the entire diocese. This would allow for fewer times when the liturgy would offer ritual instability rather than ritual familiarity and ecclesial stability. But given the way the United States Conference of Catholic Bishops has charted our course liturgically, the rule of thumb remains "when in Rome..." What needs to be kept in mind is that, by its nature, ritual is meant to be a cohesive force to foster church unity on the basis of this presumed familiarity with structure, rite, and execution. A steady diet of changing the liturgy leads to the kind of ritual that draws attention to externals and leads to an instability not compatible with the liturgy that, also by its nature, is meant to be stable, comprised of fixed prayers and rites.

At the same time, among the theological meanings of liturgical gestures is the ecclesial one that by using the same gestures and words we reflect in a privileged way who we are as members of Christ's body, the church. The GIRM has this to say about the role of the people of God in the Eucharist:

> Moreover, they are to form one body, whether in hearing the Word of God, or in taking part in the prayers and in the singing, or above all by the common offering of the Sacrifice and by participating together at the Lord's table. This unity is beautifully apparent from the gestures and bodily postures observed together by the faithful. (n. 96)

And:

> For the sake of uniformity in gestures and bodily postures during one and the same celebration, the faithful should follow the instructions which the Deacon, a lay minister, or the Priest gives, according to what is laid down in the Missal. (n. 43)

This suggests that there is a presumed, agreed-upon meaning in the gestures that the church engages in at the liturgy. We do not make them up as we wish. They are given to us to shape what we say and do in common. The liturgy is not a place for creative self-expression. The use of common gestures and the wearing of vesture carry meanings that cover uniqueness, particularity, and individual expression. They carry with them the wisdom of the ages through which we are conformed to Christ and through which we express again and again that we are members of one another as his body on this earth. Communal gestures and language are presumed in liturgy so that one's attention is not drawn to the external behavior or practice. This allows the theological meaning of what is occurring at the liturgy to emerge as what is essential, not the distraction of what different people do differently.

A particularly challenging issue today concerns the postures and gestures at the reception of holy communion. As adapted by the USCCB, the revised GIRM states:

> The Priest then takes the paten or ciborium and approaches the communicants, who usually come up in procession.
>
> It is not permitted for the faithful to take the consecrated Bread or the sacred chalice by themselves and, still less, to hand them on from one to another among themselves. The norm established for the Dioceses of the United States of America is that Holy Communion is to be received standing, unless an individual member of the faithful wishes to receive Communion while kneeling (Congregation for Divine Worship and the Discipline of the Sacraments, Instruction, *Redemptionis Sacramentum*, March 25, 2004, no. 91).
>
> When receiving Holy Communion, the communicant bows his or her head before the Sacrament as a gesture of reverence and receives the Body of the Lord from the minister. The consecrated host may be received either on the tongue or in the hand, at the discretion of each communicant. When Holy Communion is received under both kinds, the sign of reverence is also made before receiving the Precious Blood. (n. 160)

In addition to this directive is the "response" about the possibility of kneeling written by Cardinal Francis Arinze, then prefect for the Sacred Congregation of Divine Worship, that this directive did not mean that kneeling was prohibited. That communicants regularly knelt for communion when they received from Pope Benedict XVI (either at the Vatican or on worldwide pilgrimages, a practice that started with World Youth Day in Sydney, Australia, in August 2008) may well be the reason that the kneeling posture has been the cause of some debate about the proper posture for communion reception.

As already noted, I have been a weekend associate at a parish in Richmond, Virginia, for several years, I preside and preach two evenings a week at the Basilica of the National Shrine of the Immaculate Conception, which is next to the CUA campus, and once a week I preside and preach on campus. It is at the basilica where I find the postures and customs at communion to be the least uniform and thus often somewhat confusing. Given the number of tourists and business travelers who come to the shrine only occasionally, those distributing communion must be particularly attentive when communicants approach, especially to where they place their hands and whether they will remain standing (as is the norm) or kneel. This attentiveness can take its toll in terms of (dare I say it?) patience. I find it paradoxical that at the very moment when we experience the deepest *communio* through the reception of communion we sometimes find the greatest expression of diversity in terms of gestures and postures.

The Universal Prayer, or Prayer of the Faithful

In many of the debates preceding the drafting and adoption of the Constitution on the Sacred Liturgy, the restoration of the Prayer of the Faithful (*oratio fidelium*) loomed large and was almost always strongly encouraged as a way to connect the timelessness of the liturgy with today's needs and concerns.[7] That the general intercessions have been restored to almost all the reformed rites of the liturgy (except for Penance) is clear. And the texts of almost all of the rites themselves offer models for the shape and contents of these prayers.

AT THE LITURGY OF THE HOURS

Certainly among the most notable additions to the Hours are the rather expansive suggestions for the Prayer of the Faithful at Morning Prayer and Evening Prayer. I say "suggestions" because that is exactly what they are, despite the fact that many use them regularly, which is perfectly fine. The *General Instruction for the Liturgy of the Hours* (GILOH) distinguishes between the prayers in the morning, which are oriented to the (work of) the coming day, and the prayers at evening, which are decidedly intercessory:

> The general intercessions, restored in the Mass of the Roman Rite, have their place also at evening prayer, though in a different fashion, as will be explained later.
>
> Since traditionally morning prayer puts the whole day in God's hands, there are invocations at morning prayer for the purpose of commending or consecrating the day to God. (GILOH, nn. 180–81)

Given this distinction, it is also important to distinguish between using the words *prayers* and *intercessions* to describe what occurs at this part of the hours in the present American four-volume edition. At the same time, I do wonder about their "staying power." Allow me to make four observations:

First is the issue of wordiness. Are the prayers for Morning and Evening Prayer sometimes too wordy? I find myself sometimes deliberately choosing the shorter ones from Appendix II to the volumes of the Liturgy of the Hours and adding instead generous time for silence after each is prayed aloud.

Second is whether, in the haste that accompanied the revision of the Liturgy of the Hours, some of the models used were overly tied to the Eucharist and insufficiently tied to the time of day. I am thinking here of the juxtaposition in the intercessions for Morning Prayer on Sunday, week one, which propose:

Creator of the stars, we thank you for your gift, the first rays of the dawn,
  And we commemorate your resurrection.
Each Sunday you give us the joy of gathering as your people,
  Around the table of your Word and your body.

Third is the issue of the inclusiveness of the language in these prayers. While a legitimate case can be made for the use of "for us men" during the Creed to sustain the (admittedly subtle but) very real parallel between "men" and the sin of the first "man" (Adam), I think it important to eliminate language that is unnecessarily exclusive.

Fourth and last, I think it important to note that the psalm prayers, printed in the American versions of the Hours, are not found in other versions—for example, the version used in the United Kingdom. Again the GILOH states:

> Psalm-prayers for each psalm are given in the supplement to the Liturgy of the Hours as an aid to understanding them in a predominantly Christian way. An ancient tradition provides a model for their use: after the psalm a period of silence is observed, then the prayer gives a resume and resolution of the thoughts and aspirations of those praying the psalms. (n. 112)

In my own experience, these prayers are regularly not used in monastic celebrations of the Hours and increasingly are not used in other public celebrations of the Hours in favor of a generous silence to be observed after each of the psalms and canticles.

AT THE EUCHARIST

Much of what was said previously about the prayers at the Liturgy of the Hours can be said about the intercessions at the Eucharist, specifically wordiness and inclusive language. One additional comment about wordiness concerns the introduction and the concluding prayer said by the priest or bishop. Again I would argue that brevity is best. The introduction is a variation on "let us pray."

And it is certainly important to realize that this is not a prayer addressed to God; it is an invitation addressed to the gathered assembly. The concluding prayer is a variation on "we ask this through Christ our Lord." Again I would argue that brevity is recommended, especially since these intercessions follow the homily and profession of faith, which are high in word content.

In addition, it is also important to note that these are "intercessions," not prayers of thanksgiving. Further, it is important to recall and follow the structure from the more general and universal to the more particular. Here reference to the sample Universal Prayers in the Missal would be very useful to follow, at least in structure if not in some of its wording. I think it notable that in only one of the sample sets of intercessions are the pope and local bishop named. My liturgical judgment is that, given the fact that these are both named in the Eucharistic Prayer at every Mass, it is something of a duplication to have their names in each and every set of general intercessions.

Given my concern for silence and for verbal brevity where possible, I think that abiding by the number of petitions to the intercessions in the Missal's Appendix—namely, four petitions— is a wise rule of thumb to follow, especially when generous silence is allowed for personal petitions.

The wording of these prayers is always an issue and a work in progress. The more general and universal these texts, the better, as opposed to meeting individual needs. I think that divine providence can be relied on and that we do not need to attempt to tie God's hands by programming the result we desire from the petition.

The Assembly: Gathered and Sent

We do not create the church or the liturgical community. We are drawn into it by God's mysterious designs and in God's mysterious ways. The liturgy is always God's gift to us and the church's communal response to God.

While a chief characteristic of all liturgy is that it is the self-expression of the community of the church, there has been a legitimate critique of this sense of belonging when it seems self-generated or only an expression of oneself in community. For me, the words of the third Eucharistic Prayer offer an assurance and a challenge: "You never cease to gather a people to yourself..." We who gather do so at the Lord's gracious invitation, not out of our own self-will. We are made members of one another in this worldwide Catholic Church through the waters of baptism and the invocation of the three persons in the Triune God—Father, Son, and Holy Spirit.

Along with several others, I regret that after Vatican II it seemed that at least sometimes the "liturgy" folks and the "social justice" folks went in different directions—or at least were on parallel and never-to-intersect tracks. The liturgy folks were concerned with ceremonies. The justice folks were concerned with social action and service. In fact, this is to separate what is inseparable, to isolate that which should be united.[8] The liturgy is, and should be, all of a piece.

As I noted above, at the Evening Mass of the Lord's Supper on Holy Thursday, in the Prayer over the Offerings we pray that through the action of this Eucharist, "whenever the memorial of this sacrifice is celebrated the work of our redemption is accomplished." The intersection (not to say integration) of the things of this earth with the paschal victory of Christ experienced through them is underscored here and is an essential foundation for our understanding of what it means to use the things of this earth in the (eucharistic) liturgy. It is also particularly notable that on this solemn night at the Presentation of the Gifts the Missal states that "there may be a procession of the faithful in which the gifts for the poor may be presented with the bread and wine." This harkens to the time in the early church (certainly in Rome through the fifth century) when the gifts in the procession were precisely that—gifts for the Eucharist and foodstuffs for the poor. I myself saw this procession and collection Sunday after Sunday, week in and week out, when I visited churches on the outskirts of Nairobi, Kenya, some years ago. It is also notable that deacons were often responsible for the collection of the gifts. This was a particularly appropriate liturgical role since it underscores that it is the deacon's responsibility to take the gifts to those most in need. Here the ministers at the altar are the ministers of the church's charity.

One of the most poignant eschatological texts in the Gospel of Matthew is in chapter 25:31–46, the separation of the sheep and the goats. This image is sculpted above the entrance to more than one medieval cathedral. Why? Because what pilgrims do inside that church has to have its necessary complement in the way they live their lives. Like them, we will be judged on whether we fed the hungry, gave drink to the thirsty, clothed the naked, visited those in prison. We are judged on how we deal with and revere the other. We are judged on how we live life with each other in the communion of the church, strengthened by the bread of life and cup of salvation. And where do we do this? With and for each other. In an age of excessive individualism, we need to ask: If we live in isolation, whose feet will we wash? If we live in isolation, whose burdens will we help carry? If we live in isolation, whose wounds will we bind up? If we live in isolation, with whom shall we pray?

One of the main goals of the liturgy is that it prepares us for and is a foretaste of the kingdom of heaven, when we meet the Lord face to face. In the meantime, the liturgy is "heaven on earth." It is the most perfect realization of the kingdom possible this side of heaven. And again we do this in his remembrance with each other.

We pray at the Eucharist:

As we await the blessed hope
and the coming of our Savior, Jesus Christ.

Thus, the church that celebrates this liturgy here and now must then become kingdom witnesses in our world.

The dynamic of every liturgy is that we engage in communal celebrations for the sake of communal self-transcendence.

We gather in order to be sent.

We gather in order to be reshaped and reformed as God's baptized and holy people in order to be sent to live in the world as witnesses to what we have celebrated.

We, the gathered assembly, are the assembly sent forth.

What happens in between gathering and being sent is the jewel in the crown of Catholicism and makes us who and what we are: we celebrate the most sacred mysteries of our faith until "sacraments shall cease."

We call the last time we receive the body and blood of Christ *viaticum*—"food for the journey." In a sense, all communion is *viaticum*—food for the journey to live here and now what we share in the liturgy, and then food for the final journey to where there will be no more tears, no more suffering, no more mourning, and no more separation from God or one another. Then the pilgrim church on earth will have led us to the church finally and fully realized in the kingdom of heaven.

Liturgy is about church, and church is about liturgy. It's that simple, and that complex.

Conclusion

It is not a coincidence that both baptism and the Eucharist are drawn from the wounded side of Christ (see John 19:34 about the sword piercing the side of Jesus, from which flowed "blood and water"). It is worth recalling that many of the early fathers described the church as having been "born from the wounded side of Christ." As the priest places grains of incense into the paschal candle at the Paschal Vigil, he says:

> By his holy
> and glorious wounds
> may Christ the Lord
> guard us and protect us.
> Amen.

We are members of God's pilgrim church in earth. If we name our wounds and see them as healed in the wounds of Christ, we will be the stronger and more enriched pilgrim church on earth.

CHAPTER TWO

Active Participation

"Active Participation" Is Redundant

Probably no one word typifies what the liturgical reforms from Vatican II were (almost!) all about than *participation*. Adding up the number of times a word is used in any document and on that basis suggesting its importance can be very deceptive; nonetheless, that the term *participation* is used sixteen times in *Sacrosanctum Concilium*, that it is paired with the word *active* on twelve of those occasions, and that "liturgical instruction and active participation" is cited as one of the three principles on which the restoration and promotion of the sacred liturgy is based—together these are very significant.[1]

The phrases "active participation in the liturgy" and fostering "active participation" were major tenets of the Liturgical Movement's pioneers. Before the reformed liturgy from Vatican II, the liturgy was almost exclusively in Latin (although some sacraments, such as baptism and marriage, were administered in the vernacular). Then, it was not uncommon for the assembled laity to engage themselves in silent personal prayers and acts of devotion, sometimes allied with and sometimes at variance with what was said and done during the Eucharist. The literature about this is vast and examples are copious. One instance is the 1884 edition of a manual entitled *Golden Key to Heaven: A Collection of Devout Prayers and Approved Devotions for Use Among the Faithful.*[2] In addition to printing the texts of the Mass along with sketches locating the priest in the sanctuary at its various parts, the book also contains devotional prayers intended to be said before and during Mass that were not the prayers *of* the

Mass. It is therefore no surprise that the liturgical pioneers had wanted to foster hand Missals for the faithful that contained the prayers of the Mass itself: for example, the (then) famously popular *Father Stedman Missals*,[3] daily and Sunday, or the *St. Joseph Daily Missal*. But it was especially the publication of *The Bible Missal* first in Europe and then in English translation that enabled the faithful to follow the Mass, to learn about its prayers, rites, seasons, and feasts, and, not least of which, to read commentaries on the scripture readings for each day.[4] The publication of such hand Missals enabled the faithful to follow along and to understand in their native language what was happening at the altar in Latin in a liturgy largely conducted by the priest and ministers in the sanctuary. Admittedly there was a level of participation that occurred before Vatican II but it was largely by way of understanding what liturgical ministers were saying and doing, not by actively participating in the liturgy with them. This is why the following phrase of *Sacrosanctum Concilium* (n. 48) is very important: "The Church, therefore, earnestly desires that Christ's faithful, when present at this mystery of faith [the Eucharist] should not be there as strangers or silent spectators."

I wish to offer some comments about *participation*:

The phrase *liturgical participation* is redundant. Liturgy is always about our *taking part,* our *participation* in the reality of God through Christ's paschal mystery in the power of the Holy Spirit in the communion of the church. By its nature, liturgy is the church's privileged and guaranteed means of our participating in these sacred realities and events. The very term *anamnesis,* which is Greek for "memorial," means that we make memory together, and in making memory we literally *take part in,* are *partakers* in, what was once accomplished for our sakes in history and is also here and now enacted for us. We take part in what happened once in sacred history and what is experienced in the present through sacred rites even as we look for its fulfillment at the end of time. Here time—past, present, and future—intersect and eternity is experienced here and now.

Let me give an example about active participation in the revised liturgy. One of the debates that occurred in addressing how to make changes in the Eucharistic Prayers after Vatican II

44

concerned the assembly's active participation in the Eucharistic Prayer itself. From the second century, we have evidence from Justin the Martyr (*First Apology*) that the assembly called out "Amen" at the prayer's end as their ratification of it, their "So be it" to what was prayed and what occurred during the Eucharistic Prayer. Although scholars differ as to exactly when the *Sanctus* ("Holy, holy, holy") was added to the Eucharistic Prayer, it is certain that by the end of the fourth century this was in place in the West.[5] Among the ways of understanding the *Sanctus* is to appreciate that it combines our praise of the God of creation and our praise of the Christ of redemption. In it we acclaim "heaven and earth are full of your glory" (Isa 6:3) and we acclaim as well "Blessed is he who comes in the name of the Lord" (Matt 21:9). The issue before the committee (the technical term is *coetus*) charged with examining how the Eucharistic Prayer would be used in the post–Vatican II liturgy was whether the length of the Eucharistic Prayer from the *Sanctus* to the Great Amen was so long that the assembly's attention might wander during what the GIRM calls "the center and high point of the entire celebration" (n. 78). The decision was taken to add an acclamation after the Words of Institution and to provide three options for it. The texts of these acclamations concern Christ's death, resurrection, and second coming, *expressing our belief* in this central saving mystery and our *participation* in that central saving mystery. The phrase that introduces the acclamations—*the mystery of faith*—is contained in the words spoken over the chalice in the Tridentine Mass: "This is the chalice of my blood, the blood of the new and eternal covenant, *the mystery of faith*, which will be poured out for you and for many for the forgiveness of sins." The phrase *the mystery of faith* was not contained in the Last Supper account (Matt 26:27) from which this part of the Eucharistic Prayer was taken. Because it was not from the scriptures as part of the words of Jesus at the Last Supper, it was judged that it should be excised. That it became the introduction to the acclamation was fortuitous. Exactly where the phrase *the mystery of faith* came from historically is debated by liturgical scholars, many of whom hold to the theory that it was a spontaneous acclamation by the faithful upon seeing the chalice raised after the Words of Institution were said. Now the words *the mystery of faith* introduce the second of the three acclamations for the assembly's active participation in the Eucharistic Prayer—the *Sanctus*, the Memorial Acclamation, and the Great Amen.

In addition to the three acclamations found in the reformed Latin liturgy, the International Commission on English in the Liturgy (ICEL), which is charged with the translation of the revised Latin rites into English, added one more in the early 1970s for the then *Sacramentary for Mass*, based on an original composition in French. It was not a translation from the Latin texts of the acclamations in the *Missale Romanum*. The text was "Christ has died, Christ is risen, Christ will come again." It became a staple in the vernacular liturgies from after the reform through the publication of the revised edition of the Roman Missal, implemented in the United States on the First Sunday of Advent, 2011, which now does not contain it. The reason for its omission is based on the liturgy as *our expressing our belief* and our *taking part in* Christ's paschal mystery. The texts of the three Latin (now translated into English) Memorial Acclamations are affirmations of faith in the paschal mystery and how our participation in it has effects among us. Such phrases as "we proclaim your Death," and "by your Cross and Resurrection you have set us free" indicate what occurs when we *participate* in the liturgy. This is decidedly a richer set of texts about *expressing faith* and *incorporation* rather than the assertion that "Christ has died," which is not an acclamation but a declarative statement. None of the other acclamations describe the paschal mystery as does "Christ has died"; rather, they describe how we share in what we are celebrating— the paschal victory of Christ. Greater fidelity to the Latin original was a major concern in the retranslation of the Roman Missal. In the case of the acclamations, it is also a case of emphasizing our engagement in what we are doing, not our recollecting it or observing it but our *taking part* in it.

This leads to asserting a principle that is evident throughout the church's liturgical prayers, namely, that liturgical texts never *describe* God's attributes and saving work for us without also addressing how we share in the very life of God and his saving work here and now through the liturgy. Liturgical texts accompany liturgical actions. While liturgical prayers inform us about who God is and what God has done and continues to do for us, their primary purposes are to shape our belief in what we are celebrating and to underscore how we are drawn into what we believe through the liturgy. They are complemented through the actions of the liturgy and the actions that derive from the liturgy.

As I will say more than once in this book—this is what makes liturgy what it is, and what makes it unique, privileged, and above any other kind of personal or communal prayer. It is through the liturgy that in a unique way we *share in* Christ's work of redemption.

At the same time, some would argue that this acclamation is something of an interruption in the Eucharistic Prayer, stylistically and theologically. Their not-illegitimate logic is that it mars the classic structure of the Eucharistic Prayer. As the GIRM states:

> Now the center and high point of the entire celebration begins, namely, the Eucharistic Prayer itself, that is, the prayer of thanksgiving and sanctification. The Priest calls upon the people to lift up their hearts towards the Lord in prayer and thanksgiving; he associates the people with himself in the Prayer that he addresses in the name of the entire community to God the Father through Jesus Christ in the Holy Spirit. Furthermore, the meaning of this Prayer is that the whole congregation of the faithful joins with Christ in confessing the great deeds of God and in the offering of Sacrifice. The Eucharistic Prayer requires that everybody listens to it with reverence and in silence. (n. 78)

The Eucharistic Prayer is addressed to the Father and its central part delineates God's great acts of redemption, in particular through the Son's incarnation, obedient life, betrayal, Last Supper, death, resurrection, and ascension, as we await his second coming. (Depending on which Eucharistic Prayer you pray, different elements of Christ's act of redemption are articulated: for example, there is no explicit reference to Christ's second coming in the Roman Canon; more on this in chapter 3). It concludes with the final Doxology, again explicitly naming the Son and acclaiming that "through him, and with him, and in him, O God almighty Father, in the unity of the Holy Spirit, all glory and honor is yours, forever and ever"—to which the assembly responds, "Amen." The issue raised about the acclamation introduced by the words *the mystery of faith* is that in it the assembly addresses the second person of the Trinity directly: "We proclaim your Death, O Lord, and profess your Resurrection until you come again"; "We proclaim your Death, O Lord..."; "Save us, Savior of the world..." Thus it breaks the inherent logic and structure of the prayer, which till now has been addressing the Father, through the Son, in the Holy Spirit.

A second criticism concerns the placement of this acclamation. It is sometimes referred to as the Memorial Acclamation (it is debated whether this should be the way we describe it), and its coming after the Words of Institution and Consecration and not after the section of the prayer explicitly called the *anamnesis* is the reason why some call it anticipatory of what comes next, that is, the explicit assertion of the centrality of Christ's paschal mystery experienced through the Eucharist and mentioned here in an explicit way. Some argue that its placement after the *anamnesis* in the Eucharistic Prayers for children is the more logical location. The rationale there is that the assembly joins in acclaiming what has just been articulated by the presiding bishop or priest rather than acclaiming it before the *anamnesis* occurs.

"Active" Participation

The modifier *active* needs to be explored historically and theologically. The context for debates about the liturgy at Vatican II and the promulgation of *Sacrosanctum Concilium* as the first document to be promulgated from the Council was the celebration of rites as revised after the Council of Trent and in use up through 1962. That the Council fathers at Vatican II wanted to increase "full, conscious and active participation in the sacred liturgy" is clear. Where formerly the use of hand Missals (officially sanctioned by the church just over a century ago) was an option, now the use of a worship aid, hymnal, or ritual book, would become *de rigueur*. Being attentive and responding to what was occurring in and through the liturgy was to be presumed.

At the same time, even though "active participation" is a repeated refrain in the text of *Sacrosanctum Concilium*, it is important to note that encouraging such participation was not new in official church documents. From as early as the papal magisterium in 1903, in a document on music (*Tra le Sollecitudini*), Pope Pius X spoke of the value of active participation. Active participation continued to be emphasized in the papal magisterium throughout the twentieth century (for example, by Pope Pius XII in *Mediator Dei*, 1943). It was also asserted in the 1958 instruction from the Congregation of Rites about participation, which gave us the "dialogue Mass" and the singing of (usually four) vernacular hymns at Mass.

In addition, one can see why theologically active participation was at the forefront of the reasons why the Easter Vigil liturgy (in "experimental" form starting in 1951) and then all the Triduum liturgies were revised in the mid-1950s. All of these documents and rites calling for and encouraging active participation were building blocks leading to Vatican II. It was not as though someone turned on a light in 1963! The first steps toward emphasizing the reality of active participation in the liturgy were taken over a century ago.

Part of the value of insisting on "active" participation is that it respects the way we engage in the liturgy—through our bodies. Liturgy is not a cerebral exercise of the mind only. It is an experience of bodily participation and engagement. In the late second or early third century, in his treatise *On the Resurrection*, Tertullian wrote that "the flesh is the instrument of salvation."[6] In many ways the Prologue of John's Gospel (John 1:1–14)—read by Western Christians on Christmas Day and by Eastern Christians on Easter day——turns on the pivotal verse:

> And the Word became flesh
> and made his dwelling among us,
> and we saw his glory,
> the glory as of the Father's only Son,
> full of grace and truth. (v 14; NAB)

As early as the patristic era, the principle of the incarnation was summarized in this phrase: "God took flesh so we in our flesh could become God." We were and are indeed saved through human flesh. The consequence is that we in our human flesh are divinized, literally made like God, and grow in the life of God through liturgy and the sacraments.

This principle of divinization through the use of our human flesh underlies all that we do in liturgy and sacraments. It is based on the fact that the Father sent his Son to live our human life, and to suffer, die, and rise. But the Son did all of this by taking on human flesh. Therefore, in liturgy and sacraments we use our human bodies to grow in the divine life through the principle and reality of the incarnation.

That is why I much prefer the revised translation of the Creed we now use at Mass:

> For us men and for our salvation
> he came down from heaven,
> and by the Holy Spirit was incarnate of the Virgin Mary,
> and became man.

To me, saying that he "was incarnate" is preferable to the former wording that placed the emphasis on Jesus himself—"he was born of the Virgin Mary, and became man"—which phrases do not contain sufficient (any?) attention to the implications of the incarnation for us. The phrase *was incarnate* allows us to realize that his becoming flesh has implications for us who are "in the flesh" on this good earth.

When applied to the liturgy, this means that what we are and use in human life is used in liturgy and sacraments to worship God. This theology is behind the liturgy's phrase the "holy exchange of gifts," referring sometimes to the bread and wine presented to become the body and blood of Christ, sometimes to the humanity of the Son of God through whom we become divine. Sometimes the prayer refers to both, as in the Prayer over the Offerings at Christmas Mass during the Night:

May the oblation of this day's feast
be pleasing to you, O Lord, we pray,
that through this most holy exchange
we may be found in the likeness of Christ,
in whom our nature is united to you.

The implication for understanding the liturgy is that, in addition to using the things of this world to worship God (see chapter 4 on the sacramental principle), we use our human bodies to worship God. All our human faculties are brought into the worship of God—especially heart, mind, and will. Our senses are engaged—sight, sound, smell, taste, and touch. And our bodies are involved—processing, gesturing, standing, sitting, and so forth. That our bodies were and are always used in worship is clear. That the use of our bodies was somewhat limited in the rites celebrated after Trent is also clear. My own memories of those rites involved watching, standing, kneeling, and sitting. Especially at a solemn Mass this also involved the sense of smell of burning incense and sometimes of burning candles. With the emphasis on active participation in the reformed liturgy, all our senses and faculties are to be engaged much more fully. This is not for the sake of activity only and being attentive to what we are doing, although that is an important aspect. It is also more fundamentally based on the importance of our bodies in our experience of salvation in and through our use of them in liturgy.

The language of the contemporary magisterium underscores the importance of the reality of *participation* in the sacred liturgy in a number of places. For example, the assertions in both *Sacrosanctum Concilium* and *Lumen Gentium* speak of the liturgy as the "source and summit" (other translations use the terms *fount* or *font* and *apex*). *Sacrosanctum Concilium* gives great priority to the liturgy by asserting that "...nevertheless the liturgy is the summit toward which the activity of the Church is directed; at the same time it is the font from which all her power flows" (n. 10).[7] *Lumen Gentium* adjusts this to refer specifically to the Eucharist. But what is often neglected in citing this phrase is its precise wording, which refers to our taking part in it. The text reads: "Taking part in the Eucharistic sacrifice, which is the fount and apex of the whole Christian life, they offer the Divine Victim to God, and offer themselves along with It" (n. 11).[8] The theological reality and pastoral importance of *participating* in the eucharistic sacrifice is underscored to be intrinsic to the church's life.

Meanings of Participation

A PASTORAL, THEOLOGICAL LENS

More recent reflection on what exactly is meant by the phrase *active participation* has yielded rich results. We are indebted to such liturgical theologians as Cipriano Vagaggini and Edward Kilmartin for rich descriptions of what it means "to take part in" divine mysteries through prayers, rites, music, and so forth.[9] A valid criticism of the way in which some of the reforms were implemented after Vatican II concerns the assumption that one needs almost always to be engaged verbally and vocally throughout the liturgy without appropriate listening and silence. In fact, the reformed Order of Mass contains increased emphasis on pauses for silences during the liturgy for our personal appropriation of what is being enacted. This is very helpful. And that the theological emphasis is again placed on what God does for us through the liturgy, as opposed to what we do for God, is helpful, lest liturgical participation be perceived as any sort of (even semi-) Pelagianism.[10] This kind of appreciation of participation owes much to the work of Odo Casel, the important German liturgical scholar and monk who wrote during the 1930s.

Whatever rethinking is going on related to a comparatively "energetic" approach to active participation by gathered assemblies in the act of worship after Vatican II must be done in accord with the principles of sacramentality and the incarnation (among others). This is to say that, by its nature, liturgy involves the whole person—body, mind, emotions, and so forth—and all our faculties—sight, sound, smell, taste, and touch. Any reevaluating of active participation must include the full engagement of all of these faculties. Liturgy should never be confused with the passivity of a theater or television audience. This is especially difficult in an Internet age when logging on and getting instant information is the order of the day. In higher education today, the issue of online education looms large. But a major criticism of such education is that, more often than not, lectures are pretaped and chatrooms for students are where the questions surface if they do at all. It is important to recall this adage describing education: "little impression without expression." While the "expression" envisioned in a classroom is different from that in the liturgy, meaning that in a classroom often what one asks or says is not preprogrammed and occurs to students at the moment (making it an engaging, active experience), there are similarities. This is to say that by its nature liturgy requires individual and communal expression of a prepared kind in terms of speaking (responses), singing (antiphons, psalms, hymns), movement (when to process and where), and so forth, some of which remain the same and some of which change (for example, many of the texts change daily, and there is a difference in structure and movement between and among different liturgies, such as between a Sunday and a daily Eucharist and the Easter Vigil).

Clearly, the issue is that we are all the "actants" of the liturgy; the liturgy does not presuppose performers and audience. That is why "active participation" is a redundant phrase. Today, however, I am concerned that some critiques of active participation place so much emphasis on "internal" or "interior" *participation* in the paschal mystery that they can make the rites of the liturgy seem superfluous. The rites of the liturgy matter a great deal to support, insure, and sustain the adequacy and reality of *participation* in the paschal mystery. Rethinking the meaning of active participation does not mean returning to the era of hand Missals to read along and following along in a text with what the liturgy's ministers are saying and doing.[11] It should mean taking part in rites and words and, through them, in the very reality of God.

I have been known to say that "all liturgy is pastoral." By that I mean that it is always the participation of communities of faith here and now in the time-transcending events of Christ's paschal dying and rising and our incorporation—our participation—in putting to death whatever does us harm and rising through, with, and in the risen Christ to a totally new state of life and love in him.

A (MORE) THEOLOGICAL LENS

The Extraordinary Synod of 1985 is credited as being the occasion when the term *communio* was named the interpretative key to understanding the documents and the phenomenon of Vatican II. In countless Roman and other documents ever since, *communio* appears as an important and galvanizing concept for a number of things. (At the same time, however, it is to be noted that the term *communio* is not univocal and conveys at least shades of different meanings.)

What I should like to suggest is that the liturgy is an act of *communio*. Specifically I want to argue that it is the church's privileged experience of who God is, how we are incorporated into the reality of God by the liturgy, and what that means in terms of individual and communal identity.

One of the most important books I ever read about the Trinity was *The Three-Personed God* by a former colleague and esteemed Dominican theologian William Hill, OP.[12] The book is an exploration of the admittedly dense reality of what it means that we believe in the Trinity as three persons in one God. Among the things I learned was that, starting from the Old Testament scriptures through to the experience of the Trinity in our lives today, the God we believe in is a God who calls us as a people into relationship, and a God who is always "there for us."

Certainly *communio* has become an important watchword for how we should understand a number of things in the life of the church, including church-belonging itself. At the same time, I think it important to offer the caution that *communio* is not a univocal term and has been used for a variety of purposes since the Council, including how to interpret the Council itself. At baptism we are drawn into the communion of persons that is the Trinity and we are members of each other in and through the Trinity. It is the three-personed God who calls us into that divine indwelling, who sustains us in the set of relatedness and relationships that is the church, and who "again and again" calls us to worship in and through the liturgy. Whatever can be said about coming together in the Lord's name for liturgy, it is always something we do because God calls us to do it. It is not self-generated and certainly not self-sustained. It is done at the invitation and sustaining action of the Trinity among us.

But *communio* is also incomplete this side of the kingdom of heaven. Discipleship is always eschatological; "we are not there yet." *Communio* is always incomplete and needs to be fulfilled. In this "in between" time between Christ's paschal mystery and his return at the end of time, eschatology has to lead to caring for one another in love, sometimes specified in social justice ministry.

Think about it: Again and again in the Hebrew scriptures we are told that God is always with us, that God is "there for you." While the contrast between the God of the Greeks (God in godself and described by nouns) and the God of the Hebrews (God as there for us and described by verbs "I am who am") can be overdrawn, there is something to be said for the fact that the emphasis in the Hebrew notion of God is of a God who is active among us, always inviting and sustaining us. This is the God continually revealed to us through word and action in the liturgy. The God revealed in the liturgy is less a God who is able to be defined than a God who is unfathomable and into whose very being we are drawn by the liturgy.

The words of Preface VI in Ordinary Time ring true:

[I]n you we live and move and have our being,
and while in this body
we not only experience the daily effects of your care,
but even now possess the pledge of life eternal.

The first phrase, "In you we live and move and have our being," is from St. Paul's speech on the Areopagus (Acts 17:28), appealing to those whose understanding of God (or "gods") is undifferentiated and needs refinement. And while it is debated whether St. Paul used here a phrase from a pagan source, the reality expressed has staying power for us. Certainly in and through the liturgy we are drawn into and are incorporated in the very being of the three-personed God. The God we believe in is a God of relationship and relationality. Participation in the liturgy insures this again and again. We share in the *communio* of the three divine persons through the *communio* of the liturgy. The greeting at the start of Mass is helpful when it states:

> The grace of our Lord Jesus Christ,
> and the love of God
> and the communion of the Holy Spirit
> be with you all.

When this greeting is used it articulates how what we are about to enter into is an act of "communion." (The Latin term here is *communicatio*). When it is used as the first thing the presiding priest or bishops says to the gathered assembly after the Sign of the Cross, it is a theologically rich gesture, for what is the church but a *communio* of persons who derive their life from the *communio* of the Trinity? By using the term *communion* here, we emphasize that the church is not of our own making.

At the end of the Eucharistic Prayer (recall again that this was the first documentable acclamation of the people to the prayer), the Doxology (now) reads:

> Through him, and with him, and in him,
> O God almighty Father,
> in the unity of the Holy Spirit
> all glory and honor are yours,
> forever and ever.

While theologians and liturgists comment on this in a number of rich and varying ways, for me the issue of "in the unity of" is very important. It underscores for me (again) how the liturgy is an act of *participation* in the three-personed God, the Trinity. At the same time Josef Jungmann (among others) will emphasize that "unity" here refers to the reality of the gathered assembly as the church drawn into the mystery of the Trinity through the liturgy. The use of "in the unity of" at the end of every Collect at Mass (rather than the former translation "who lives and reigns with you *and* the Holy Spirit") not only is more literal, but it also allows us to realize that through such a phrase the reality of what liturgical participation is all about is underscored.

PARTICIPATION FOSTERED BY FAMILIARITY

In some ways liturgy is a refined taste! I mean that, by its nature, it is a learned set of behaviors and actions, not all of which are immediately obvious and not all of which can ever be totally explained. That is because liturgy is a ritual. By its nature it is *multivalent*: it has many meanings. *Multi* comes from the Latin (*multus*) for "many." *Valence* also comes from the Latin (*valere*), one of whose meanings is, in fact, "meaning." (Dare I try to recall my high school chemistry lab, whose wall was adorned with the "periodic chart of the elements," on which a couple of letters indicated the "valence," that is, the chemical bond formed by the atoms of a given element—its contents and meaning?) Put those two Latin words together and we have the term *multivalence*, signifying that liturgical terms and words often have more than one meaning. One of the most enriching results of a study of liturgy's words and rites is to discover a number of things that are signified by the use of a single word.

Novelty for the sake of novelty is the polar opposite of what the liturgy is. Liturgy is predetermined and has a set structure, some parts of which are always the same (the Order of Mass); some of which change by church decision (the structure of the *Lectionary for Mass*, for example, means that the scripture readings change from day to day by church decision); and some of which change by the determination of the local liturgical leadership (for example, music at the liturgy).

Some argue today that there is too much flexibility and that we should return to "one Roman Rite." While some liturgies may have too much that is unfamiliar, which can hinder immediate and obvious participation, the assertion that there was and should be "one" way of doing the Roman Rite is ahistorical and untrue. At the risk of overgeneralizing, this means that from as early as the fourth century the liturgy as celebrated at Rome had the same structure, but that there were differences among the papal liturgy, the liturgy celebrated in parishes, and the liturgies celebrated at cemeteries. It is also the case that in the Middle Ages we have evidence at Rome of liturgy celebrated by the pope in the Sistine Chapel and when he visited parishes (called "stational" liturgy),[13] and also the liturgy of parishes under the leadership of their pastors. There was and is the important distinction between monastic liturgy and what is called "cathedral" or parish liturgy. And even after the Council of Trent, liturgical practices that were in existence for two hundred years were allowed to continue, such as the Dominican liturgy or the Ambrosian liturgy celebrated in Milan and northern Italy. "One size fits all" has never been the case when it comes to the Roman (Western) liturgy.[14]

Yet, it can also be said that "one *structure* fits all" in the sense that the eucharistic liturgy always has the same basic outline: Gathering, Introductory Rites, Liturgy of the Word, Presentation of the Gifts, Eucharistic Prayer and Consecration, Communion, and Dismissal. What remains different are the ways this is fleshed out given the variety of assemblies that celebrate it.

It is here that some legitimate debate can and should occur. It was nothing less than a herculean task to implement the reformed liturgies after Vatican II. The fact that all the liturgical rites were changed within a relatively short period of time naturally caused its own set of disturbances and a loss of liturgical equilibrium. But what should eventually occur is that the liturgy's rites and prayers become so well known that they are experienced as "second nature." By that I mean that drawing attention to one or another aspect of the liturgy, either by changing texts and rites or by the way they were enacted by liturgical ministers who draw attention to themselves, can cause a certain ritual instability. This is not desirable, simply because by its nature liturgy is fixed and stable, and ritual familiarity is meant to foster engagement with God on a far deeper level than the noticing of externals. The use of familiar phrases and rites in the liturgy allows for a deeper engagement in the reality of God. Noting liturgy's externals can mar such a deep and profound experience of the divine. Liturgical changes for the sake of greater participation after Vatican II was and is highly desirable. Change for the sake of change in the liturgy and continuing to change it goes against its very nature.

This is one of the reasons why I was glad that the implementation of the revised translation of the Roman Missal was preceded by catechesis and has now been implemented. (Whether the catechesis was sufficient or always as accurate as possible is open for debate.) That the Missal is in place will hopefully lead, over time, to a deeper and ever-fuller appreciation for its contents. That we are noticing particular phrases and words at Mass now should hopefully lead to less attentiveness to critiquing texts and more to an experience of being able to focus on the kind of participation in the divine that the liturgy envisions.

Even as we evaluate what may in some cases have been an over-energetic emphasis on active participation, I am concerned that the theological reality of what participation means must be emphasized; among other things, this means taking part in the life of the Trinity in the community of the gathered assembly at liturgical prayer. And again, externals matter. They reflect the doctrine of the incarnation and of sacramentality—important bases for active participation in and through the liturgy.

Acknowledging Critical Voices

That there are dissenting voices about the ways in which the stated goal of active participation in the reformed liturgy has been implemented is clear.[15] That they have been dismissed by some out of hand has, in my opinion, not added to what I believe should be an assessment of strengths and weaknesses of the liturgical reform. While others have undertaken a serious, detailed, and careful analysis of the critics,[16] the issue I should like to raise here concerns the assertion that the reform of the liturgy was influenced by a post-Enlightenment mentality and method. Specifically, this critique argues that understanding both what occurs through the liturgy and the intelligibility of its rites has led to an overly didactic form of liturgy, in which the practice of ceremonies and rites have been diminished in favor of commentaries containing explanations and descriptions of what is occurring. In effect, the result is more instructional than formational, more intellectual than holistic, more about hearing descriptions than about being assimilated into the mystery of God revealed and disclosed in a unique way through the liturgy. It seems to be that a certain flatness and didactic emphasis in liturgical celebrations have characterized some of the reform.

While there may have been a rush to an (over-)energetic emphasis on active participation, more recently what is now called the *ars celebrandi* has moved us toward a more reverential approach to liturgical celebration that emphasizes the variety of elements that comprise liturgy and differentiate it from a lecture, a classroom, or an event of theater. These include vesture, movement, and symbolic engagement as well as an emphasis on beauty and aesthetics, which should always characterize the liturgy (more on this in chapter 7).

My own quibble with some critics is that they cite the influence the Enlightenment had on the pioneers of the nineteenth- and twentieth-century Liturgical Movement. My sense is that the Liturgical Movement was fueled by a deeply held passion for the pastoral life of the church and the ways in which the liturgy could enhance it. From a more academic perspective, the discovery of ancient liturgical manuscripts and their being edited (largely by Benedictine monks) into accessible printed form meant that those treasures (texts and rites) could be used in the reform of the liturgy. For example, Pope Paul VI stated in the apostolic constitution *Missale Romanum*, which introduced the revised Roman Missal of 1970:

> One ought not to think, however, that this revision of the Roman Missal has been improvident. The progress that the liturgical sciences have accomplished in the last four centuries has, without a doubt, prepared the way. After the Council of Trent, the study "of ancient manuscripts of the Vatican library and of others gathered elsewhere," as Our predecessor, St. Pius V, indicates in the Apostolic Constitution *Quo primum*, has greatly helped for the revision of the Roman Missal. Since then, however, more ancient liturgical sources have been discovered and published and at the same time liturgical formulas of the Oriental Church have become better known. Many wish that the riches, both doctri-

nal and spiritual, might not be hidden in the darkness of the libraries, but on the contrary might be brought into the light to illumine and nourish the spirits and souls of Christians.[17]

That these texts were very influential on the post–Vatican II reformed liturgy is clear. That sometimes liberties were taken with the revised liturgical books is also clear. Sometimes, wordy and didactic explanations of what was taking place, or the assertion of "themes" for a particular liturgy, also occurred. The music used at liturgy in the first generation or so of the reform was clearly not always of the best quality (more on this in chapter 9). These are all worth debate and discussion.

But at the same time I also want to observe that some of the rhetoric that pits the excesses of the celebration against the forms of the rites as revised after the Council of Trent can be guilty of caricature and misrepresentation. The emphasis on *active participation* was absolutely necessary in order for the liturgy to be the liturgy and not a passive experience for the gathered assembly, or an act of a preconciliar notion of the church with the laity passively receiving from the ordained what the sacred rites confer.

My own sense is that underlying the ways we can appreciate the term *active participation* is the principle that liturgy is never totally understandable or comprehensible. In fact, the liturgy always articulates and enacts what is incomprehensible, astounding, and, yes, fascinating (in the Rudolf Otto sense in *The Idea of the Holy* as *mysterium tremendum et fascinans*). By their nature, liturgical rites are multivalent, are comprised of a number of things, and should engage all of our senses. They are not simply the speaking of the right words over the right elements to produce predetermined results. Liturgy is always that astounding complexus of ideas, images, sights, sounds, silences, people, ministers, buildings, and much more, all of which contribute to a multisensory and multidimensional experience. Liturgical understanding is more about appreciating and revering what occurs on many levels by many people, in a variety of settings. The liturgy invites us into experiences that deserve understanding and exploration, realizing at the same time that they can never be fully explained. But *understand-*

ing what occurs is always secondary to *experiencing* in ever-new ways what occurs uniquely in and through the liturgy.

Every liturgy is a unique and particular experience. While in every act of liturgy we use what we have used before—texts, rites, gestures, music, and so forth—no act of liturgy is ever repeated or the same. It is the unpredictable confluence of the liturgical rites being celebrated in particular places on particular occasions that cannot be predicted, preprogrammed, or defined. Just as we experience the liturgy in ever-new ways, the liturgy itself unfolds in ever-new ways based on ever-ancient forms.

I do not believe that calling for more "mystery" and "transcendence" in the reformed liturgy is at all illegitimate—provided that the rites conform to the guidelines set by *Sacrosanctum Concilium*:

> The rites should be distinguished by a noble simplicity; they should be short, clear, and unencumbered by useless repetitions; they should be within the people's powers of comprehension, and normally should not require much explanation. (n. 34)[18]

Examples of ways in which the liturgy can become too didactic are excessive wordiness and sound-bite explanations. I am thinking here of the presider's using far too many words at the introduction to the Penitential Rite at Mass or at the Dismissal, or in commentaries about the scripture readings to be proclaimed or in comments before the Eucharistic Prayer. An example of a sound-bite explanation would be saying before immersing or pouring water at baptism what its effects are rather than to rely on a clear and careful articulation of the prayer for the blessing of water, which contains a host of examples from salvation history about what water meant, all of which comes to bear on what the water can and does "do" in the act of baptism. Facilitating the many meanings of what baptism can and does do can only be enhanced by a clear proclamation of this blessing prayer, whose presence in the revised rite is a decided improvement over the former rites for baptism.

I think it could be said that respecting the liturgy as multivalent is crucial and that the rites of the liturgy should never be appreciated or made more understandable at the risk of lessening their potential and enormously rich effects. Understanding that liturgy is a multivalent act is meant to serve its less definable or describable results—an ever-progressive assimilation into the mystery of God and the appropriation of his saving deeds into our own broken and still not yet fully redeemed persons.

Active participation in the sacred liturgy is the *means* to serve unimaginable and indescribable goals. Letting the liturgy be the liturgy is a first step in all its complexity and beauty toward the real goals of the liturgy—assimilation into God in the communion of the church for the sake of our witnessing in the world to what we celebrate.

Conclusion

As a conclusion to this chapter it is hard to improve on what *Sacrosanctum Concilium* reminds us of:

> The Church, therefore, earnestly desires that Christ's faithful, when present at this mystery of faith, should not be there as strangers or silent spectators; on the contrary, through a good understanding of the rites and prayers they should take part in the sacred action conscious of what they are doing, with devotion and full collaboration. They should be instructed by God's word and be nourished at the table of the Lord's body; they should give thanks to God; by offering the Immaculate Victim, not only through the hands of the priest, but also with him, they should learn also to offer themselves; through Christ the Mediator, they should be drawn day by day into ever more perfect union with God and with each other, so that finally God may be all in all. (n. 48)[19]

CHAPTER THREE

Making Memory Together

Neither Reenactment, nor Memorial

I spend a good bit of time in a part of the world outside of Washington, DC, where Civil War reenactments are common. Several parishioners spend time preparing for them, gleaning and cleaning costumes from the Civil War and Colonial eras and meeting to discuss how to do what they will do. It is exciting for them to engage in historical reenactments and to tap into that part of our nation's history in that way. It is especially opportune when reenactors live in or near Richmond and Fredericksburg, Virginia—understandably so, because for them to walk where the soldiers walked, to dress as they dressed, and to reenact what they did is a great thrill.

To continue the liturgical thought beneath this example, I offer another:

It is not uncommon these days that instead of prescribed funeral rites, such as the Catholic funeral Mass, "memorial services" are requested for loved ones at which their lives are recalled and esteemed. The deceased are "remembered" by having family and friends invoke their past.

When at the Last Supper Jesus said, "Do this in memory of me," he established a command that would be observed in countless times and places and ways.

But there is a real difference between reenactments and memorial services on the one hand and what "Do this in memory of me" means and is on the other. In a sense, the former reflect the old television series *You Are There*. This series was hosted by the famous broadcast journalist Walter Cronkite, who, at the beginning of the program, would set in historical detail the scene that was about to take place. This was followed by the reenactment of such events as the signing of the *Magna Carta* or the Boston Tea Party. In effect, these plays went back in history to help us envision what happened then and thus appreciate those events. This is a reenactment. It is not what the biblical notion of what "Do this in memory of me" means. Similarly, there is a world of difference between conducting a "memorial service" for the deceased, like the one just described, and celebrating the funeral Mass, which does what Jesus asked us to do at the Eucharist.

What is the difference? While reenactments and memorial services are "you are there" in the past, the liturgy always celebrates "the future present" and takes us "back to the future."

This is to be faithful to the biblical notion of "memorial" (the Greek term is *anamnesis*, frequently used in liturgical literature, as in the last chapter), whereby we recall the past in the present in order to summon the future. St. Thomas Aquinas tells us that sacraments are *commemorative* of what happened once for all in saving history. They are *demonstrative* in that they are present experiences of the great deeds of salvation done once for all in history on our behalf. And they are *prognostic*, that is, anticipatory of their fulfillment in the future, in other words, eternity in heaven. Or in the words of the Magnificat Antiphon on the Solemnity of *Corpus Christi* (the famous *O sacrum convivium*): "How holy this feast in which Christ is our food; his passion is recalled; grace fills our hearts; and we receive a pledge of the glory to come."

Making memory together is not a historical reenactment. There are a number of reasons for this, one of which is that it is not only a looking back but is always a looking forward.

Making memory together is not a memorial service in the customary use of the term. It does not engage us through costumes and artifacts of a bygone period in recollections of a historical event but is an experience in which we "do" things that engage our total selves and through which we are brought into those unique and saving events here and now, based on the past and also based on their promise of fulfillment—"next year in Jerusalem" for the exodus or "thy kingdom come" for the Christian liturgy.

Making memory together requires that we appreciate the way the biblical authors and our liturgical tradition "tell time." Time-telling in the liturgy is not merely a chronology according to which central saving events happened, such as the call of Abraham and Sarah, followed by the exodus, followed by the birth of Jesus, or his death, resurrection, and ascension. Rather, the additional and particular notion of time that is operative in the liturgy is one in which a saving act that occurred once and for all (the Greek word for this is *ephapax*, as seen, for example, in Hebrews 7:27) at a time and place in saving history is experienced still, here and now, in a new experience until it is fulfilled at God's saving initiative and in God's good time at the end of time.

This helps explain why I normally shy away from using words such as re-*enact*, or re-*actualize*, or re-*present* to attempt to explore what the liturgy does. For me, the prefix *re-* denotes doing something again. The liturgy, on the other hand, does not do over or again what was once accomplished in history; rather, it offers us the opportunity of experiencing these selfsame saving events here and now in the present as we look toward their ful-fillment. It is through making memory together in and through the liturgy that we "enact" or "actualize" the same gracious deeds God accomplished for us and for our salvation. The fact that we make memory again and again is for our sakes. By engag-ing in them again and again, we hope to grow in the holiness that is of and from God. And as we engage in them day in and day out, they are for us the selfsame act of redemption God accomplished, experienced anew here and now as we await its fulfillment.

Another helpful phrase for describing what making memory together means comes from St. Leo the Great: all that Christ accomplished, Leo said, has passed over into his mysteries, namely, the liturgy and sacraments.[1] The theological issue at stake can be illustrated through the example of lenses used in eyeglasses or in contacts through which we see things. The lens through which the church views any experience of the past is the lens of Christ's res-urrection and ascension. Precisely because we live after Christ's resurrection and ascension and because we believe in them as an essential part of the paschal mystery, we do not act as though they did not happen. In fact, in the liturgy we always view Jesus's earthly life, suffering, and death through the prism of the resurrection. We do not put blinders on and pretend that the resurrection and ascension have not happened. This is another way of saying that in *making memory together* we always make memory of Christ in light of all that he accomplished for our salvation—accomplished once in history and experienced here and now in a cosmic moment.

In its genius and uniqueness, the liturgy is not going back in history and trying to repeat what was done then and there, as if we ever could. It is, rather, appropriating what was done once and for all then and there, commemorating it here and now as we pray for its fulfillment at a time of God's own choosing at the end of time when time will come to an end. Liturgy is not dramatizing events of the Palestinian past of the first century. Rather, it is making memory of those saving events through word and sacrament in the present as we look for their fulfillment in the kingdom of heaven when words will not be necessary and sacraments shall cease. Liturgy is not turning back the clock so that we can be at the cross or the empty tomb. Rather, in commemorating the cross and resurrection we are made free here and now, and in inviting the Lord's coming-in-glory we can put life in the here and now into proper perspective. Liturgy and sacraments are not an enclave to escape to; they are the threshold of heaven.

The Paschal Triduum

ALL OF SALVATION IN EACH DAY

When applied to the liturgical celebration of the Triduum[2]—from the Evening Mass of the Lord's Supper on Holy Thursday through the Mass of Easter Sunday—what we commemorate is not the unfolding of a passion play that begins with betrayal and ends with triumph. Rather, what we do in the Triduum is to commemorate the entirety of Christ's saving deeds accomplished once for all through successive liturgies; yet through each of them we experience at the same time the entirety of the paschal mystery and of Christ's salvation in the church all at once and again and again. While each day obviously has a different emphasis, we never enter into any one facet of the Triduum without the sure hope that comes from Christ's resurrected life—his resurrection from the dead and our resurrected life in and with him. No, we were not there "when they crucified my Lord." But we are here in "this year of Our Lord" commemorating that unique death through the lens that is the resurrection.

We do not reenact anything from saving history in and through the liturgy; rather, we make memory of it all together as one event of redemption with and for each other as members of each other. We do not separate Holy Thursday night from Good Friday or Holy Saturday, the Easter Vigil or Easter Day; rather, we enter into each of those liturgies knowing that Christ has indeed risen. He does not need to rise again. We commemorate his paschal mystery because we have to rise again, and again, and again. The liturgy is not a biography of Jesus. It is the placing of our lives into Christ's very life and love and the experience of all that life and love really means this side of heaven.

While there are dramatic elements to the liturgy—sights, sounds, smells—they are not dramatic effects of reenacting the life of Jesus. The dramatic effects surround our commemoration of the paschal mystery through the ritual's prayers and actions. This is to say that while we may wash feet on Holy Thursday, we do so in the context of the Eucharist, the memorial of Christ's paschal mystery through the word proclaimed from the ambo and the eucharistic sacrifice enacted at the altar. We do not do so by reenacting the Last Supper in the Upper Room. The title of the liturgy for this evening says as much—Thursday of the *Lord's* Supper, not his *last* supper.

The same word *Lord* is used in the title for the Good Friday liturgy—Friday of the Passion of the *Lord*. It does not say "of Jesus" because Jesus died once for all. What we make memory of is his paschal triumph, accomplished by a death that takes away all deaths forever precisely because it was followed by resurrection and ascension. Death has been made whole in Christ's resurrection; our rising through him to new life is at the center of our faith. We make memory of this in and through every liturgy because all liturgy is paschal—Christ's paschal triumph and our passing over to new life through him. We (dare to) call it the paschal *mystery*, not that it is a problem to be solved but simply because it is too rich, too unfathomable, too profound ever to experience or understand completely or entirely.

The two options for the prayer (the Latin used is *oratio*, not *collecta*) with which the Celebration of the Passion of the Lord on Friday of Holy Week (Good Friday) begins are illustrative in this regard. The first says:

> Remember your mercies, O Lord,
> and with your eternal protection sanctify your servants,
> for whom Christ your Son,
> by the shedding of his Blood,
> established the Paschal Mystery.
> Who lives and reigns forever and ever.

Here the shedding of Christ's blood is juxtaposed with the establishment of "the Paschal Mystery," meaning the entire sweep of betrayal, obedience, suffering, death, resurrection, and ascension. The second option reads:

> O God, who by the Passion of Christ your Son, our Lord,
> abolished the death inherited from ancient sin
> by every succeeding generation,
> grant that just as, being conformed to him,
> we have borne by the law of nature
> the image of the man on earth,
> so by the sanctification of grace
> we may bear the image of the Man of heaven.

While the term *passion* is used here, note that it is accompanied immediately by words that modify it in an important theological way. We do not address "Jesus" here, or in any liturgical prayer, for that matter, without adding the important theological terms *Christ* or *Lord*. This is to suggest that the liturgy is always a commemoration of the whole paschal mystery through which he became the Christ and Lord and of our incorporation into it.

This is also evident in the Prayer after Communion on (Good) Friday of Holy Week:

Almighty and ever-living God,
who have restored us to life
by the blessed Death and Resurrection of your Christ,
preserve in us the work of your mercy,
that by partaking of this mystery,
we may have a life unceasingly devoted to you.

The operative phrase here is "who have restored us to life by the blessed Death and Resurrection." The prayer does not speak of passion or death only. It bespeaks what we always commemorate—death and resurrection together.

There are at least two implications to be drawn from these assertions about making memorial together and about Good Friday. One has to do with devotions that focus exclusively on only one element of the Triduum; the other is on preaching during this period.

THE INCOMPLETENESS OF NONLITURGICAL DEVOTIONS

While I will treat devotions separately in chapter 10, I simply point out here that there is a theological and liturgical incompleteness to devotions about the passion that do not at least refer in some substantial way to the hope that comes from appropriating Christ's resurrection as well as his death. Precisely because we believe in death *and* resurrection, our prayer needs to focus on both, even if in the Triduum the emphasis might be on death, sin, and distance from God on a particular day, and on another day resurrected glory, forgiveness, and reconciliation with all of humanity and creation. Obviously I am thinking here of the Good Friday *tre ore*, the three-hour devotion from noon to three o'clock in the afternoon. There are also street processions following Jesus as he walks to Calvary, or following the weeping Madonna as she accompanies the corpse of her crucified Son to the tomb.

There is an inherent hopefulness and optimism that comes from making memory together and experiencing the paschal mystery in and through the liturgy that is not conveyed when suffering and death alone are the center of the devotion. To view Mel Gibson's *The Passion of the Christ*, for example, is not to engage in the liturgy of Good Friday. The difference is reenactment (in a cinematic or stylized way) over against making memory together.

PREACHING ON GOOD FRIDAY

Any preaching on Good Friday that even hints that this day was or is tragic, or that we are in mourning, or that grief should swamp us, or that we are watching Jesus die again is inaccurate theologically and misguided pastorally. We preach Christ crucified, says St. Paul in 1 Corinthians 1:23, and indeed we do. But we do so by asserting that he is the Christ, the resurrected Lord, the Messiah, and the Anointed One. On Good Friday, we do not preach solely about Jesus' dying. We preach about his new life and ours in his, accomplished through his death and resurrection. That his death had to occur is clear. But that it is commemorated on Good Friday in isolation from his resurrection is not what occurs in the liturgy, and our preaching should not hint at that. What our preaching might well speak about is how his death has saved us, inspired by the first reading from the Book of Isaiah— "It was our infirmities that he bore, our sufferings that he endured....He was pierced for our offenses...[and] by his stripes we were healed" (Isa 53:4–5). Or it could address how the obedience of Christ Our High Priest brought an end to what we inherited from the disobedience of Adam and Eve (second reading from the Letter to the Hebrews). Or it could mirror the theological vision of the Gospel of John proclaimed on Good Friday, emphasizing the exaltation of Christ to the throne of the cross. But whatever is preached, it should not indicate that on Good Friday we are only part of the way to redemption. Good Friday is about the totality of our redemption as much as is Easter Sunday, the Solemnity of the Ascension, Pentecost, or Christmas.

The Triduum climaxes with the Easter Vigil, called the "mother of all vigils." Like the other Triduum liturgies, this one has very dramatic elements involving earth, air, fire, and water. That the liturgy begins outdoors in the open air says a great deal about the earthiness and primal character of all of our liturgy (more on this in chapter 4). The soaring new fire shatters the darkness of the impending night. The procession following the flickering paschal candle offers us a glimpse (literally) of what even the light from a candle can mean in the pilgrimage of our life on this earth. The sounds of bells and organ bring their silence during Lent to an end in the Glory to God and Easter alleluias. The immersing in water gives new life to catechumens and the liturgical renewal for the already baptized is in water blessed and generously sprinkled. The placing of fresh bread and wine for consecration at the altar is a reminder that all is indeed new in and through the paschal celebrations (see the second option for the second reading on Easter Day, 1 Corinthians 5:6–8 about the yeast in the dough). What better complement to all of this than the words of the first Easter Preface:

> For he is the true Lamb
> who has taken away the sins of the world;
> by dying he destroyed our death,
> and by rising, restored our life.

In the first chapter, I indicated the importance of checking and being attentive to the pronouns in the texts of the liturgy. In my opinion, the second most important thing in understanding liturgical prayers is the verbs and the way the verbs connect us with what happened in Christ's paschal mystery. All of that is happening to us through the liturgy. This Preface is poignant in the way it subtly confirms what the liturgy always accomplishes—putting an end to death and inviting us to rise to ever-new heights by enabling us to put to death that which is death-dealing in our lives and to embrace what is really life-giving, always from God through his Son.

It seems to me that one of the real "success stories" of the liturgical reforms after Vatican II is that the reality of Triduum is seared in our consciousness in a way that it was not prior to the reform (it started in experimental form in 1951, was published in 1955, and was first celebrated in 1956, then revised after Vatican II). That we are very careful about how we celebrate it is crucial in order that it not appear as a reenactment or a "memorial service" of our own doing.

Christmas Celebrations

If the Triduum with its attendant preparation in Lent and its extension through the Easter season is a real "winner," the liturgical celebrations of Advent and Christmas can be judged less so, because what are largely factors from our (American Protestant) culture so influence attitudes and behaviors at this time of year. The juxtaposition of Thanksgiving at the end of November followed in four weeks by Christmas and then New Year's makes for a very full end-of-the-year "holiday" season. The idea and ideal of families gathering more than once in this short period of time make for logistical challenges and sometimes nightmares, especially given the number and variety of family units in society today. In addition, a post–World War II prosperity in America has enabled many people to spend far more when exchanging gifts than ever possible before.

SECULAR ANTICIPATION VS. LITURGICAL FULFILLMENT

There is also the issue of the ways we often anticipate things and events. Theologically, the liturgy rests on many premises, among which is *hodie*—"*Today* Christ is born for us" (Christmas Antiphon); and *haec dies*—"This *is the day* the Lord has made" (Easter Antiphon). But the reality is that, especially at Christmas, we "anticipate" the feast in a number of ways. In our culture, Christmas decorations, music, and parties abound, beginning immediately after Halloween, so that the day of the feast itself can sometimes seem redundant, and we ask, "Haven't we done that already?" Strictly speaking, no, we have not celebrated Christmas yet.

With this in mind, I think a number of issues might well be raised about how we celebrate the liturgies of Christmas.

Obviously there is important historical and theological background as to how and why the liturgies on Christmas Day and of the Christmas season evolved.[3] Up through Vatican II, there were three eucharistic liturgies for Christmas Day and there was (and is) the Liturgy of the Hours from First Vespers through Second Vespers on Christmas Day. As in all such cases, comprehending what a feast or a season means theologically and liturgically means taking into account all of the scripture readings, euchological texts, antiphons, psalm selections, and patristic readings from the Office of Readings from all the liturgies in order to try to grasp the breadth of what is being commemorated. Historical insights about what set of texts evolved, and when, are also important parts of the equation.

For Christmas, this means that the scripture readings for the Mass during the Day—Hebrews 1:1–6, about God speaking now through his Son, and the Prologue to the Gospel of John (1:1–14), about the preexistence of the Incarnate Word and the Word become flesh—are really two convenient lenses through which to view this feast. Like any other feast, Christmas is not a biography of whose feast day it is. This is to suggest that the retelling of the accounts of Jesus' birth from the Gospel of Luke at the Mass at Night (Luke 2:1–14) and the Mass at Dawn (Luke 2:15–20) should be understood in such a way that, through word and sacrament, we are incorporated into what we celebrate. That is the theological reality of what it means that the Messiah was born in order to begin the work of our redemption and our continual appropriation of that reality, not the details of human birth alone. In the words of Raymond Brown, what we look forward to during Advent is *The Birth of the Messiah* and the coming of *An Adult Christ at Christmas*.

That this is the theological reality of what we celebrate is underscored by the "O Antiphons" used at Evening Prayer and as the Gospel Acclamations from December 17 to 23. The antiphons are named for the O that begins each: "O Wisdom of our God Most High," "O Leader of the House of Israel," "O Root of Jesse's stem," "O Key of David," "O Emmanuel," "O King of all nations," and "O Radiant Dawn" (all of these here as they are listed in the *Lectionary for Mass*). Each of these titles is worth study and reflection. All of them taken together help us focus on Christmas as a feast of the incarnation through which we commemorate "the beginning of our redemption" (from the Prayer over the Gifts, Christmas Vigil Mass).

The pastoral challenge occurs when all this "liturgical anticipation," rich in its theology, comes face to face with the cultural reality that the celebration of the Christmas Vigil or Midnight Mass has replaced the celebration of Mass during the Day on Christmas. In classic Roman liturgy, vigil Masses occurred only for a feast with a high rank, such as the Solemnity of John the Baptist, of Saints Peter and Paul, or of the Assumption of Mary. The vigil was celebrated, and then on the next day the liturgy for the feast proper was celebrated as well.

What about what we now customarily call the Vigil Mass for Sunday that is celebrated on Saturday night? The term is really not accurate. What we actually celebrate is the Sunday liturgy itself but on the evening before, in accord with the Jewish telling of time, with a new day starting at dusk.

All of this is to say that what we now have in place for the scripture readings on Christmas Eve should be seen as leading up to our *returning* for the Christmas Day Mass. In fact, these texts for the Christmas Vigil Mass were added to the Missal after Vatican II; they were not from any prior liturgical tradition in the church. They are Isaiah 62:1–5, about the Lord's relationship to his people; Acts 13:16–17, 22–25, in which Paul bears witness to the Son of David, respecting his genealogy; and the genealogy itself from Matthew 1:1–15, accompanied by the description of how Christ was born. As such, they brim over with meaning about the human genealogy of Jesus' family tree and how his human birth came to be. That this is then complemented by the scripture readings the next day and the theological implications of what that human birth means by reflecting on the Hebrews and Johannine texts is important theologically.

The mystery of the incarnation includes the human birth of Jesus the Messiah. But liturgically the celebration of Christmas is about the divinization of the human race through God's divine Son. In other words, the liturgy celebrates the reality of our becoming like God through the Son of God, who became one of us. Liturgical celebrations are about our being incorporated into what Christ accomplished for us once and for all, and then our experiencing his saving acts anew—and hopefully in a deeper manner—here and now as we await their fulfillment in the kingdom of heaven. The famous phrase of St. Leo the Great in the

Christmas Collect prayer (also said on December 17) should resound in any and every celebration of Christmas:

> O God, who wonderfully created the dignity of human
>   nature
> and still more wonderfully restored it,
> grant, we pray,
> that we may share in the divinity of Christ
> who humbled himself to share in our humanity.

This incarnation emphasis can be ascertained from the fact that the earliest Gospel passage employed for the celebration of Christmas was the Prologue to St. John's Gospel (John 1:1–14), which, in contrast to the Gospels of Matthew and Luke, concentrates not on the physical birth of the Lord but rather on the theological idea of the incarnation of the preexistent Word. The sermons of Pope Leo the Great (mid-fifth century) indicate that John 1 was the Gospel read at the eucharistic liturgy on December 25. The companion text for it—used to this day—is Hebrews 1:1–6, about how God spoke in times past in various ways, but now and forever speaks in a definitive way through his Son.

THREE MASSES, ONE LENS OF THE INCARNATION

Eventually, not one but three Masses were provided for Christmas. The remote origins of this practice can probably be found in the celebration of the Jerusalem church, which began on the Vigil of Epiphany (Jerusalem's original nativity celebration), with a eucharistic liturgy celebrated at Bethlehem, followed by a procession back to Jerusalem for a Eucharist on the following day. By the latter part of the fifth century, Rome had its own "Bethlehem," the Basilica of St. Mary Major, which housed the crib of the Lord that had been transported from the Holy Land.

There "at the crib," the pope celebrated a eucharistic liturgy during the night of December 24 to 25. (It is notable that this Mass has never officially been called "Midnight Mass"; hence, an appropriate critique of "It Came upon a Midnight Clear" is that it is too "chronological" compared with the title of "the Mass during the Night," not to mention the fact that Masses celebrated before midnight have recently become more prevalent.) The next morning the pope celebrated the Eucharist at St. Peter's Basilica on the Vatican Hill. The celebration at St. Peter's had been the first form of the Christmas liturgy and had been introduced in the fourth century. St. Peter's was an apt spot for it, since the Vatican Hill overlooks the city of Rome. In other words, one can see the rising sun coming up over the city's horizon from this location.

The third Mass of Christmas was added some time during the sixth century. The Byzantine court had taken up residence on the Palatine Hill. On the return procession to St. Peter's from St. Mary Major, the pope and his entourage stopped at the Church of St. Anastasia at the foot of the Palatine Hill for the Mass at Dawn, also called the Shepherd's Mass, because that portion of St. Luke's infancy narrative was read at this liturgy. There is some evidence that one reason why the pope celebrated this Mass was that the community there refused to celebrate Christmas and preferred to celebrate the Epiphany. The pope's celebration of Christmas with them was akin to "the family that prays together stays together."

The Johannine Prologue clearly emphasizes the creation and re-creation of the world through the Word becoming flesh (v 14). It does not describe the events of Jesus' human birth. But when the other Gospel texts about the human birth of Christ are read through this lens, that part of the Gospel assigned for the Christmas Mass at Night—when the infant is called "Messiah and Lord"—stands out, as does the phrase in the second reading, "the appearing of the glory of the great God and of our Savior Christ Jesus...who sacrificed himself for us." In a sense, the Responsorial Psalm of the Christmas Mass at (Mid)night says it all because it combines the liturgical celebration in "this year of our Lord" with the mystery of Christ appearing in the flesh, and we sing, "Today is born a savior, Christ the Lord." Again note the importance of *hodie*: "today."

A useful exercise in itself is to review both the scripture texts assigned for Christmas and its vigil, and the Missal's prayers for Christmas Day and its vigil, to see the names used to describe who it is who was born for us. The name *Jesus* only appears once without a modifier, and that is in the Gospel for the Christmas Vigil

Mass: "You are to name him Jesus...." Otherwise, the name appears with modifiers; for example, "Jesus Christ" (twice in the Gospel, Vigil Mass); "Savior Christ Jesus" (second reading, Mass at Night), and "Jesus Christ our Savior" (second reading, Mass at Dawn). The rest of the references are to "Christ the Lord" (Responsorial Psalm, Mass at Night); and to "God with us" and "first-born son." In the Gospel for the Mass during the Day, *Word* is used four times, and *Jesus Christ* is used once toward its end. This spare usage of the name *Jesus* is reflected in the rest of the Roman Missal (and in the tradition of the liturgy of the Roman Rite), in which it is never used except with a modifier; in the Missal, *Jesus* is used on its own only in antiphons quoting the scriptures.[4]

With this exercise in mind, I would like to make three theological points:

First, the term *Jesus* on its own means "the one who saves us from our sins." If you have ever seen a sign saying, "Jesus saves," that sign is, in fact, redundant because *Jesus* means "savior."

Second, the spare use of this term in the *lex orandi* and the broad use of other terms and modifiers tells us that the church's wisdom invites us to reflect on the breadth and depth of the wonder of the incarnation by offering us a kaleidoscope of images to describe the indescribable and unutterable manifestation of God in human flesh. The term *Jesus* is totally insufficient according to what we pray in and through the liturgy.

The third point is a bit more delicate and subtle. If *Jesus* is never used in the church's *orandi* and only sparingly in the scripture readings, then should we not evaluate how often, where, and in what manner we use *Jesus* in the music we sing at the liturgy and in the comments made by presiding priests during the liturgy? (For example, is it really correct theologically to choose such songs as "Alleluia, Sing to Jesus," or "I Heard the Voice of Jesus Say"?)

The intention of those charged with assigning scripture selections for the Lectionary was that the use of these selections at the Vigil presumed that the assembly would celebrate another Christmas liturgy—during the night or at dawn or during the day. In fact, that is a rare occurrence. Some parishes wisely eschew the vigil scripture readings for the (Mid)night Mass texts. But even here it takes a skillful preacher to invite the gathered assembly to hear more than the events of Jesus' birth and to experience the inherent divinization that Christmas celebrates. That the Johannine Prologue offers a key insight about what Christmas means is reflected in the fact that, according to the *Lectionary for Mass*, these same texts from Isaiah, Hebrews, and John assigned to the Day Mass can be used for any of the Christmas Masses—its vigil, at night, and at dawn. This might well be a way of keeping our theological lenses on straight even as we allow the liturgy of the vigil to be the liturgy of Christmas for a large number of those in our assemblies.

That the incarnation is the theological center of the solemnities of Christmas and the Annunciation is reflected in the rubrics requiring that on these days we kneel during the part of the Creed that mentions the incarnation. That we bow at these words each time we say them in the Creed is its own statement about their importance. (Interestingly, there is a parallel here with the rubrics for the Tridentine Mass: when the priest recited the Prologue as the "last Gospel," he had to genuflect at the words "and the Word became flesh and dwelt among us.") I think a good case could be made that the fact that presiders bow to the assembly before and after their incensing at Mass, and that monks bow to the altar and then to each other in some monasteries, reflects a thoroughly incarnational principle: we meet Christ in each other.

The issue here is to rediscover incarnation—not "just" the nativity—as a principle of the Christmas liturgy. Again, the Creed (now) reads:

> For us men and for our salvation
> He came down from heaven,
>   was incarnate of the Virgin Mary
>   and was made man.

The liturgy of Christmas is about the incarnation of the Word made flesh and the implications of that incarnation for us in our human flesh. Both the Johannine Prologue and the first words of Genesis are "in the beginning." These are not chronological references but an invitation to luxuriate in the events annually recounted through those texts—the creation of every living thing and that the Word became flesh and dwelt among us who share in his glory—especially at Christmas. The Prayers over the Offerings at Christmas put it this way:

> that through this most holy exchange
> we may be found in the likeness of Christ
> in whom our nature is united to you, (Mass at Night)

And also:

> that, just as Christ was born a man
> yet shone forth as God,
> so may these earthly gifts
> confer on us what is divine. (Mass at dawn)

In light of what I argued at the beginning of this chapter—that the liturgy is not a reenactment or a memorial service—and of this exposition of the theology and liturgy of Christmas, a number of issues and questions arise. For example:

- What happens when Christmas carols replace the antiphons for the Masses at Christmas? What does that say about the theologically significant realities of salvation and redemption? Do they send us back like an episode of *You Are There*?

- What happens when the preaching at Christmas is about "having no room at the inn" rather than about our being made like God? This is seen dramatically in the pivotal verse from the Johannine Prologue:

> And the Word became flesh
> and made his dwelling among us,
> and we saw his glory,
> the glory as of the Father's only Son,
> full of grace and truth. (v 14; NAB)

- What happens when we use candles at the Christmas Vigil Mass when in fact the paschal candle is the only required addition to sanctuary décor? (Candles are a baptismal symbol and are used by all who participate at the Easter Vigil.)

- What happens when we dramatize the proclamation of the Gospel at the Christmas Vigil Mass, most often by (understandably) restive children, so that the performances and costumes of shepherds and angels preoccupy parents whose (understandably) restive little ones "perform" the gospel at the Vigil Mass, which gospel needs the Johannine prologue (and all the others as well) to help draw out the full meaning of Christmas?

- What happens when some groups choose to celebrate the Mass of Christmas for the nine days preceding December 25? What happens to the Advent liturgy from December 17 to 24, which recounts the events leading to Christ's human birth and includes several personages from "the root of Jesse" in the history of salvation, most prominently St. John the Baptist?

Eschatology

In *Sacrosanctum Concilium* we read:

In the earthly liturgy we take part in a foretaste of that heavenly liturgy which is celebrated in the holy city of Jerusalem toward which we journey as pilgrims, where Christ is sitting at the right hand of God, a minister of the holies and of the true tabernacle; we sing a hymn to the Lord's glory with all the warriors of the heavenly army; venerating the memory of the saints, we hope for some part and fellowship with them; we eagerly await the Saviour, Our Lord Jesus Christ, until

He, our life, shall appear and we too will appear with
Him in glory. (n. 8)

Liturgy and sacraments are seen in this light as privileged but provisional experiences of God's presence that will be finally and
fully realized only in the kingdom. They are regarded as unique,
but they are not the exclusive locus for communicating with God,
who is revealed in all life. The eschatological nature of the sacraments and the pilgrim nature of the church as underscored since
Vatican II have helped theologians reemphasize how the sacraments are intense experiences of the risen Christ and the kingdom, while also serving to point believers beyond the present
sacramental experience to a yearning for their full realization in
God's kingdom.

This is simply to draw out an intrinsic aspect of liturgy's
memorial nature as we make memory together. All liturgy is
paschal in that it is the church's commemoration and experience of
being drawn into Christ's paschal dying and rising *until he comes
in glory*. This is to draw out the not-yet-ness of the liturgy even as
we commemorate through the liturgy our present experience of the
past redemptive deeds of God for us and for our salvation.

I am not the first to suggest that the Western liturgy is far
more attuned to experiencing the (real) presence and action of
Christ in the present based on the past, rather than to appreciate
the liturgy only as "the future present,"[5] always eschatological in
its nature and in its fullness. I can remember reading Geoffrey
Wainwright's *Eucharist and Eschatology*[6] in the early 1970s, with
his heavy reliance on exposing and explaining the eschatological
parts of liturgies of the Eucharist, both East and West, and have
since been forever challenged to see the liturgy's incompleteness,
as well as its reality as the fullness of our experience of redemption here and now. Almost all of our reformed prayers of blessing
for water, oils, and chrism, and in particular the Eucharistic
Prayers, refer specifically to the eschatological nature of our faith
and its celebration in and through the liturgy.[7] At times their
inclusion helps to overcome the lack of explicit references to
Christ's second coming in such revered texts as the Roman Canon
itself. In the present Eucharistic Prayer III, we now pray:

Therefore, O Lord, as we celebrate the memorial
of the saving Passion of your Son,
his wondrous Resurrection
and Ascension into heaven,
and as we look forward to his second coming,
we offer you in thanksgiving
this holy and living sacrifice.

And in Eucharistic Prayer IV, we pray:

Therefore, O Lord,
as we now celebrate the memorial of our redemption,
we remember Christ's Death,
and his descent to the realm of the dead,
we proclaim his Resurrection
and his Ascension to your right hand,
and as we await his coming in glory,
we offer you his Body and Blood,
the sacrifice acceptable to you
which brings salvation to the whole world.

RITES FOR THE SICK AND DYING

Allow me to suggest something we Catholics have done well:
the rites for the anointing of the sick and the prayers for the
dying. If there were ever a "sleeper" among the liturgical reforms
from Vatican II when compared with the previous liturgy, it is the
anointing of the sick. The fact that four of the chapters of the *Rite
for the Pastoral Care of the Sick and the Dying* are dedicated to
visiting the sick, bringing them communion, and praying for the
faith-filled passage from this life, and that these activities can be
performed by both ordained and nonordained ministers, means
that this richness is opened far more than the previous experience
of "extreme unction."[8] My own assessment is that the prayers for
the dying are among the most beautiful of the reformed liturgy
and deserve wide exposure and usage.

The communal anointing of the sick (which is celebrated
three or four times a year in the parish where I regularly preside
and preach) can be an extraordinary experience of consolation

and healing for the sick and for those whom we think are well. Whenever I preach at a communal celebration of the anointing of the sick, I always distinguish a physical "cure" from a "healing" and emphasize that the sacrament is about a spiritual healing and integration of life as we prepare for the journey to the kingdom of heaven. I have also been known to say that, as much as it is a privilege to impose hands on and anoint the foreheads and hands of the aging and the terminally ill, it is also the case that they who are obviously physically weak and aging and who suffer from terminal illnesses really anoint us, in fact, in the sense that their obvious disability or debilitating illness should reveal to us what really matters in life.

In 1986, Senator Jacob Javits from New York died of Lou Gehrig's disease. A convention center being constructed on the west side of Manhattan was named in his honor. Despite the ravages of the disease, Senator Javits attended the dedication. He was in a wheelchair and was on oxygen most of the time. He was allowed to speak for fifteen seconds at the dedication. He thanked the assembled crowd for the honor, admitted his disease, and then said, "I'm the lucky one. I know my life is terminal. But all life is terminal."

I often think that those we anoint at such communal celebrations reveal to the rest of us that, in effect, all life is terminal. They can and should be signs to us of what really lasts—signs that this good life leads to an even better life in the kingdom of heaven.

Sometimes the sacrament of the sick cannot be celebrated at a communal Eucharist for a number of legitimate pastoral reasons, not to mention emergencies. But if possible, it is always accompanied by the reception of communion. Again this can be administered by both ordinary and extraordinary ministers of the Eucharist. When administered for the last time, we call it *viaticum*—"food for the journey" to eternal life. But in a sense the Eucharist is always *viaticum*, food to strengthen us for the journey of life as well, with all of life's trials, sufferings, and defeats. The Eucharist is called the real presence, and it can heal us as we deal with the sense of God's absence when life's sorrows wear us down. The fact that communion to the sick can be administered regularly and frequently is another of the post–Vatican II liturgical "winners."

ORDER OF CHRISTIAN FUNERALS

Catholics do funerals right. The post–Vatican II funeral rites have legitimately been acclaimed as a major pastoral success, and legitimately so. The fact that the rite is now called an "order" means that it has successive stages: vigil, Eucharist, and burial. These three "stations" also signify the movement from grief (especially noted at the vigil), to hope in the deceased's passage through Christ's paschal victory (in the Eucharist), to final resting (burial). The presumption is that all three stages are observed. Pastorally these are very effective when taken together; they shape and form how we humans deal with suffering, sorrow, and death. We should never underestimate the value of the way the liturgy shapes our commemoration of the deceased and the way it confirms the faith of those who mourn their loss.

Along with weddings, funerals are often among the most sensitive pastoral situations for the celebration of the liturgy. They are often occasions to minister to both those who practice their faith regularly and those who practice sporadically if at all (the numbers of which are sadly on the increase). All funerals call for pastoral patience and sensitivity, some more than others.

Most often, pastoral ministers and priests find it enormously helpful when they can meet with the family of the deceased, or even with the soon-to-be-deceased themselves to prepare the funeral liturgy. Some family members find that when they have a terminally ill family member, praying over the possible scripture readings that can be used at funerals is very consoling and helps them put the impending death of their loved one in the proper faith perspective. It also helps in the selection of the texts to be proclaimed at the Eucharist. Insights about the deceased's background or life story that can help the preacher appreciate who he or she was can obviously be very important.

It is sometimes the case, however, that requests will be made that are not in conformity with the funeral liturgy. Often these concern music and eulogies. Recall what I mentioned in the

What We Have Done, What We Have Failed to Do

Introduction: Just because it has been done elsewhere does not mean it is right. When someone views a funeral on television, often what occurs is seared into that person's memory and not infrequently is used as data on which to base a request for music, or the number and content of the eulogy or eulogies, or the content of the general intercessions. Parish wedding coordinators and those who assist with funeral planning (musicians, for example) all have their stories of things requested on the basis that they were "seen elsewhere"; not all of these things should be imitated. Allow me simply to note three instances of what was done at a funeral but that might have better been done differently.

The first is the account from a music minister friend who watched the televised funeral in Boston of the wife of former Speaker of the House Tip O'Neill. One of the music selections during the funeral was "I'll Be with You in Apple Blossom Time." Whether another family member wanted this piece of music or Mrs. O'Neill herself, what this did was establish for some the impression that such music was acceptable for funerals. It is not.

Second, when Senator Ted Kennedy was laid to rest after a long and very debilitating illness, his grandchildren all offered prayers at the Prayer of the Faithful during the funeral Mass at the Church of the Holy Trinity in Washington, DC. In addition to the fact that some of the children were barely able to read, all of the prayers were "in thanksgiving" for attributes or deeds done by the Senator. These should have been prayers of petition, not of thanksgiving.

Third, several years ago, a priest friend was savagely murdered in the rectory in the middle of the night. The funeral Mass was attended by hundreds of family and friends of this extraordinary priest. The bishop who presided began the liturgy by reading a letter from the former archbishop of Washington, Cardinal Baum. The Mass proceeded and ended in just about an hour. It was then that we were asked to be seated. Four eulogies ensued, despite the archdiocesan regulation that only one eulogy is allowed. The eulogies ended, close to a second hour later.

My own sense of the eulogy is that it "fits" better theologically at the vigil for the deceased, where it is allowed according to the revised rite. Through the eulogy or eulogies, aspects of the person's life and shared remembrance can help fill out his or her biography and good deeds. The setting allows the time for stories to be open-ended. Such is not the case in a funeral Eucharist. The funeral Mass is the time for attention to be placed less on the biography and personality of the deceased and more on that person's death and hope for new life in eternity. If eulogies are given at the end of the funeral Mass, the gathered assembly is wrenched back to the biography and the individual, rather than the person now joining all those who have gone before us in faith, who also lie in death awaiting final resurrection.

A few years ago, I was invited to preside and preach at the funeral Mass of a retired Air Force lieutenant colonel at the chapel on the grounds of Arlington National Cemetery. I was pleased to do so. But the practice was that there was no prior viewing and that the time in the chapel was forty-five minutes, no more. That meant I was unable to invite family and friends to share reminiscences at the vigil service. One son asked whether he could deliver a eulogy. I said, yes, provided that it be two minutes in length and be delivered before the Collect prayer. The length was so that I could preach for slightly more time (depending on the actual length of his eulogy). And I asked that it be done at the start of the liturgy so that the theological movement from biography and grief to hope because of our faith in Christ's resurrection would be maintained.

A final comment concerns the words that those who preside often say at funerals (with more to be said in chapter 8). I am concerned when well-meaning presiders indicate in their comments at the start or the end of the liturgy that the deceased is now with God in heaven. In point of fact, the funeral rites speak of passage and hope. The (Catholic) consoling doctrine of purgatory is that we who remain have the privilege of praying for the deceased who may well still await final passage into heaven.

"AS WE AWAIT THE BLESSED HOPE..."

The theology of the liturgical year is simply ignored when we neglect its inherent eschatological dimension and celebrate the liturgy as though it were historical reminiscence. Through the liturgy, we do not engage in a "you are there" activity. What we celebrate is "the future present" by means of going "back to the future" and celebrating these eternal mysteries *today, on this day*. If we do not get this eschatological dimension of all liturgy right, then we will always suffer from not having been there when they crucified the Lord, or at the Last Supper, or at the empty tomb. We were never meant to be there physically or historically. In God's providence, we were and are meant to be here and to commemorate the liturgy as the past, present, and future of our redemption with an eye to its complete fulfillment in heaven. Liturgy is always heaven *on* earth even as we acclaim that heaven *and* earth are filled with God's glory.

When my Australian students used to complain that their celebration of the liturgical year was predicated on the seasons as celebrated in the northern hemisphere, I was initially stuck and challenged. But it did not take me long to think it through a bit and to offer a few thoughts. The first was that their celebration of Christmas just after the longest day of the year (this being the southern hemisphere) allowed them to experience "the Light of the World" in a very different way than we did. I also pointed out that the whole church celebrates the Triduum when it does because it is about the same time of the calendar year when Jesus died and rose, not because it is springtime in the northern hemisphere. And finally I suggested that their celebration of the Triduum when much of the earth was going into dormancy was a reminder for all of us that Easter is not about the return of life in creation at springtime but new life in Christ, no matter the weather. Their experience of Easter was decidedly eschatological compared with ours when it coincides with spring. Then again, all liturgy is supposed to be decidedly eschatological, no matter the seasons of the cosmos.

CHAPTER FOUR

The Sacramental Principle

"Sign Language"

Especially in an Internet world of "breaking news," IMs, and constant Twitter feeds, we are inundated with words. Yet we often say that "actions speak louder than words." Human beings communicate through both—and so does the liturgy. This chapter concerns how God speaks to us and we speak to God through the words and actions of the liturgy.

While I do not agree with the fiercest attacks on the revised liturgy that argue it is too cerebral and reflects a post-Enlightenment concern for understanding and comprehension,[1] I do want to observe that some of the ways in which we may have implemented the revised liturgy have made it a highly verbal, didactic, and (overly) wordy experience. I will deal with words in worship more directly in chapters 5 and 6. Here I want to address the way the liturgy uses words as well as signs and actions, and their substratum—what I call the sacramental principle. In what follows I will use the terms *sacramentality* and *sacramental principle* interchangeably. While I understand these terms to be equivalent, of late I have become increasingly aware that the phrase *sacramental principle* might be better since it denotes exactly what sacramentality is, namely, the substratum (a "principle") upon which liturgy and sacraments function. It is something that is pervasive in any and every act of liturgy. Theologically and liturgically, the sacramental principle is directly related to the incarnational principle. This is to say that we humans worship God by using our bodies, minds, and hearts, and by using all that lives and moves on this good earth and all that exists in the cosmos.[2]

In the fifth century, St. Augustine coined this pithy yet profoundly insightful phrase: "A sacrament is a sign of a sacred thing." That this phrase has taken deep roots in Catholic teaching on sacraments is evidenced by the fact that, in the thirteenth century, St. Thomas Aquinas used it to introduce the section of his *Summa* dealing with the sacraments, asserting that "a sacrament is a kind of sign."[3]

When the Western church started to be concerned about describing what sacraments "do" or "effect," the language of "sign" (used as early as St. Augustine) continued to be used and the word "cause" was added by Peter Lombard in the mid-twelfth century (*IV Sententiarum* d. 1, n. 2). Thomas Aquinas combined these two words into the phrase *significando causant* (*De Veritate* q. 27, a. 4 at 13). This phrase continued to be influential on Scholastic and subsequent theologians.[4]

In the liturgy, we communicate with God and God communicates with us through signs, not through words only. A primary category for understanding sacraments is that they are "sacred" signs. In a very real sense, sacraments are the church's official "sign language," engaged in by humans and expressive of the way human beings interact with God and with one another.

It is often said, especially today when we look for the chief characteristics of Catholicism, that we belong to a "sacramental church." This is quite correct. But some commentaries on this phrase misfire when they turn immediately to the celebration of the liturgy and the seven sacraments as external expressions of Catholicism's uniqueness. While this is not at all wrong, I want to argue that it is the principle of sacramentality—or the sacramental principle—that undergirds Catholicism's uniqueness and that also undergirds the celebration of the liturgy and the sacraments. "The story behind the story" of sacramentality is as important a Catholic doctrine as the ritual celebration of the liturgy on which it is based. My own sense is that this key doctrine has been eclipsed in the post–Vatican II reform of the liturgy and is something that we Catholics can bring to the table in ecumenical discussions of liturgy and sacraments and why they matter.

An Incarnational and Sacramental Worldview

Sacramentality is a worldview. It is a way of looking at life. It is a way of thinking and acting that values and reveres the world. Sacramentality is a prism, a theological lens through which we look at creation and all that is on this good earth as revelations of God's presence and action among us here and now. The premise of sacramentality means that in fact we do not live in two different worlds, the sacred and the secular, but that we live in one graced world named "good" by God in Genesis 1:3. At the same time, this principle admits that there are moments of particular sacredness—created in the liturgy—that enable us to experience the divine in the human and on this good earth. ?

Sacramentality is a worldview that invites us to be immersed fully in the here and now, on this good earth, and not to shun matter or avoid the challenges that such earthiness will require of us, even as we pray through liturgy and sacraments (and other means) to enter into heaven when this earthly pilgrimage has ended. Since the human being is the pinnacle of God's creation (Gen 1:26–27), part of what is called "dominion" is to value and revere the things God has created and to see human beings as part and parcel of that created world. The theology of the goodness of creation and of human beings in light of the incarnation is reflected again and again throughout the liturgy, although not always described as such. Created human beings use other aspects of the created world to worship the God of creation, the God of the covenant, and the God of redemption. It is all of a piece and is a continuum—or should be.

Closely allied with this is the theological reality that we use our bodies in worship. It is the genius of the liturgy that we celebrate the mystery of faith with the very flesh and blood that God created as "good" in Genesis. As mentioned earlier in chapter 2, it was Tertullian who asserted that "the flesh is the instrument of salvation"[5]—Christ's taking on our own flesh and blood and our using our flesh and blood to worship God. The Catholic liturgical ? experience is always a *mediated* experience. It is mediated by the things of this world and human beings. Our direct encounter and experience with the saving deeds of our salvation is through creation—created things and created human beings. From St. Augustine onward, a sacrament has been described and defined as a "sign of a sacred thing"; we also have Augustine's famous adage that "the word is brought to the material element and it becomes a sacrament."[6] The Catholic sacramental imagination is always one that embraces and uses the world; it does not take us out of the world. We live in one graced world where Jesus lived and died.

From the perspective of the theology of the liturgy, I wonder whether at times the reform has been not only too cerebral but, dare I say it, "dis-incarnate." I wonder whether the way we use, or do not use, our bodies in worship reflects a disconnect with our world and our everyday lives. In fact, Catholic liturgy is especially anthropologically apt—by which I mean that it respects our human lives on this earth and the things of this earth. An integral vision is presumed and is the basis for all liturgy. The very life relation of the liturgy is at stake here.

The American liturgical pioneer Fr. Martin Hellriegel of St. Louis authored the popular hymn reflecting this life relation: "God's Blessing Sends Us Forth."[7] Hellriegel would find himself in good company with Pope Benedict XVI, who added two forms of dismissal from the Eucharist in the revised Missal to underscore its life relation, to live what we have celebrated: "Go and announce the Gospel of the Lord," and "Go in peace, glorifying the Lord by your life."

I do wonder, however, whether we should also emphasize today that God gathers us to celebrate the liturgy, the blessings of creation on this good earth, and human beings on this earth made in God's very image and likeness. One result of misunderstanding the intrinsic sacredness of the liturgy is to think that there is a *separation* between what is often termed the *sacred* and the *profane*. In point of fact, precisely through the sacramental principle and the mediation to us of sanctification and salvation through the use of created and manufactured means, there is a continuum at work here. We live in a graced world. The liturgy sets us in proper order and reshapes us in God's image and likeness through this act of redemption, so that we can be sent forth to live, in the world, what we worship. Dare I suggest that we might adapt another song used at liturgy and say, "God's Blessings Gather Us In"?

I believe there could well be a convergence of the Catholic principle of sacramentality and today's ecological consciousness that could be a paradigm for delineating nothing less than sacramental theology itself. Put differently, I wonder whether our classic approaches to the sacraments were *fostered by reacting to errors* (such as the canons of the Council of Trent being reactions to the heresies of the time), or *fostered by exploring underdeveloped aspects* of liturgy and sacraments (such as Vatican II's Constitution on the Sacred Liturgy, as well as Pope Benedict's post-synodal exhortations *Sacramentum Caritatis* and *Verbum Domini*), but that these approaches stayed within the Western church's frameworks of emphasizing what sacraments cause.

While I have learned much from the notions of "the church as sacrament" (from Karl Rahner, among others) and "Christ as sacrament" (Edward Schillebeeckx, among others)—both ideas being popularized in theological literature since the 1960s—I do wonder whether each idea in its own way is not also very "sacral" and deals with the fundamental language of sacraments, the sacramental principle. What would happen if *causality*, or any other contemporary paradigm for sacramental theology, such as Christ or the church as "sacraments," might be replaced by what I would argue is more foundational—*sacramentality*? My recent musings in this area are pushing me toward trying to articulate that ecology and the environment are a basis for the central Catholic sacramental principle that is presumed but not readily expressed as the source of the reality of liturgy and sacraments. For me, there is an integration at work in sacramentality that encompasses the created world, human beings, the word of God, and the enactment of the sacraments as the ongoing work of our redemption so that we can live redeemed lives in our world.[8] Put succinctly, is there a theology of Catholic sacraments that can be articulated from a theology of creation and today's concern for the environment that uses sacramentality as its basis?

Several of the pioneers of the Liturgical Movement took for granted the intrinsic relationship between the worship of God and the world in which we live. In the American context, Virgil Michel exemplified this point of view. Michael Woods, SJ, also argues that the Liturgical Movement was intrinsically related to the National Catholic Rural Life Conference.[9] That the liturgy is rooted in the land was clear to our forebears in the Liturgical Movement. That it is less clear to us is cause for theological and pastoral regret.

Liturgy is "heaven on earth" and at the same time also the threshold of heaven. It is the most sacred thing we do, because through and in it we humans touch God and are embraced by God. Liturgy is the breaking into our world of all that is of God and of the kingdom of heaven. It is the fullness of the divine offered to us, but precisely because it is sacramental it is offered through created means and human beings. Until we are called from this good earth to a new heaven and a new earth (Rev 21:1), we use the things of this earth and of human life to commune with God through the liturgy, which is always based on the sacramental principle. Sacramentality presumes engagement in the world and things on this earth; this engagement in and through the sacred liturgy leads us to experience that which transcends this world.

Sacramentality is based on the goodness of creation and the engagement of humans in worship, especially through the primal elements of earth, air, fire, and water as reflective of God and revelatory of God. They are constantly used in worship as the means of naming God, experiencing God, and worshipping God—but in relation to words and texts, lest their use be perceived to be a pantheism of any sort. (More on this follows.) The point to be made here is that our appreciation of creation and all created reality is not unfettered or a psychological "free fall." Rather, an integral part of humans engaging in the act of worship is that we use our minds and intelligence. In addition to using things of this earth in worship, we place them in relation to actions and words that tether their possible meanings to rich avenues for reflection and deeper appropriation of what is occurring. The God of creation, of the covenant, of revelation, and of redemption is the very same God we worship through the liturgy. One needs all these dimensions of sacramentality to try to be grasped by God and to attempt to "grasp" God. *Lex orandi, lex credendi* means that we "say" many things in and through the liturgy—sometimes with words.

At the risk of oversimplification, it can be said that there was a certain presumed robustness in the way liturgies in the patristic period were celebrated, and that at their heart they "used" the things of creation and "the work of human hands" in recognizably engaging ways. Reading the mystagogic catecheses of the great mystagogues Saints Cyril of Jerusalem, Ambrose, and Theodore of Mopsuestia, among others, reveals instructions on the sacraments based on the use of light and darkness, water, bread and wine, and oil and chrism by human beings in the community of the church. That these were unself-consciously used to worship God and to explore how God works through them is clear. While I would take issue with calling the patristic era a "golden age" of church life and worship (as I would the thirteenth, "the greatest of centuries"), since there were serious, church-changing theological and pastoral issues that had to be dealt with (think of St. Augustine facing into Pelagianism and Donatism, or the spate of christological and trinitarian controversies over which people debated fiercely)—there was and still is something paradigmatic about the way the mystagogues used the liturgy as the primacy catechesis for sacraments. The very fact that many of our revised liturgical rites derive from early church and patristic sources (e.g., the three eucharistic prayers added to the Missal in 1968 and the structure of the Rite for the Christian Initiation for Adults) indicates their import for us today, not for imitation necessarily (as if that were possible) but for the depth of their texts and the beauty of their rituals. That we are still in the process of recovering some of that depth and breadth is clear.[10]

These rites evolved and changed in later centuries, so that by the time of the Scholastics a number of distinctions had been made and a certain condensing of the rites had taken place. But even then (and since), Catholicism upheld the importance of "signs" in the liturgy by insisting on the "matter" and "form" of sacraments. Another way of saying this is that "matter matters." Catholicism has never wavered from ensuring that in and through liturgy and sacraments the world and all that God created was part of praising, thanking, petitioning, and being sanctified by that ever-steadfast God of creation, of the covenant, and of redemption.

At the same time, this is to admit that there was a certain minimalism that infected liturgical and sacramental practice. It was hard to experience and thus to maintain the value of, for example, the coming of the light to begin a new day in the (then) Divine Office at Lauds and the onset of darkness at Vespers when the Office could be "said" at any time of day. That the revisions to the Liturgy of the Hours in the Breviary intend it now to be celebrated as much as possible in accord with the actual hours of the day is a move toward placing the cosmos before us. Among the clearest examples is the Canticle of Zechariah (Luke 1:68–79), which welcomes the new day with these references to light and darkness:

> In the tender compassion of our God
> the dawn from on high shall break upon us,
> to shine on those who dwell in darkness and the shadow
> of death,
> and to guide our feet into the way of peace. (vv 78–79)

That Evening Prayer is meant to reflect the ending of the day is clear in several of its prayers. I do regret, however, that the use of the hymns in the Latin edition of the Liturgy of the Hours about the days of creation at Vespers is regularly jettisoned in the American four-volume edition in favor of other hymns. A more regular singing of them at Evening Prayer would simply underscore the theology and reality of this important creation motif of separating light from darkness to the creation of the human being in all of the liturgy. I am heartened to learn that, in fact, in the revision of the American edition of the Hours these creation hymns will be restored.

A certain minimalism in celebrating liturgy and sacraments also occurred when the requirement for baptism was the mere pouring of water and the saying of the baptismal formula. This has been replaced by very fulsome revised rites for infant baptism and adult initiation with the Liturgy of the Word leading to sacramental initiation and the Eucharist for adults at the Easter Vigil, and to sacramental initiation for infants and children when baptisms take place at Sunday Mass. That in the revisions the option for immersion is placed before infusion can be read as a decided preference for returning to the patristic usage of immersion.

We make theological (and other kinds of) statements about water during baptism. Water is the only element without which we cannot live. Hydration is not just an "end of life" issue. It is the key issue of human life and survival. If we cannot live without water, then what more proper element from the world to use to usher us into new life in Christ?

An essential element of the church's *lex orandi* of baptism is water. The value of its use is obviously maximized when we immerse for baptism. Immersion is rich in symbolic and theological content—it is a multivalent act. Baptism is about entrance to eternal life through the element that sustains us in human life, and much more besides.

The sacramental principle allows us to experience this multivalence of water. And that means respecting water's potential to create both life and death. Not enough water on the earth causes drought. Not enough water, and plants, animals, and humans die. Too much water causes flooding, destruction, and death. Water is experienced as refreshing and yet also as a place where one can drown. For me, this life-and-death struggle in water mirrors the life-and-death struggle we all engage in throughout our lives in terms of sin and separation from God, and reconciliation and union with God.

At the same time, if we extend *lex orandi* and *lex credendi* to include and involve *lex vivendi* (what we pray is what we believe is how we live), then I think we need to look at human actions that pollute water and the political machinations that limit access to water. I often wonder to what extent the issues in the ever-volatile Middle East are about water rights and access to water. And for anyone of us who has ever traveled to the Holy Land, how much more poignant is our praying Psalm 62, a classic "morning psalm" about "a dry weary land without water" (v. 1), or the adaptation of this sentiment in Matthew 5:6 about "hungering and thirsting for the living God"? The theology of baptism is as much about water and the need of all God's creatures for it to live as it is about the words we use to describe what water is and does in the sacrament—hence the value of the blessing prayers we have used in the reformed liturgy over baptismal fonts and over water itself. (Again, more on this follows.)

The sacramental principle reflects valuing and revering human labor. Besides the products of nature, the liturgy uses "the work of human hands," which furnishes other things we use in worship—bread, wine, oil, and so forth. The ingenuity and resourcefulness that go into the work of humans are part and parcel of these "signs" that we use in worship. For example, the sacramental principle takes very seriously the cycles of planting and harvesting, and then the baking of bread and making of wine for the materials we need for the celebration of the Eucharist.[11] In addition to the same cycle of planting and harvesting, pressing olives for the oils we use at worship is also an important substratum for anointings in the liturgy. There are paschal processes involved here—dying and rising—to manufacture the "matter" used in worship in order to experience, again and again, the dying and rising of Christ and our own dying and rising through, with, and in him.

The sacramental principle also reflects valuing and revering the human artistry needed for designing the vessels we use in worship, designing the fonts, ambos, and altars, the vesture, and liturgical books. And they value the human work necessary to produce them. All of these help to ground the doing of liturgy and sacraments, and none should be ignored or even forgotten in trying to comprehend what the liturgy is and does.

The process of making such materials reflects and respects humanity's creativity and ability to work. Humanity's work is offered back to God in worship. The reminder that all that we do and are comes from God ensures that what we do in worship must not be perceived to be Pelagian in any way. Human work is initiated by God and sustained by him. And humans respond by producing what is needed to return thanks back to God. "The work of our redemption" is enacted through "the work of human hands."

Part of this aspect of the sacramental principle includes the issue of beauty and aesthetics. While this topic is much debated, it has been advanced by the leadership of recent popes (whose support is akin to the times and places in papal history in which the popes were significant patrons of the arts and artists). More recently these include Pope Paul VI, who supported the designing and making of many contemporary works of art (including the doors of St. Peter's Basilica in Rome by Giacomo Manzu). Pope John Paul II's concern for fostering the work of artists is reflected in a number of his writings, including his "Letter to Artists" (1999).[12] As an interest of Pope Benedict XVI, it has been reflected in many of his sermons and talks, most notably his repeated concern for beauty in the liturgy.[13] When crafted and used in the liturgy, "the work of human hands" should always reflect the intended beauty of the created order and beauty as an attribute of God. This is often the theological grounding for asking some questions about what we use in the liturgy and whether the pragmatic sometimes takes precedence over what should be beautiful as well as useful.

The sacramental principle also means that we take things we do in human life and use them in the act of worship to experience God. Among these are the "daily and domestic acts" of washing and dining. The "bath" of baptism is like other baths in that it cleanses and refreshes us and, as mentioned above, draws us into the very life of God through the primal element that sustains life. The sacred meal of the Eucharist is like other meals in that we take food and share it. It is also the sacred meal through which we dine again and again on the "bread of life" and "the cup of eternal salvation." The anointing of the sick involves oil and human touch. In and through it, we pray that the Divine Physician might dwell in the fragile bodies of the anointed in order that they might experience a measure of healing (not necessarily physical) through oil that salves and through human touch that reminds them that they are not alone and that their bodies—as made in the "image and likeness of God"—are no less valuable or sustained in life, especially in their illness. The sacrament of penance takes such words as *forgiveness* and *reconciliation*, which we use to remain members of one another in our human community, in order to insure that God is with us and that it is God who restores us to life after the fracture of our relationship with God by our sometimes self-inflicted wounds of division and scandal. Matter matters. Words matter as well.

At the same time, the sacramental principle reflects that our experience of God this side of heaven is, in fact, always through a glass darkly—always veiled (1 Cor 13:12). Signs disclose only as much as they are able and as much as we can appropriate of God. But they never disclose the total reality. Even in and through what is the "source and summit" of the church's very life, there is always more to yearn and long for. Even the liturgy will never be a totally satisfying or a full and complete experience of God. That happens in the kingdom when we see God face to face. But in the meantime we use the things of the earth to worship God, who is both revealed, disclosed, and incarnate, as well as unrevealed, totally other, and utterly transcendent. Thus, the things we use in "worldly worship" both reveal and at the same time leave hidden the whole of what they symbolize.

The sacramentality of the world means that the world's works can be invested with worth, but that their ultimate worth as expressions of God's creation and presence will always be inadequately achieved and expressed.[14] In effect, then, the celebration of liturgy and sacrament is an action that symbolizes, expresses, and accomplishes the interaction between God and the human person, as mediated by the things of the natural world or of human manufacture and productivity; it is expressed through words and interactions that are nothing less than divine and human activity occurring at the same time in the community of the church. Such celebrations have meaning and consequences beyond what we can ever immediately grasp or measure. Any individual act of liturgy can never fully express the totality of this reality and interaction.[15] And every act of liturgy leads to the next until all liturgies have been done, "sacraments shall cease," and the elect will have met their Lord in the kingdom of heaven.

Sacramentality is a chief characteristic of Catholicism. While it is not particular to Catholicism alone, I suggest that the sacramental principle is at the heart of Catholicism, so much so that it is often not defined or adverted to: it is presumed. However, in the celebration of the reformed liturgy, I do wonder whether (perhaps by unintended osmosis) Catholics have imitated the emphasis placed by most American Protestant denominations on the Bible and preaching. Clearly, we Catholics are indebted beyond words to the experience of American Protestants. They had the vernacular and we learned much from them about how to use it. But has the implementation of Catholic liturgy been Catholic enough?

Without being anti-ecumenical, I wonder whether a certain wordiness has crept into Catholic worship when, in fact, its primal nature and sacramentality are chief among Catholicism's strengths and true characteristics. I am thinking here about the length of overly long preaching, the overreliance on the singing of hymns at the Eucharist when antiphons and selected verses of psalms are envisioned, the presider's insertion of too many words when the rubrics say to use "these or similar words," and other ways of not allowing the multivalence of the liturgy to occur in as unfettered a way as possible. I am also thinking here about the implementation of the revised translation of the Roman Missal. I stand with many others in insisting on the theological and liturgical premise of *lex orandi, lex credendi*. For me this includes words, but also more foundationally, signs, symbols, gestures, music, silence, movement, and so forth, all of which are intrinsic to and comprise the act of worship.

There is a primal-ness to Catholic worship that stands alongside our use of prayers that contain concepts, images, and metaphors about God and our human condition. But to lose or even to eclipse the earthiness of liturgy is to cut ourselves loose from what is a characteristic mooring for the way we have always worshipped God—through things from this earth.

While admitting our debt to the Protestant churches in helping us to shape the implementation of the reformed liturgy, I question the depth with which other Christian churches share our commitment to the sacramental principle.[16] In other words, for others who share our "liturgical tradition," is the substratum of sacramentality and the goodness of creation evident in the way they celebrate? Issues of anthropology and valuing creation are part of this reflection and, I think, should be part of our ongoing ecumenical dialogue. Put differently, although the shape of the reformed liturgies is the same among the liturgical churches—for example, the Anglican, American Episcopal, Lutheran, and Methodist Churches—is a shared worldview and anthropology operative, even as we use remarkably similar words and actions in the liturgy? The sacramental principle refers to a theology and appreciation of creation, of all that dwells on this earth—an essential part of which is that we revere human beings made in

God's image and likeness, and that we revere the way human beings interact and work.

Problems with the Word *Symbol*

What we use inside and outside of worship are the same. What we do in the liturgy is really anthropologically fitting. Tertullian's adage that "the flesh is the instrument of salvation"[17] involves the bodiliness of worship, but it also includes gestures, postures, and processions—all are part of the anthropological fittingness and substratum of the liturgy. They are all part of its sacramentality.

Up until now I have not used the word *symbol*, even though that word has a rich history and a revered place in our Catholic sacramental vocabulary. In fact, one could argue that it is more important and more traditional than *sign*. But I have not used *symbol* yet because of the way the term lost its reality content, simply because language has evolved. Originally *symbol* was taken from the Greek verb *symballein*, meaning "to unite," or, more literally, "to throw together." For several centuries, the church relied on the word *symbol* to mean something rich in reality and in the ability to unite us to what is beyond reality—to God and the things of God. But because language changes and the meanings of words sometime change, it is imperative that the church's teaching documents keep up and try as best they can to articulate in ever new concepts and words the truths of our theological and magisterial tradition. A case in point is the word used to describe what the Eucharist is.

At the risk of oversimplification, it can be said that for close to ten centuries the teachings about the Eucharist in the West concerned what the Eucharist *did*—build up the body of Christ, give food for the journey of life, and so on. That it was a "symbol" and a "figure" of Christ was acceptable theological vocabulary. But once attention started to be given to what the reality of the Eucharist was and is in itself (the true body and blood of the Lord), debates arose about how best to describe an essentially indescribable reality. Words that sustained rich reality content like *image, likeness,* and *type* (among many others) were judged inadequate to reflect this reality. It was then that the language of *substance* and *accident* entered Catholic sacramental vocabulary to describe the fact that the Eucharist looked like bread and wine, while in fact after the consecration it was the real body and blood of the Lord.

Although the word *symbol* originally derived from the Greek *symballein* meaning "to unite"—in that the symbol united us to the mystery being celebrated—this level of understanding was unfortunately lost, and *symbol* started to mean "less than real."

In our day and age, *symbol* and *symbolic* almost always mean "less than real," or worse, refer to an act that is empty or false. In the city where I live, commentators will often regard something done by a politician as "merely symbolic," which can often mean not only less than real but something tinged with deception. In fact, the exact opposite was the case when "symbol language" was the preferred language of sacraments and sacramental theology. For this reason, I judge "symbol language" to be best confined to contexts in which it can be explained and explored as a term meaning involvement and engagement in what is being celebrated.

(This is one of the reasons why my partners in the United Methodist–Roman Catholic dialogue in 2009 to 2011 would often ask whether the term *sacramentality* was itself able to carry the meanings I would often presume to associate with it, such as those reflected above. These are very good questions in an age when what is deemed "true" is only what is scientifically verifiable. What is not scientifically verifiable is deemed "false." In fact, as acts of faith, sacraments are "really real" and "as good as it gets" despite the fact that what is tangible is often perceived to be what matters. I will return to this in chapter 10 on spirituality and devotions, and on the "staying power" of devotions, largely because they use what is tangible as objects of prayer.)

Despite today's evolution of language, I want to suggest that there can be a decided diminishment in not using the word *symbol* as opposed to the word *sign* (or at least what is meant by it) simply because there is a multivalence and pluriformity of meanings conveyed through all the means of communication at work in the liturgy as symbolic—so much so, that one cannot and should not point to any single definition of what any single liturgy does or accomplishes. This is to assert that symbols always function on many levels, even symbolic words. Dare I suggest that there is a level of participation in and through the liturgy that does not rely on particular words alone but that respects a union with God accomplished through the use of verbal and nonverbal ways?

Premises and Practices

There may well be some pastoral liturgical practices that should be assessed in order that the sacramental principle might stand out more evidently and clearly. Along with what has been argued above, another guiding principle is that the most authentic, best materials and the finest of human workmanship should be offered back to God. Sometimes what is decreed in law and judged to be restrictive can be based on the sacramental principle and thus be seen to sustain this important substratum for all liturgy. Among the possible points for discussion, for ongoing liturgical catechesis, and for pastoral ritual adjustment are the following:

PARTICIPATORY GESTURES

Shortly after the Rite for Infant Baptism was implemented (1970 in English), the editors of the journal *Lumen Vitae* conducted a survey of parents about their experience of using the rite for the baptism of their children. When I started reading the article, I mused that perhaps they would have noticed the blessing prayer for the water that was recovered from ancient sources—certainly a major change from the previous rite. But in fact, what scored the highest was their appreciation for the fact that they made the Sign of the Cross on the foreheads of their children after the priest (or deacon) did it at the beginning of the ceremony. I then realized what I should have realized all along—that the gestures in which people participate, and not only the ones they watch others perform, are going to be especially remembered. Ways in which we all use our bodies in worship matter a great deal.

One gesture that we all engage in regularly at the Eucharist is bowing. This is a sign of reverence for the object at hand or for the meaning of the words we say. As ministers process to the altar in church, they bow to the altar as a sign of reverence for Christ himself and the place where the sacrifice will be offered. My own sense is that a very useful catechesis for this gesture can be taken from the Prayer of Consecration of an Altar, which is part of the Rite for the Dedication of a Church. Certainly one of the most beautiful of the revised liturgies, the Rite for the Dedication of a Church deserves catechesis and reflection because of its theological depth and imagery. If one were to offer a mystagogical *lectio divina* on the following prayer, I think it would go a long way in emphasizing why we bow to the altar and why the priest kisses it at the beginning and end of every Eucharist.

> Father,
> we praise you and give you thanks,
> for you have established the sacrament of true worship
> by bringing to perfection in Christ
> the mystery of the one true altar
> prefigured in those many altars of old.
>
> Noah,
> the second father of the human race,
> once the waters fell and the mountains peaked again,
> built an altar in your name.
> You, Lord, were appeased by his fragrant offering
> and your rainbow bore witness
> to a covenant refounded in love.
>
> Abraham,
> our father in faith,
> wholeheartedly accepted your word
> and constructed an altar on which to slay
> Isaac, his only son.
> But you, Lord, stayed his hand
> and provided a ram for his offering.

What We Have Done, What We Have Failed to Do

Moses,
mediator of the old law,
built an altar
on which was cast the blood of a lamb:
so prefiguring the altar of the cross.

All this Christ has fulfilled in the paschal mystery:
as priest and victim he freely mounted the tree of the cross
and gave himself to you, Father, as the one perfect oblation.
In his sacrifice the new covenant is sealed,
in his blood sin is engulfed.

Lord, we therefore stand before you in prayer.
Bless this altar built in the house of the Church,
that it may ever be reserved for the sacrifice of Christ,
and stand for ever as the Lord's table,
where your people will find nourishment and strength.

Make this altar a sign of Christ
from whose pierced side flowed blood and water,
which ushered in the sacraments of the Church.

Make it a table of joy,
where the friends of Christ may hasten
to cast upon you their burdens and cares
and take up their journey restored.

Make it a place of communion and peace,
so that those who share the body and blood of your Son
may be filled with his Spirit
and grow in your life of love.

Make it a source of unity and friendship,
where your people may gather as one
to share your spirit of mutual love.

Make it the center of our praise and thanksgiving
until we arrive at the eternal tabernacle,

where, together with Christ,
high priest and living altar,
we will offer you an everlasting sacrifice of praise.

We ask this through our Lord Jesus Christ, your Son,
who lives and reigns with you and the Holy Spirit,
one God, for ever and ever.

R. Amen.

Brothers and sisters, our community rejoices as it comes
    together
to bless this altar. Let us ask God to look kindly on the
    Church's offering
placed upon it and to receive his people as an everlasting
    gift.

Blessed are you, Lord our God,
who accepted the sacrifice of Christ,
offered on the altar of the cross
for the salvation of the world.

Now with a Father's love,
you call your people to celebrate his memory
by coming together at his table.

May this altar,
which we have built for your holy mysteries,
be the center of our praise and thanksgiving.

May it be the table
at which we break the bread which gives us life
and drink the cup which makes us one.

May it be the fountain
of the unfailing waters of salvation.

Here may we draw close to Christ,
the living stone,

and, in him, grow into a holy temple.
Here may our lives of holiness
become a pleasing sacrifice to your glory.

R. Blessed be God for ever.

In another familiar gesture, we all regularly bow at these words in the Creed:

...and by the Holy Spirit was incarnate of the Virgin Mary, and became man....

We also genuflect at these same words on the solemnities of the Annunciation and Christmas. The catechesis here should be about the incarnational principle enunciated above. It can also focus on the Prologue of the Gospel of John, especially 1:14, in which case part of the catechesis can be about why this is the Gospel proclaimed on Christmas Day. The fact that in many monastic communities the monks process into the church for the major hours and bow two by two to the altar and then to each other as they enter the stalls can be used to illustrate the showing of reverence both to the altar and to each other as the liturgy begins.

The catechesis on bowing before receiving communion—to show particular reverence for the eucharistic species—can be accompanied by encouragement that, as we approach the communion minister, we focus on singing the accompanying music and recollecting ourselves in such a way that we do not greet the other worshippers. There is a time and place for everything. This is the time to focus on eucharistic participation in the act of communion through our bodies as well as our recollected minds and hearts.

At the actual reception of communion, sometimes mixed signals are given, and this can cause confusion or unease at precisely the moment when there should be a certain ease borne of familiarity in the use of gestures. The USCCB offers important catechesis on communion reception on its Web site.[18] The communicant, not the minister, decides whether to receive communion in the hand or on the tongue. A certain confusion can occur when communicants cross their arms over their breast as a bodily sign of reverence. The problem is that ever since the 1998 publication of *One Bread, One Body*, guidelines for communion written by the Bishops' Conference of England and Wales, people who do not intend to receive the Eucharist may now come in procession with their arms over their breast to indicate their desire to receive a blessing, but not the Eucharist itself. However, not all ministers are aware of this practice and may try to offer the host to someone who does not intend to receive it. (*One Bread, One Body* is an extremely useful document accompanied by a slightly longer pamphlet with more theological explanation. This is the best thing I know of in English to deal with assemblies with people from different faiths.)

Other practices that can cause at least some awkwardness include when people want to receive communion in the hand but try to take the eucharistic bread from the minister with their fingers instead of placing their hands out, and when people kneel for the reception of communion. The American bishops have consistently taught that the posture for communion is standing and that when the recipient is one person away from the communion minister, he or she should make a bow to show reverence. At the same time, the bishops have said that communicants who kneel should not be refused communion but should be catechized about the value of the standing posture. More recently, their Web-site directive indicates that communicants may kneel for reception. The problem with people kneeling is that it disrupts the flow of the communion procession and can cause a person to fall if he or she is unaware that the communicant in front of them will kneel for reception. It also mitigates the value of the principle in the GIRM that "uniformity of posture is a sign of the unity of the body of Christ" (n. 42).

My own pastoral experience is that in the parish almost everyone stands to receive. At the evening Masses at the Basilica of the National Shrine of the Immaculate Conception, about 10 percent of those receiving communion do so in the kneeling posture. While it might seem that this would be because people come to the basilica on pilgrimage and are accustomed to kneeling, in fact, the communicants who kneel for communion are regular worshippers at the shrine.

LIGHT AND DARKNESS

The fact that light and darkness figure into so many of our liturgies is important, even in an age of electric lighting. Again the multivalence of each should be respected: for example, the importance of sunlight for things growing on the earth. Or of "the light at the end of the tunnel" for someone facing an economic downturn. Or of the flickering light of hope for a person dealing with the gloom of depression.

The *Exsultet*, or Easter Proclamation, reminds us of the value of candles when it asks that God to

> accept this candle, a solemn offering,
> the work of bees and of your servants' hands,
> an evening sacrifice of praise,
> this gift from your most holy Church.

Later on it continues, describing it as

> a fire into many flames divided
> yet never dimmed by sharing its light
> for it is fed by melting wax,
> drawn out by mother bees
> to build a torch so precious.

Here the work of human hands is accompanied by a reference to the work of God's other creatures to manufacture what we use in worship. This text articulates what is always the case: that it is not only the flame of fire but what stands behind the candle—creation, the work of creatures, and the work of human hands.

The reference to the fire in the *Exsultet* links nature with saving history in the Exodus. It also reflects unity in diversity in the communion of the church through those who carry candles during the Easter Vigil Mass. This section can lead to a reflection on "the light of Christ" as acclaimed at the procession that precedes the *Exsultet*, or a reflection on how Christ is "the light of the world" (John 8:2).

110

The implication here for the principle of sacramentality is that there should be no "fake" candleholders for candle oil to replace the beeswax candles required by the liturgy.

VESTURE

That the newly baptized are clothed afterward in a white garment is as traditional as when baptisms first occurred by immersion at the Easter Vigil, as evidenced in the mystagogic catecheses in the fourth and fifth centuries. This custom has been revived in the revised rituals for adult and infant baptism. The reference to being "clothed in Christ" is derived from a number of New Testament texts: for example, Romans 13:14, which is an admonition on how to live the life of Christ. This is especially poignant since it comes after Romans 12, which contains several admonitions about how to offer our bodies as a living sacrifice (Rom 12:1). Another example is Colossians 3:1–17 with its reference to putting on a new self and putting aside what leads to death and destruction. Both of these chapters deserve prayerful reflection as they draw out what it means to die to self and rise to newness of life, a continual battle, but one that has been overcome in the risen Christ.

The vesting of liturgical ministers in albs is based on the theology of these baptismal robes. They are liturgical garments over which deacons, priests, and bishops wear vesture of different colors—dalmatics for the deacons and chasubles for the priests and bishops. That these outer garments have come to be designed in a number of ways attests to human artistry and ingenuity based on a faith perspective on what we celebrate in the liturgy. But fundamentally these are garments, not signs or signboards. To reflect the sacramental principle they should be made of real cloth materials, such as linen, wool, and cotton, and not from polyester. The issue here is respect for the authenticity of the fabric and where it comes from, the earth and those who dwell on it.

BOOKS

The presumption of using a number of books for the celebration of the sacred liturgy is a hallmark of the reform, especially when compared with the use of the single-volume Roman Missal (containing scripture readings, prayers, antiphons, verses of psalms, and the ritual for other sacraments).

But not all liturgical books carry the same "theological" weight. One of the advantages of the liturgical reform has been to unpack and separate parts of the *Missale Romanum* that resulted from the Council of Trent. This means specifically the placing of scripture readings in separate books—the *Lectionary for Mass* and the *Book of the Gospels*. The *Book of the Gospels*, because it contains the words of Jesus through the inspired word of God, is carried in the Entrance Procession. It is placed on the altar at the end of the procession to signify, among other things, the unity of "Word" and "altar" as being one act of worship (*Sacrosanctum Concilium*, n. 56). It is then carried in procession to the ambo, from which the Gospel is proclaimed. After the proclamation, the deacon or priest kisses the book. At a Mass at which the bishop is presiding, the book is brought to him at the chair, where he reverently kisses it. The presiding bishop may bless the assembly with the Sign of the Cross using the *Book of the Gospels* after it is kissed. This is the regular practice at major papal liturgies. All of these are signs of special reverence for it. The *Lectionary for Mass* is also revered because it contains the word of God, but it does not carry with it the same protocols for signs of reverence toward it. But it also reminds us that "we are people of the book." The Roman Missal and other ritual books have also never received the same signs of reverence, but these are important books because they reflect the church's patrimony of prayer texts and protocols for the conduct of the liturgy.

The artistic attention and extreme care devoted to the production of all of these books goes as far back as scribes copying scrolls for the Torah, monks illuminating manuscripts in the scriptorium, and printers setting type in more recent times. Reverence for them is also demonstrated by the choice of their bindings and the quality of the paper for their pages. Again, issues of beauty and art are sustained (presumed?) by the human manufacture of books for worship.

It is for these reasons, among others, that strong objection has been voiced against the use of disposable worship aids, such as Missalettes. While these may contain the same texts of the rites, they do not inspire the same level of respect for the words, especially God's word, that is inspired by a beautifully produced book. The recent prohibition of the use of iPads and tablet computers for worship is based on this same reasoning.[19] Again, the prohibition derives from the church's concern to sustain the principle of sacramentality, specifically "the work of human hands," as well as aesthetics and beauty.

A final word concerns the possible criticism that these prohibitions might lead to the sense that the liturgy ought to be marked by opulence and excessive expenditures when stewardship is and should be very much on our minds. The issue here is not opulence or excess. It is an issue of using genuine materials and of having respect shown for those who design and manufacture these things. In the end, the Roman Rite should be marked by a "noble simplicity," part of which is to use materials that are germane to the peoples who celebrate with them. But it should not be materials that are shoddy or ephemeral. At the same time, what costs a bit more at the initial outlay stands the test of time and is the more economical in the long run. This is to underscore that stewardship matters. In a culture that disposes of many things, these liturgical materials should not be disposable. They should be shown reverence and respect.

CHAPTER FIVE

Liturgical Translations

"Every Translator Is a Traitor"

T his Italian proverb rings very true for any of us who deals
with more than one language in conversation, business,
reading, or academic research. It has also been very much
on my mind of late since we have implemented the revised
Lectionary for Mass and, more recently, the Roman Missal. At
the outset, let me say that issues of translation are so complex,
and the evolution of the vernacular translations in the liturgy
since Vatican II such an unprecedented challenge, that I am not
going to say whether or not I "like" or "dislike" them. The issues
are far more wide-ranging and complex than that. To be sure, I
have found what I think are less-than-accurate translations in the
Missal, and even some that reflect poor theology. At the same
time, a principle I use about liturgical texts is that, as ritual language, "they are what they are"—and I have no right to change
them. Ritual language fosters comprehension because of its reli-
ability. For any individual to change them during a liturgy disrupts the ritual and draws unnecessary attention to the one doing
the changing.

My purpose in this chapter is not to list what I judge are difficulties with any translation, while at the same time realizing the
wisdom of the Italian proverb "every translator is a traitor."
Instead what I hope to do is to explore how we got here and how
to use well what we have. Because we have recently implemented
the Missal and because it is a prime example of the evolution to
this point of the how and why of translations, this will be my
principal example. Like most Catholics, as attested in the surveys,

114

I regard the vernacular liturgy as one of the gifts of the post–Vatican II liturgical reform.

Catholicism is a theological tradition. The words we use to describe God, the three Persons in one God, the human person, our need for God, the church, how God works in history and in our lives, and so forth, are all very important. Creeds are filled with words—precisely crafted and finely tuned. So is the liturgy. The very important maxim *lex orandi, lex credendi*—"what we pray is what we believe"—reminds us of the importance of the words of the liturgy. Therefore, it is imperative that our liturgical texts reflect as accurately as possible what we believe. In the end, they are nothing less than words about the living God and the things of God. The implication is that what we say and do in the liturgy can and will continue to shape what we believe.

The Richness of Our Multivalent Liturgical Texts

As I said before, liturgical texts are *multivalent*; in other words, more often than not, they have more than one meaning. This term should be at the back of our minds as we deal with liturgical translations in order that the manifold meanings of a term or a phrase or a whole prayer can be upheld and used as a source of reflection. In addition, the science of *hermeneutics* attempts to interpret texts as accurately as possible, with the understanding that a wide range of possibilities exists and that allowance for this variety is part of the complexity involved in translations. Trying to uncover the inherent breadth and depth of texts can be challenging, but rarely do I find that it is not worth the effort.

An example from everyday life might help to underscore why *multivalence* is important. Many engaged and married women wear diamond rings. Diamonds come in a variety of sizes measured in carats. They also come in a variety of shapes (such as square, oval, round) and in a variety of settings, sometimes with other stones, sometimes alone set in gold, silver, platinum, and other precious metals. They also are often cut in a variety of ways in order to emphasize different facets of the diamond, especially given the different ways that light can shine on them. Some of the resulting shapes are simple, others are very complex and ornate. When a light shines on such rings from different angles, different aspects of the stone shine forth, are emphasized, and are appreciated. It often takes a few minutes to look at a particular diamond to appreciate its depth of beauty. More often than not, the wearer also sees in the ring an external manifestation of commitment in deep and abiding love to another person. This depth of meaning is revealed when we reflect on the length of time a person has been engaged or is married. And sometimes it is the imperfections in the ring and scratches from years of wear and tear that can mean the most to a married couple. The intrinsic beauty of a gem is one thing; its having been worn for years is another. A ring is one thing; to appreciate what a ring means is another. Reflecting on the ring in its historical *context* in the lives of the engaged or married couple is a study in depth and breadth derived from its context. One ring can and does often have many meanings. This is *multivalence* at work.

The phrase *Agnus Dei*, "Lamb of God," illustrates well the importance of *taking liturgical texts in context*. We sing it (at least) three times as the eucharistic bread is broken into parts for communion. It recalls John the Baptist's acclamation at the sight of Jesus, "Behold, the Lamb of God" (John 1:36) and underscores that the celebration of the Eucharist is our participation in the sacrifice of Christ offered once for all for our salvation. The *agnus* in *Agnus Dei* also reflects the Latin for St. Agnes (*Agnete*), whose name as part of the Roman Canon reminds us of those who gave their lives in martyrdom ("Graciously grant some share and fellowship with your Apostles and Martyrs...Marcellinus, Peter, Felicity, Perpetua, Agatha, Lucy, Agnes, Cecilia, Anastasia, and all your saints"). As the gathered assembly sings this acclamation, it cannot but affirm its faith in the one Lamb of God whose sacrifice "takes away the sins of the world," even as it then processes to partake in that sacrifice by the means of sacramental communion.

Although I have already discussed the importance to the Mass of music, the engagement of the senses, posture and gesture, sign and symbol, and so on—and will discuss other aspects of these later—I want to emphasize again that the liturgy is far more than texts alone. The liturgy is the church's ensemble of prayers, rites, actions, signs, and gestures that together comprise its central act of worship. In that sense, texts are a part of the liturgy's structure and contents, its rhyme and reason, but they are not the whole of the liturgy. Therefore, the texts of the liturgy should be appreciated in the context of all the other things that occur when the liturgy is enacted. And the word *enacted* is important. The liturgy is an *experience* of the paschal mystery of Christ as expressed through the means of communication that humans use in all of life—words, gestures, actions, things, and so on. Liturgy is enacted prayer. Liturgy is experienced theology. And when it comes to any individual word, gesture, or rite in the liturgy, the entire liturgical context needs to be recalled.

I will use three examples as at least an initial indication about the range of issues involved in liturgical translations.

1. *Kyrie, Eleison*

Normally translated as "Lord, have mercy," the *Kyrie, Eleison* is the last instance of the use of Greek in the Roman liturgy. On one level, to say or sing the *Kyrie, Eleison* at the start of the Eucharist in the Penitential Act is to acknowledge our sinfulness and need for forgiveness. But historically, before this phrase was used in the Christian liturgy, the word *Kyrie* was used to acclaim the Roman emperor. And so our liturgy, too, at this point has a level of meaning in which we acclaim: "You are the Emperor!" It is akin to "Long live the Queen." Christians first adopted it in the liturgy as a response to a litany prayer of the faithful,[1] and the Roman liturgy kept it in its native Greek. The *Kyrie, Eleison* is less about naming personal sins than it is to acclaim who Christ is and that it is his saving mysteries we have the privilege of entering into and sharing through the liturgy. In addition, the term itself, *Kyrie*, is significant: We are not addressing "Jesus," but, as is the custom in the Roman liturgy, we are calling out to the exalted Christ, Lord of all. In effect, "Lord, you are the ever powerful and merciful One" might be a stab at a (more accurate?) English translation.

2. Invitation to Communion

The now-familiar text for the priest's Invitation to Communion is:

> Behold the Lamb of God.
> Behold him who takes away the sins of the world.
> Blessed are those called to the supper of the Lamb.

On one level this is an obviously literal invitation since the priest says these words as he holds up the eucharistic gifts, and the people's response is about their literal reception: that they are not worthy that the Lord "should enter under [their] roof." On another level, the priest's invitation refers to the "supper of the Lamb" from the Book of Revelation 14:4 (and the people's response to Luke 7:6). And, on still a third level, the not-yet character of every Eucharist is expressed even as we now approach the reception of the Lord's very body and blood.

That this last motif finds its way into some of the prayers after communion is a helpful reminder of the eschatological nature of all liturgy. *Maranatha*, indeed.

3. Rule of St. Benedict

For a number of professional and personal reasons, I have been influenced a great deal by Benedictine monasticism. One of the classics of Western spiritual writing is the *Rule of St. Benedict*, which is read daily in monasteries throughout the world and as spiritual nourishment by countless lay and religious. One especially poignant section of the *Rule* (chapter 4) refers to the fact of death and how it should affect the life of the monk. In one translation the text reads, "Have death daily before your eyes." Another (more recent) translation reads, "Remind yourself daily that you are to die."

Personally I prefer the older translation—"Have death daily before your eyes"—because for me (here I am engaging in the work of interpretation and am likely bringing my own perspectives to bear on the text), the newer one is descriptive of the reality of death, whereas the older allows us to make the reality of death a prism through which we look at and evaluate life. I judge

118

that the older text is more about the deep perception that insight and contemplation give us about what matters in life. It is less about seeing with our eyes and more about seeing through contemplation about the very mystery of life and death, where, for the Christian, death leads to real life.

The Evolution and Contents of the Revised Roman Missal

As is well known, *Sacrosanctum Concilium* announced "that holy Mother Church desires to undertake with great care a general restoration of the liturgy itself" (n. 21) and that "the liturgical books are to be revised as soon as possible; experts are to be employed on the task, and bishops are to be consulted, from various parts of the world" (n. 25).[2] Thus was initiated the most complete reform of the liturgy ever undertaken at one time in the history of the church. For all practical purposes, the most authoritative work detailing this process is by Annibale Bugnini, *The Reform of the Liturgy (1948–1975).*[3] Bugnini worked tirelessly in the Curia for all those years as secretary for a variety of curial groups responsible for this reform, the principal of which was the committee called the Concilium. That there were a number of "study groups" involved with the reform of the Roman Missal under the Concilium from the mid-1960s to 1970 attests to its supreme importance and to the vast amount of research, study, dialogue, and consensus building that would occur as the Missal came to be.[4]

That the process was not without roadblocks and wrinkles is both documentable and a cause for concern today, especially since some of the issues that surfaced about the liturgical reform in the late 1960s have resurfaced and the strategies put in place to deal with them then were obviously not totally satisfying. In a now famous address to the Roman Curia on December 22, 2005, newly elected Pope Benedict XVI spoke of ways in which the documents of Vatican II had been interpreted. That day, he introduced into our church vocabulary the now common phrases "hermeneutic of continuity...of discontinuity" and "hermeneutic of reform...of rupture." While it is often asserted that the pope contrasted conti-nuity with discontinuity, in fact, he paired continuity with reform and asserted that these were important values from the Council—*ecclesia semper reformanda*. He chided those who judged that the Council was a "rupture" with what went before, and insisted that we should not understand the Council as such.[5]

A similar debate took place in the Roman Curia regarding the structure of the new Order of Mass. Although it was hoped that the Order of Mass would be published in 1968, it took another year to get beyond the allegations that, as proposed, it was "heretical" and so to secure papal approval.[6] Here Bugnini offers an insightful, succinct summary of what went on during those months.[7] There were those who insisted that an additional document was required to "justify" the new Mass. Pope Paul VI countered that what would be more effective was the addition of an introduction to the *General Instruction of the Roman Missal* (GIRM) to deal with these concerns. Subsections of that Introduction are titled "Testimony of an Unaltered Faith" (nn. 2–5), "Uninterrupted Tradition" (nn. 6–9), and "Accommodation to New Conditions" (nn. 10–15). These are among the most fully footnoted paragraphs of the GIRM, a significant number of which were taken from the Council of Trent. I believe that these paragraphs need to be read and digested again and again and could well be utilized to assert how and why the Missal needed to be revised after Vatican II. These paragraphs are clearly from the pen of Cipriano Vagaggini, *peritus* at Vatican II and founding president of the Pontifical Liturgical Institute at Sant'Anselmo (Rome).[8] Clearly, too, some similarly well-informed and moderat-ing voices are needed today.

There is at least a hint of defensiveness from the pen of Pope Paul VI in his apostolic constitution *Missale Romanum* approving the Missal. He wrote: "[H]owever, it should in no way be thought that this revision of the Roman Missal has been introduced with-out preparation, since without any doubt the way was prepared by progress in liturgical disciplines these last four centuries."[9] He then went on to say that, in the intervening years since Trent, ancient liturgical manuscripts were discovered, both Eastern and Western, containing extraordinary richness in their number and theological depth that could now be incorporated into a new Missal—texts that were simply unavailable at the time of the publication of the previous *Missale Romanum* in 1570. The principal innovation, he stated, was "the restoration concerning the Eucharistic Prayer," specifically the addition of over eighty Prefaces and the additional Eucharistic Prayers, some of which were based on Eastern liturgical sources.

The post–Vatican II Missal was distinguished from the post-Trent Missal by the absence of scripture readings. But its companion volume, the revised post–Vatican II *Lectionary for Mass*, was and remains a major achievement of the liturgical reform across denominational lines. That the Roman Catholic series of scripture readings at Mass has been adopted, if somewhat adapted, by other Christian churches is itself an attestation of the esteem in which it is held and a statement of ecumenical convergence about this newly restored and emphasized part of the Mass.[10]

According to Pope Paul VI, when Pope Pius V promulgated the 1570 *Missale Romanum*, he did so

> as an instrument of liturgical unity and as a monument of true and reverent worship in the Church. We, too, no less, even though We have accepted into the new Roman Missal "lawful variations and adaptations" our own expectation in no way differs from that of our predecessor. It is that the faithful will receive the new Missal as a help toward witnessing and strengthening their unity with one another by means of which, in the variety of so many languages, one and the same prayer of all will rise up, more fragrant than any incense, to the heavenly Father, through our High Priest Jesus Christ, in the Holy Spirit.[11]

At this point in the evolution of using the post–Vatican II Missal for these forty years, and in light of recent initiatives about changes to the translation, I offer the following observations about the Missal and its implementation.

BOTH TRANSLATED AND
NEWLY COMPOSED TEXTS

Almost all of the contents of the then English-language *Sacramentary* were a translation of the 1970 *Missale Romanum*. Among the most notable additions to the *Sacramentary* were the alternative Opening Prayers for Sundays. The initiative to compose such prayers was undertaken by the International Commission on English in the Liturgy (ICEL) in light of the 1969 document governing translations, *Comme le prevoit*,[12] which indicated that original texts for the liturgy could be composed. The same issues were in play when the second edition of the Italian version of the *Missale Romanum* added the newly composed Collect prayers based on the three-year cycle of Sunday scripture readings at Mass.[13] The intention was to offer an introduction to (what I might call) a "liturgical hearing" of the word of God. These were clearly a popular innovation. The project did have its detractors, however. At least two questions emerged: First, would a steady diet of these alternative prayers diminish the potential for the Missal to be a universally prayed series of texts? Second, were these prayers too didactic and wordy, especially as a prelude to the obviously lengthy Liturgy of the Word?[14]

The Concilium also judged that some of the Tridentine Missal's contents needed reworking. For example, its members asserted that the prayers and rites of the Offertory were most in need of a revision in order to remove any expression that anticipated ideas proper to the Eucharistic Prayer itself.[15] After the revisers of the Missal finished their work and produced the Latin *Missale Romanum*, ICEL went a step further to draft original texts for the Opening Prayer, the Prayer over the Gifts, and the Prayer after Communion. The project about the Prayer over the Gifts was especially notable because it would change the church's *lex orandi*, one of whose premises is the inherent multivalence of many liturgical texts. The newly composed Prayer over the Gifts assiduously avoided any proleptic reference to what the gifts would accomplish after consecration. As such, they collapsed possible meanings of the proposed texts into one possible meaning and thus diminished the multivalent potential of liturgical texts.

TWO MISSALS IN COMPARISON

The comparing of texts from the Tridentine Missal with those in the present Missal makes for a fascinating project. This can entail, for example, comparing which texts from the previous Missal remain in the new one, whether prayers that have remained in the new Missal are used on the same day as in the old one, and whether—and which—words in the former Missal change in the new one. Work on the revision of the Missal and on all the post–Vatican II liturgies was anonymous in the sense that we do not know who decided what about texts and on what basis. We do, however, know which members of the study groups were assigned to particular tasks.[16] For the prayers of the Missal, the group was headed by the famous Belgian liturgical scholar Fr. Placide Bruylants on the basis of his classic two-volume study of the prayers of the Roman Missal.[17] Also on the committee was Antoine Dumas, who, by all accounts and because of his numerous journal articles published at the time about the prayers of the Missal,[18] was one of the chief architects of the arrangement of the prayers in the new Missal.

My own methodological presumption is that the contents of the new Missal are normative and that in any comparison the benefit of the doubt should go to the revised Missal unless compelling arguments suggest the contrary. Other authors, however, argue that the new Missal should be judged against the normative Tridentine Missal, and where changes were made in the new edition, one should be suspicious in favor of the Tridentine Missal. This is part of the methodological platform of Dr. Lauren Pristas of Caldwell College.[19] In effect, we have agreed to disagree about the premises of our research.

Allow me to illustrate a case in point about the value of comparing texts from the two Missals. The current Missal's Prayer over the Offerings for Ash Wednesday is taken from the previous Roman Missal, in which most of the present text was prayed on the First Sunday of Lent. Two sets of phrases have been added to that prayer. Not found in the former prayer was an explicit reference to "works of penance and charity." While we do not know with certainty why this phrase was inserted, I would venture to guess that it was to make the prayer conform to the stated ancient disciplines of Lent of penance, prayer, and almsgiving—themes that occupy the Gospel proclaimed on Ash Wednesday (Matt 6:1–6, 16–18). The other addition is at the end of the prayer, which now refers to the end of the Lenten season when we pray that we "may become worthy to celebrate devoutly the Passion of your Son," a phrase taken from the eighth-century Bobbio Missal, which is normally dated from the seventh century. The Latin phrase *Filii tui passionem* ("Passion of your Son") is rich in meanings simply because the word *passion* in English and *passio* in Latin can cover a range of meanings—from the physical passion of Jesus to his paschal triumph. As a literal rendering, *passion* is adequate as far as it goes, but there is a level of meaning about our passing over—through, with, and in Christ—that is also carried by the use of *passio*.[20]

In my opinion, what is lost in praying this text in the Prayer over the Offerings is that the former prayer on Ash Wednesday, then called the "Secret" and prayed in near silence, is not used. That prayer contains a reference to Ash Wednesday as "the beginning of the venerable sacrament," that is, Lent—*venerabilis sacramenti exordium*. I would have wished that this use of the word *sacrament* could have been retained because it recalls the time before the thirteenth century when the seven sacraments were explicitly numbered by Peter Lombard, whereas calling Lent a "sacrament" goes back at least to St. Leo the Great.

THE TRIDENTINE MASS: THEOLOGY AND CULTURE

The issuance of Pope Benedict XVI's *Summorum Pontificum* in July 2007[21] and then May 2011's clarification of its application in the instruction *Universae Ecclesiae*[22] set into play permission for a somewhat wider use of the previous *Missale Romanum* under specified circumstances and under the direction of the diocesan bishop and the Sacred Congregation for the Doctrine of the Faith, specifically the Pontifical Commission *Ecclesia Dei*. That these documents have spawned intense interest by some and equally intense scrutiny by others is clear. From a theological standpoint, it is at least worth noting that the initial inspiration for allowing the use of this form of the Mass was to be a factor in trying to reconcile the followers of Archbishop Lefebvre with the rest of the Catholic Church.[23] At issue was and is reconciliation, a supreme goal of any celebration of the Eucharist and of the church in any and every age. In addition, a related issue involves what this new Missal contains theologically. Father Patrick Regan, OSB, of the faculty at Sant'Anselmo in Rome authored an important book laying out a comparison of these two forms of the Mass. I judge that this work will be very important in discerning why the Council fathers at Vatican II decided to reform the liturgy in the first place and why they decided to call for a reformed Mass in particular.[24]

There were and are compelling theological reasons why the Tridentine Missal was changed. And it is for good reason that Pope Benedict repeatedly called it "the extraordinary form" of the Mass. What does concern me, however, is the statement in his letter accompanying the issuance of *Summorum Pontificum*[25] that "the two Forms of the usage of the Roman Rite can be mutually enriching: new Saints and some of the new Prefaces can and should be inserted into the old Missal."[26] However, who would be authorized to do this and on what basis? After all, liturgy is quite unlike the troubadour at the start of Leonard Bernstein's *Mass* who plaintively invites us to "sing God a simple song" and "to make it up as we go along." One of the purposes of a Missal is to present us with texts and rites *precisely so* we do not make it up.[27] Otherwise, would this not be a 2014 version of the 1960's *Experimental Liturgy Book*, with the Xerox machine in overdrive? Is this not the very thing that church documents have tried to avoid?

Worth noting in this regard is today's use of the phrase "the reform of the reform." The Sacred Congregation for Divine Worship has not used the phrase, nor did Pope Benedict XVI, nor has Francis since becoming pope. With this phrase, nothing less than confidence in the liturgical reform of Vatican II is at stake— this despite the fact that "the reform of the reform" was recently used by Cardinal Klaus Koch in a lecture in Rome and in some recent publications in Italy about the future shape of the revised liturgy.[28] None of these uses of the phrase has official sanction.

I also wonder whether the theological climate and the culture that produced the Tridentine Mass can or should be replicated. The world that spawned the Roman Missal of 1570 was post-medieval, post-Reformation. We live in a postmodern, post–nuclear bomb, postmillennial, post–Gen X world in which a revised Missal was judged to be and still is necessary. Church teachings that have evolved since Trent are reflected in the Roman Missal of 1970 and now of 2002. While a premise in compiling prayers and texts for the new Missal was "back to the future"— in the way that some ancient (especially patristic) texts have been revived and are in the new Roman Missal—the principle that we should go back to the era of the Council of Trent just for the sake of going back is to drive the bus backward. As a theological tradition, Catholicism is never about "the way we were," save for how "the way we were" shaped our history and also enables us to look at the present and rearticulate what we believe in ever new contexts and ways. In fact, "back to the future" and our collective future in God is what matters—not nostalgia or a seemingly "pristine" form of liturgy for its own sake.

THE ROMAN MISSAL, OTHER MISSALS, AND THE CELEBRATION OF MASS

It is a well-worn but lucidly clear dictum that unity does not mean uniformity. The "substantial unity of the Roman Rite" as a value is cited in *Sacrosanctum Concilium* (n. 38) in the context of four paragraphs about adapting and inculturating the liturgy (nn. 37–40). There are several other Missals in use today that supplement the *Missale Romanum* for a variety of religious communities and new ecclesial movements. These include, for example, the Jesuit, Dominican, Franciscan, and Benedictine rites.[29] Sometimes they contain texts for feasts (the Jesuits, for example) or chants (such as in the *Dominican Sacramentary*), or parts of the rite that are different (for example, the *Statutes* of the Neocatechumenal Way).[30] These are notable in that they are Missals in their own right and are officially sanctioned by all the requisite ecclesiastical authorities. Rather than regarding these as exceptions, I would prefer to view them as post–Vatican II examples of the kind of permission granted after Trent to religious communities or geographical territories that had their own Missals in use for two hundred years and were allowed to retain and use them. Among these were the Dominican and Carthusian liturgies and the Ambrosian liturgy celebrated in and around Milan to this day.

The point to be made here is to be careful about thinking that there was and is only one accepted way of celebrating the Roman Rite, either after Trent or after Vatican II. One clear example of the substantial unity of the Roman Rite is in the texts of the prayers. The art and craft of celebration well reflects legitimate diversity, often epitomized by the choice of music.

THE NEW MISSAL: GUIDELINES—OR A SCRIPT?

One school of thought holds that we should see the Missal as a model but not as a set of texts to be used. It should be a guide only, and presiding priests and bishops should either compose prayers spontaneously or craft them ahead of time with evocative language, images, and metaphors that are more reflective of our time and culture—not the classical world from which the prayers came—and of the needs of the assembled community. Even as I say this, I am reminded of the famous statement in the late 1960s of Father Clarence Rivers, who said that "spontaneity takes a great deal of practice."

Something of this was noted by liturgical scholar John Baldovin, SJ, at a lecture in March 2011. He offered the comment that his stated preference was for newly composed prayers. One of the issues raised here is that ancient texts are just that and sometimes the Missal's prayers fail to inspire. Several pros and cons are worth debating here. I am thinking of some Collects assigned for Sundays in (what is now called) Ordinary Time, which were composed to reflect contemporary cultural or religious crises in the city of Rome that have long since been settled. One example is the Collect in the present Missal originally prayed at the time of the Roman feast of Lupercalia in mid-February.[31] This midwinter festival was to avert evil spirits, purify the city, and release health and fertility. While one might find traces of St. Valentine's Day here, Valentine never made it into the Roman euchology, and Lupercalia is officially a dead feast. But the sentiment of the prayer—to follow the light and to reject what is contrary to the Gospel—obviously still stands. At the same time, while some prayers from the tradition may be judged deficient, I would suggest that some of the alternatives themselves are also theologically thin and with less rhetorical style than should be expected. For example, the alternative Opening Prayer for this same Sunday in Ordinary Time reads:

> Father,
> let the light of your truth
> guide us to your kingdom
> through a world filled with lights
> contrary to your own.
> Christian is the name and the gospel
> we glory in.
> May your love make us what you have called us to be.[32]

I, for one, did not shed a tear when this text found its way to the floor of the scriptorium and not into the revised Roman Missal.

Overall, I judge that we are far better served by using traditional sources and voices from our family album, like Leo the Great on Christmas, than by searching for the novel and contemporary.

Translation of the Missal

The vernacular English translation of the Missal and of all other post–Vatican II liturgical documents is intertwined with the establishment and continued efficient operation of the International Commission on English in the Liturgy (ICEL), founded by ten (eventually eleven) English-speaking bishops' conferences just prior to the promulgation of *Sacrosanctum Concilium* in 1963. The first text produced by the young translation body was the Roman Canon in 1967. It was only subsequently in 1969 that the Holy See issued the document *Comme le prevoit* (which I alluded to previously) that would govern the unprecedented and herculean task of translating the liturgy into English through to 2011.

This document contains several principles for translation, among which the best known is probably that of "dynamic equivalence" as opposed to "formal equivalence," meaning that in translating from the Latin, certain liberties could legitimately be taken for the sake of comprehension in the "receptor language." For example, in the third Eucharistic Prayer, the new Missal used the words "so that from east to west a perfect offering may be made to the glory of your name." The scriptural reference was to the Book of Malachi 1:11—"So that from the rising of the sun to its setting, a perfect offering may be made to the glory of your name"—but the exact wording was lost. "From east to west" was judged a more adequate way to describe this cosmic reference, but that it was geographically focused meant that any reference to the offering of an ongoing, eternal sacrifice in which an individual celebration of the liturgy participates would be diminished if not lost altogether. But even as I say this, I want to be clear that ICEL was following its "marching orders" with this kind of "dynamic equivalence," as well as in its composition of original texts for the liturgy.

At the same time, actual mistakes were made in the translations. How could there not be? There was no precedent in the Catholic Church for such a wholesale revision of all of our liturgies at one time, which now had to be translated in rather quick succession into English acceptable to all eleven bishops' conferences. ICEL was the first to admit that a better translation was needed and undertook a revision that culminated in what is now often called the *1998 Sacramentary* (translated by ICEL and approved by all its member conferences). The years before the final approval of the *1998 Sacramentary* saw increased interest in and oversight of the texts by individual bishop-members of the ICEL episcopal conferences. On this side of the Atlantic, the debates were at times intense, and unfortunately name calling and personal attacks were not absent.

The history of the evolution toward the revision that culminated in the new Missal can be documented easily enough, and has already been done well by others.[33] These were, however, very important years for establishing parameters for translating, for evaluating texts, for experiencing what a vernacular liturgy could be like, as well as for assessing where some initiatives misfired and needed correction.

There was one underlying "subtext" operative during these years: "English is the new Latin." While all liturgical translations into the vernacular should have been made from the Latin, it became clear that some vernacular texts translated after Vatican II into languages other than English were, in fact, inspired by the ICEL English translations and were not as faithful to the Latin as was presumed. Hence, greater scrutiny would now be exercised over the ICEL English texts for at least two reasons: because they influenced other translations and because faithful translations of the liturgy are required to reflect accurately the faith professed through the liturgy's prayers.

At about the same time, there were three other translation projects that influenced the new Missal and its eventual approval:

1. The Order of Christian Funerals

The first edition of the Order of Christian Funerals was published by ICEL in 1970, followed by a revised edition by ICEL in 1985. Some of the debates that ensued before the approval of the revised edition by the then-called National Conference of Catholic Bishops (NCCB) and by Rome in 1987 were well publicized at the time, with many arguing that Rome should have approved the ICEL text "as is" and not required some adjustments for more accurate translations and adjustments in the wording of original texts. They number almost a dozen. Eventually the matter was settled, the texts were approved, and the revised funeral rites were implemented on All Souls Day, 1989. In hindsight, it is clear that Rome was exercising increased oversight of the English-language liturgical translations.

2. Rites of Ordination of a Bishop, of Priests, and of Deacons

The first Latin *editio typica* for the Rites of Ordination was issued in 1968 and subsequently translated by ICEL in 1969. Almost immediately, the NCCB requested approval from Rome to use this interim translation provided by ICEL, and permission was granted. ICEL provided a revised translation in 1975, and again the NCCB requested Rome's approval to use it. This was granted in 1977.[34] A second *editio typica* (*altera*) of the ordination rites was issued in Latin in 1989,[35] which was also to be translated by ICEL. However, this was a protracted process that involved ongoing discussions among the ICEL constituencies, among which were the NCCB Bishops' Committee on the Liturgy and officials in Rome. In effect, Rome rejected ICEL's first effort at translation in a document dated 1997. ICEL worked toward a revised text that itself was debated by the Bishops' Committee on Liturgy, its advisors, and the bishops' conference. In 2002, the now-named USCCB approved the final text, and Rome approved it for use in 2003.[36]

3. The ICEL Psalter

Part of the original mandate for ICEL from as far back as 1964 was to prepare a Psalter suitable for liturgical use.[37] But because of the heavy work demands involved in translating liturgical texts, the real work involved in preparing such a Psalter was not undertaken until 1978.[38] In that year, the Episcopal Board of ICEL appointed a subcommittee charged with this task, composed of specialists in Hebrew language and poetry, liturgical history and theology, music, English poetry, and literary and language theory. In 1984, twenty-two psalms were prepared and subjected to extensive consultation. In 1987, twenty-three psalms were published with the title *Psalms for All Seasons*. Subsequently, four working groups were charged to complete the translation. This was done and the texts were approved by the ICEL Episcopal Board and forwarded to the NCCB Ad Hoc Committee for the Review of Scripture Translations.

In 1995, Cardinal William Keeler granted an imprimatur to the ICEL Psalter. While this text was printed "for study and for comment," one of the versions published by Liturgy Training Publications was entitled *Psalms for Morning and Evening Prayer*, with the psalms arranged for the four-week liturgical cycle.[39] In addition, all one hundred and fifty psalms were published as *The Psalter: A Faithful and Inclusive Rendering from the*

Hebrew into Contemporary English Poetry.[40] Among other things, to recommend this translation for liturgical use was that it was done in light of the need for psalms to be translated for singing. But despite the granting of the imprimatur, this Psalter was not authorized for liturgical use.

Starting in February 1996, the leadership of the NCCB and officials in the Congregation for the Doctrine of the Faith undertook discussions in which the latter raised questions about doctrinal issues related to the Psalter. As early as April of that year, Cardinal Joseph Ratzinger notified the then president of the NCCB, Bishop Anthony Pilla, that the imprimatur was to be withdrawn. The Vatican assessment, which came through the Congregation for Divine Worship, was that the text was "doctrinally flawed."[41] After consultation with the bishop chairmen involved with the Psalter, the Administrative Committee of the NCCB, and all the bishops, the imprimatur was withdrawn in 1998.

Not coincidentally, in 1995 the Congregation for the Doctrine of the Faith issued a document *Norms for the Translation of Biblical Texts for Liturgical Use.* I suspect that one of the dominant reasons for the withdrawal of the ICEL Psalter's imprimatur was that some uses of inclusive language in translating the psalms would eliminate liturgical use of the Psalter as christological—that is, the possible understanding of a verse to refer to Christ,[42] to help us understand who Christ is. For example, in Psalm 8:5, the ICEL Psalter reads:

> What is humankind
> that you remember them,
> the human race
> that you care for them?[43]

The same verse from the officially approved *Revised Grail Psalms* reads:

> [W]hat is man that you should keep him in mind,
> the son of man that you care for him?[44]

ICEL Itself Is Revised

Starting in 1998, three changes occurred that have been very influential on the processes, policies, and personnel involved in approving liturgical books in English:

1. In October 1998, the prefect for the Congregation for Divine Worship, Cardinal Medina Estévez, wrote to then president of ICEL Bishop Maurice Taylor, stating, among other things, that

- ICEL's role was as a translation agency, not an agency to compose original texts for the liturgy;
- the office of executive secretary of ICEL was different from that of the bishop members;
- ICEL employees should have fixed terms of employment, with the Congregation for Divine Worship holding the right to grant dispensations;
- members of the ICEL Advisory Committee would now need to receive a *nihil obstat* from Rome on all translations; and
- the statutes governing ICEL needed to be revised within six months.

In effect, what resulted was a less "American"-centered ICEL office and focus. The election of Bishop Arthur Roache from Leeds (UK) and the subsequent hiring of Msgr. Bruce Harbert and now Msgr. Andrew Wadsworth (both from the UK) attest to this. As of this writing, the bishop chair of ICEL is Bishop Arthur Serratelli, an American with an earned doctorate in biblical theology.

2. The publication of *Liturgiam Authenticam*[45] in April 2001 and its consequent *Ratio Translationis*[46] in 2007 replaced *Comme le prevoit* (1969) to govern vernacular translations. That the 2001 document was additionally titled *"The Fifth Instruction" for the Right Implementation of the Constitution on the Sacred Liturgy* indicates its importance. If *Comme le prevoit* was the document that allowed

133

for "dynamic equivalence," this new document was to insist on "formal equivalence"— that is, a more literal translation from Latin to English. This document has obviously been the object of much heated debate within our church for a decade.[47] Whether or not the entire document has been implemented and with strict consistency is a question. For example, while *Liturgiam Authenticam* does allow for the substitution of another word or phrase in the Creed for the term *consubstantial* (nn. 21 and 53), in fact what we all say now is that Christ is "begotten, not made, consubstantial with the Father."

3. Also in 2001, the Congregation for Divine Worship announced the formation of a committee named *Vox Clara*, which added, in effect, a new level of consultation in the process of evaluating and approving liturgical books. It is comprised of an international committee of bishops from the English-speaking countries (presently chaired by Cardinal George Pell) with a number of non-bishop consultors. Its role is to give advice to the Congregation for Divine Worship regarding translations from Latin to English, thus its competency includes an evaluation of ICEL's work.[48]

A "NEW" MISSAL FROM A "NEW" ICEL

I will now try to summarize the process of the American approval of English-language liturgical translations of the Missal. It was an enormous undertaking, given the number of texts to be translated, and the vast number of people involved. The American bishops have been quite engaged in the process ever since the beginning.

In November 1993, the American bishops voted to reject the first segment of the translation of what eventually would become the 1998 *Sacramentary for Mass*. In the autumn of 1998, the bishops did vote to approve the revision of the presidential prayers of the Missal and forwarded the *Sacramentary* to Rome for approval. Approval was denied, one reason being that the then-forthcoming third edition of the Latin *Missale Romanum* was expected to be published in the Jubilee Year of 2000 (it was published in 2002), and that it was this new edition which would need to be translated. An underlying reason, however, was that the Vatican had grown increasingly concerned about the accuracy of the vernacular English texts. Official notification of the rejection of the decade-long, ICEL-led revision of the presidential prayers for the Roman Missal came in 2002. In that same letter, the Congregation expressed dissatisfaction that the ICEL Statutes still had not been revised, three years after the due date. This was finally accomplished only in the autumn of 2008.

In effect, the process by "the new ICEL" to retranslate the Roman Missal took the better part of a decade. It is an understatement to say that its evaluation was a major preoccupation of the American bishops. From the beginning, these ICEL texts had their critics for various reasons, including verbosity and literalness. At the same time, the ICEL texts have also had their supporters, on the principle that "what we pray is what we believe" and that these texts should be as accurate as possible.

Compare the Opening Prayer for Christmas morning in the *Sacramentary for Mass*:

> Lord God,
> We praise you for creating man,
> And still more for restoring him in Christ.
> Your Son shared our weakness,
> may we share his glory.

with the version in the new Missal:

> O God,
> who wonderfully created the dignity of human nature
> and still more wonderfully restored it,
> grant, we pray,
> that we may partake in the divinity of him
> who humbled himself to share in our humanity.

Liturgical Translation: An Ongoing Task

The challenge of translating the Latin liturgy into the vernacular is a task that will be with us for generations to come. Revised rites will be published in Latin, and some translations in the various languages will undergo the same retranslation that ICEL undertook for the English texts. I believe that some of the resistance encountered by the revisions to the English translations of the Missal's texts was largely due to the familiarity that presiders and the gathered assemblies had presumed better, simply because of the repeated use of the former texts. This is, in fact, an important value in the liturgy in general and for liturgical texts specifically. In my opinion, the more we can hear a text and say to ourselves, "Oh yes," rather than, "Oh my" (meaning that we notice differences), the better off we are. This is because texts serve the liturgy and our incorporation into the very mystery of God experienced through the liturgy. That experience is fostered by liturgical prayers and liturgical language; it is not controlled by it.

I will now return to the issue of the ICEL Psalter, its rejection, and the work done by Abbot Gregory Polan, OSB, and the monks of Conception Abbey in Missouri on a revision of the Grail text (for inclusivity, among other reasons). I look forward to the day when the recently approved Grail Psalter will be incorporated into all English-language liturgical texts. This is not because I want to relearn well-worn, memorized phrases. In fact, given the experience with the revised Missal, I know I will make mistakes and on some level not like the revision. Again, the issue here is familiarity, which leads to the likelihood of better appreciation of what is said and celebrated.

The reason why I would like to see the same Psalter in all the English-language liturgical books is that at present we have competing translations for antiphons, refrains for Responsorial Psalms, the Responsorial Psalms themselves, and the psalms in the Liturgy of the Hours. Dare I envision a day when the Psalter is so restored to the church's liturgical prayer that we can know the psalms almost by heart? That would certainly allow the possibility of greater familiarity, so that our imaginations would be engaged in the divine mysteries—not controlled by, but instead tethered to, the texts of the liturgy.

Liturgical rhetoric and the Christian reality are always paschal. Even when liturgical language is decidedly incarnational, as it obviously is at Christmas, it almost always refers to the way Christ's birth leads to his death and resurrection. Liturgy always celebrates paschal triumph in the midst of what is sometimes much more obvious: suffering, diminishment, and loss.

All that we can ever expect from a liturgical text is the least inadequate expression that humans dare to use to worship God in speech. All that a liturgical text can be expected to do is to guide and offer insight. All translations will fail to grasp that the real rhetoric of liturgy and the depth of Christian life is always about dying and rising and how in and through the liturgy we die and rise again and again. That is a paschal process; it is not about speechmaking or debates about words, phrases, capitalizations, or commas. All any translation can try to do is to tether our imaginations and invite us to focus on one or another of God's attributes enacted among us liturgically through Christ in the enlivening and sustaining power and action of the Holy Spirit. Liturgical texts are not about mind control; they are about opening minds and hearts to what is really and always unfathomable. They are about repeatedly turning minds and hearts—our very selves—over to God. The act of liturgy is nothing less than giving voice to our faith in the Triune God when words fail us, as all human words eventually will. It is about giving voice to our Christian faith in the face of our dying and rising, our need to die to some things that are not life-giving or life-sustaining, and our rising again and again until one day we see God face to face.

When it comes to liturgical texts, I rejoice that the ICEL translators assigned the translation of the *Exsultet* from the Easter Vigil to Dame Maria Boulding of Stanbrooke Abbey in England, the author of the book *The Coming of God*[49] and translator of several of St. Augustine's writings, including *On the Psalms*. As Maria Boulding lay dying in Stanbrook Abbey on November 11, 2009, the assembled nuns and some friends, including Bishop Arthur Roache, prayed over her the words of her own translation of the *Exsultet* for the revised Roman Missal.

What We Have Done, What We Have Failed to Do

Every Easter, we too sing these human and yet stellar words, translated by this humble monastic servant of her Lord:

> This is the night
> when Christ broke the prison-bars of death
> and rose victorious from the underworld.
> Our birth would have been no gain,
> had we not been redeemed.
> O wonder of your humble care for us!
> O love, O charity beyond all telling,
> to ransom a slave you gave away your Son!
> O truly necessary sin of Adam,
> destroyed completely by the Death of Christ!
> O happy fault
> that earned so great, so glorious a Redeemer!
> O truly blessed night,
> worthy alone to know the time and hour
> when Christ rose from the underworld!
> This is the night
> of which it is written:
> The night shall be as bright as day,
> dazzling is the night for me,
> and full of gladness.

A liturgical translation doesn't get any better than this!

CHAPTER SIX

The Proclamation
of the Word and the
Liturgical Homily

Proclamation Is Enactment

I t is not my intention here to repeat what I have written at some length in other books about the value, importance, and implications of the Proclamation of the Word at every liturgical rite reformed after Vatican II.[1] What I should like to offer are simply two thoughts derived from those insights—specifically about the theology of the enacted word proclaimed at the liturgy and about preaching—and in light of them.

There is a world of difference between an individual's reading of the scriptures (for example, *lectio divina*) and the liturgical Proclamation of the Word. In the liturgy, words effect what they say; they do something. They may contain familiar stories, events, and phrasing. But when the scriptures are read in the church, *they happen*.

Pope Benedict XVI, among others, spoke of the strengths and also the limitations of the historical-critical method of biblical interpretation, and I have followed his thoughts with great interest. While I find merit in his critique, I also want to be cautious and not to jettison the benefits of the historical-critical method. To ignore the insights gained from it could collapse the important edifice built on a scientific and rigorous examination of exactly what the texts "say" and what they "do not say." I am thinking here of how Pope Benedict XVI himself lays out the differences in the way, for example, the Synoptic Gospel authors and the author of the Gospel of John lay out their chronologies of Holy Week. It is also interesting to see how he argues which he prefers as more historically accurate.[2] All of this suggests to me a wise use of a most valuable methodology.

At the same time, I want to suggest that in looking for additional and complementary ways of interpreting the scriptures, consideration be given to what I call "a liturgical hermeneutic" of the proclaimed scriptures. The very proclamation of the scriptures in the liturgy is what I deem to be a significant "success story" of the post–Vatican II liturgical reform. I cannot help but think that attention to where and when biblical books are assigned in the post–Vatican II lectionaries for the liturgy and the sacraments are important factors in understanding how an ecclesial hearing of the word is undertaken. I also think that the way biblical texts are juxtaposed in the lectionary (Old Testament, New Testament, and Gospel, with the corresponding Responsorial Psalm and Gospel Acclamation) should shed light on the way the church understands and interprets the scriptures.

For example, to this day the Prologue to the Gospel of St. John is proclaimed in the Roman liturgy on Christmas Day, but in some Eastern rites it is proclaimed on Easter morning. Another example is the placing of the three Johannine Gospel texts on the Third, Fourth, and Fifth Sundays of Lent: the Samaritan woman, the man born blind, and the raising of Lazarus, with their accompanying first and second readings, also specially designed for the Lenten Sunday Lectionary.[3] On weekdays of the year, when there is a two-year cycle of scripture readings for the first reading at Mass and a one-year cycle for the proclamation of the Gospel, this liturgical hermeneutic is most clearly evident.[4] This is to say that the liturgical proclamation of these texts invites us to appreciate the breadth and depth of each reading individually, as well as the breadth and depth they reveal when proclaimed at the same liturgy in relation to each other. This is how these texts are "heard"—in the liturgy. My argument is that how we interpret them should also be influenced by the liturgy. A principal way in which this hermeneutic is brought to bear and applied is in the way the preacher studies the scriptures and prays over the texts (in the specific liturgical context where he and the gathered assembly will hear the texts proclaimed), and as he prepares to write a homily that extends and expands on that proclamation.

A basic principle of such a hermeneutic is that when the scriptures are proclaimed in the liturgy, they are not about what happened once in history but rather about what happened then and there and occurs still as we hear and experience these events anew. They are always a new event. Even when we proclaim the same set of texts together, there is no such thing as a repeated liturgy. The Liturgy of the Word insures that the texts are always a new experience of redemption, here and now, for our sakes and for our salvation. Scriptural words are unique in that in and through the liturgy *they happen.*

Some Initial Questions about Preaching

Priests rank the celebration of the liturgy and preaching as the highest sources of their "job satisfaction." At the same time, surveys of American Catholics indicate poor "approval ratings" for the preaching they hear and express their heightened interest in and expectations from preaching at the liturgy.[5] Priests (as well as bishops and deacons) are aware of the central assertion of the Decree on the Ministry and Life of Priests of Vatican II:

> The People of God are joined together primarily by the word of the living God. And rightfully they expect this from their priests. Since no one can be saved who does not first believe, priests, as co-workers with their bishops, have the primary duty of proclaiming the Gospel of God to all. (n. 4)[6]

In light of this serious responsibility and opportunity, I will begin by offering the following questions and issues related to preaching.[7]

- *What is our operative theology of grace in preaching?*
  Is it "naming grace in everyday life"? Is it that the word

141

of God comes like an unexpected bolt from outside the everyday to sanctify us? Might it be a theology of "memorial" in which *anamnesis* refers to the whole liturgical event and not "just" to words of blessing and consecration? Is preaching part of the "act of memory" that constitutes the liturgy? If we believe that sacraments cause grace, is the Proclamation of the Word and preaching part of sacramental causality?[8]

• *Do we know what a good liturgical homily is or should be?* There is important, growing literature about, and a call for, mystagogical preaching. A classic definition of this would be "initiation into the mysteries"—of Christ through the liturgy. This could well be a very fruitful avenue for preachers to raise for self-examination. What is the operative result a preacher seeks to offer through the homily? Deeper experience of God through the paschal mystery as experienced in the liturgy is hard to beat.

• *Put more practically, do the words of our homilies contain some reference to the rest of the liturgy?* Why do we need to move from ambo to font or to altar, or to *anoint* the bodies of the sick, or to hear the sins of penitents? The issue is, how do Word and Sacrament form one act of worship? If we could bracket out the homily or when it refers back to the Proclamation of the Word only, and not the Sacrament part of the rite, then I think we are not being faithful to the Catholic vision of sacramentality.

• *Is our preaching too much about "results" rather than about its function as a means of grace given to us to transform and sanctify?* It should not be—if we allow that a proper appreciation of the liturgy places the emphasis on what God does for us uniquely through the liturgy, as opposed to what we do for God at the liturgy. Perhaps a preacher could devote several weeks to emphasizing what the proclaimed word is doing among us. Put simply: less moralizing, more emphasis on what God does for us.[9]

- *Can we use the familiar to enliven the new?* We hear the same Gospel texts in the daily liturgy year after year, the same first readings every two years, and the same Sunday readings every three years. But there is no such thing as a "repeated liturgy." It is our privilege to give voice to those words here and now in each new church and world situation. The liturgy is always a new event; it is always these same texts and rites celebrated in new contexts for us, the church, and the world.

- *Are we able to examine, even overturn, cultural assumptions and practices when needed?* For example, in a culture that prizes individual initiative and work, the recent downturn in the economy has caused serious burdens for many among us. Parishioners who are out of work or burdened by decreased income should be on preachers' minds and in their prayers as they preach important Catholic social themes, such as the common good. Fidelity to the Gospel, especially in such a context, is a challenge and a responsibility.

Contemporary Challenges

While numerous aspects of contemporary American culture need to be factored into an approach to preaching, the following insights are offered to remind preachers of the issues that influence the contexts in which the liturgy is celebrated today:

MOBILITY OF PARISHIONERS

In many parishes today, one cannot presume that the liturgical community is the same week after week. In one sense, this *mobility* of parishioners means a change of their physical locations. Countless people in urban areas move rather frequently, seeking employment or accepting business transfers. Some major

American cities have planned suburbs surrounding them so that frequent movers can find in their new home the same amenities they experienced in their former locations. At other times, mobility simply means that people *choose where* to worship. For many, parish boundaries are no longer an obstacle to choosing where to celebrate Mass and to attend to their other spiritual needs.

Mobility of parishioners can also mean a change in time, in that people choose to attend Mass less frequently. In recent sociological surveys, some American Catholics characterize themselves as "occasional" Mass-goers. Some attend about once a month. Pastoral ministers deal with this regularly in the course of pastoral ministry. They deal with it most poignantly in sacramental preparation programs when they encounter baptized "non-practicers." The presumption that people belong to parishes, are regular participants in liturgy, and regular contributors to parish collections can no longer be sustained.

These phenomena mean that preachers cannot presume that the congregation necessarily knows him or that he knows them and that allusions or explanations offered in previous homilies are remembered. It also means that while preachers and many parishioners can rely on the continuous reading of a book of the Bible (*lectio continua*) to foster an ever-deepening awareness of the richness of that book, many other people experience each Eucharist as a unit distinct from those that preceded it and will follow it.

FEWER PRIESTS

The other side of the coin about the mobility of parishioners is the mobility of clergy. The decline in the number of the ordained and the phenomenon of clustering parishes mean that the stability offered by a regular priest staff at a given parish cannot be presumed. It is not uncommon today for a single priest to celebrate several Masses (sometimes in several parishes) on a weekend. This places an immediate strain on him in terms of getting to know the parishioners. Also, when priests cover parishes on a rotation basis or infrequently (if at all), the question of "liturgical familiarity" needs to be raised. This means that especially at Sunday Eucharist there should be a presumed rapport within and among the assembly and a familiarity with what goes on liturgically at Mass. A change in presiding priests can disturb that kind of "at homeness" that the ritual of liturgy would normally presume. It also means that preachers are truly challenged to learn the strengths and weaknesses of the liturgical community they are serving, sometimes on an infrequent basis. This means that even more effort than usual needs to go into assessing what to say and what not to say in a homily, simply because it is meant to respect and reflect the particular liturgical community assembled for worship. Paradoxically, as the frequency and demand for quality preaching increases, the decline in the number of priests may well mean that they have less time to devote to preparing homilies.

To "fill the gap" caused by the decrease in American priests, many dioceses often rely on international priests for pastoral ministry and service. While *Preaching the Mystery of Faith* notes the challenge this affords in a positive way,[10] anecdotal evidence, at least, indicates that an inability to understand what a preacher is saying causes increased disappointment with homilies, especially at a time when there are heightened expectations about what parishioners expect from them.

MULTICULTURALISM

The still-burgeoning awareness of the multicultural nature of most of our liturgical communities offers both a real challenge and a real opportunity for pastoral ministers today. Those who deal with the more obvious culturally diverse communities (with various ethnic groups in one parish) realize only too well that "multicultural liturgy" is a work in progress. Some parishes celebrate Masses in several languages. What happens when there is but a single liturgy for a given occasion, such as the Easter Vigil? Deciding which languages to use and at what points during a given liturgy is its own challenge for such a parish. Determining the appropriate idiom for the homily is another.

At the same time, our multicultural awareness has led to profound respect for the variety of ethnic groups that comprise a local parish. It also serves as a constant reminder that we need to be aware of exactly who populates our liturgies and to ask ourselves continually how best to minister to these people effectively.

It is notable that the American bishops cited the practice of preaching in African American communities as an example of how "particular cultures often have their own preferences for which style of preaching they find most compelling."[11] That this statement can lead to a respect for a variety of ways of preaching in multicultural settings is something that pastoral ministers will find both encouraging and challenging. In preaching, as in much of the liturgy, "one size does not fit all," despite the fact that the structures of the liturgy and the lectionary selection of the proclaimed scriptures in the same.

CATECHETICAL BACKGROUND

It is fair to say that the catechetical challenges that resulted from Vatican II were not always met with universal success; some were not even welcomed at all. Catholic literacy remains a work in progress. Pastoral ministers realize only too well that sacramental-preparation programs are often opportunities for engaging in practices surrounding the new evangelization. Those who teach at Catholic colleges and universities are often struck by the lack of theological preparation and depth that new students bring to campus. Many American preachers find themselves faced with the same situation that Pope John Paul II addressed in his post-synodal exhortation about the church in Europe (*Ecclesia in Europa*: "Everywhere, then, *a renewed proclamation is needed even for those already baptized*. Many Europeans today think they know what Christianity is, yet they do not really know it at all" (n. 47).[12]

This can also mean that terms used to describe lived realities from former generations can no longer be used without adjustment. Specifically, this means that while mystagogy in the patristic era was the presumed consequence of the catechumenate and its intellectual and spiritual formation, today we are faced with the challenge that many who are baptized are still in need of the basic formation in the faith into which they have been baptized.

HIGHER EXPECTATIONS OF PREACHING

And yet another challenge: American Catholics today have higher expectations than former generations in terms of the content of the homilies they hear, their contemporary relevance, and their application to their real lives. Across the board, American Catholics are (much) more highly educated than even a generation or two ago. They expect more from preaching.

This is well documented in recent sociological surveys of American Catholics. In the 2001 survey presented in *Young Adult Catholics*,[13] young people aged between twenty and thirty-nine stated that what was positive about their experience of liturgy was homilies, music, and a vibrant sense of community. (They rated the liturgy negatively when it was "boring," "mechanical," or "unwelcoming.") Other surveys point to the quality of preaching and give priests fairly high marks. In *Catholicism in Motion*,[14] when graded in report-card language, priests receive a grade of B. One-third of laypeople report that homilies are excellent. Forty-five percent say they are good. Twenty percent rate homilies as only fair to poor. A summary of other (earlier) surveys[15] indicates that homilies are very important to the quality of the experience of the liturgy and that good preaching helps lay Catholics understand the meaning of the proclaimed scriptures and the teaching of the church (especially from Vatican II).

Obviously preaching matters. It matters so much that those who preach need to challenge themselves continually to work on even more effective, carefully constructed, and well-delivered homilies. It is a matter of justice and professional integrity that those to whom the ministry of preaching is given act responsibly in the ways they fulfill that ministry.

In effect, these (and numerous other) examples of contemporary challenges for preachers are noted simply to remind preachers that to be effective they need to be aware of the liturgical communities they serve. Learning and relearning who they are is an important first step in determining what is adequate for preaching a homily today.

147

Preachers Are Fellow Listeners

"SPEAK, LORD, FOR YOUR SERVANT IS LISTENING"

This text is very familiar to us because it is often used as an acclamation to accompany the procession with the *Book of the Gospels* that precedes our hearing of the words of the Gospel. The text's origin is the call of Samuel in the Old Testament (1 Sam 3:1–10, 19–20), which is proclaimed every other year right after the Christmas season.[16]

The original context for this passage is a time when revelations from God were few. Eli and young Samuel were asleep. Three times Samuel heard the voice of God, roused Eli from sleep, and three times was sent back to bed. Only after the third try did Eli and Samuel realize that it was indeed the Lord who was calling Samuel to spread his word and thus to renew the dynamic of God's speaking to Israel and leading them as his chosen people (see 1 Sam 3). The fact that this text of Samuel's "call" is read during the first week of the liturgical year is always poignant and pertinent. After the appropriate festivities of the Christmas season, we celebrate the beginning of Jesus' earthly ministry by commemorating his baptism in the Jordan by John. Then the very next week we hear a text that can equally apply to us all as those who hear and respond to God's call in our day and age. The call of God to Samuel is God's call to us to do two things: *to listen and respond* to God's call. Is it any wonder that we find the summary phrase "Speak, Lord, for your servant is listening" as an acclamation before our hearing of the good news of salvation? It reminds us that God's speaking is a direct address and invitation to us to "listen up" and respond to the power of God's revelation.

It is also worth noting that the full text of the proposed acclamation is "Speak, Lord, for your servant is listening; you have the words of everlasting life." This second part of the acclamation is from John's Gospel (John 6:69, the end of what is often called the "Bread of Life" discourse), indicating that what we are about to hear are words that lead us to everlasting life. Not surprisingly, the liturgy juxtaposes texts to reiterate a main point—

God's speaking makes things happen and our hearing and living of God's word lead us to everlasting life.

"ONLY SAY THE WORD AND MY SOUL SHALL BE HEALED"

This text is familiar to all of us as we say it each time we celebrate the Eucharist and are invited to communion. That this text makes an explicit link between the Proclamation of the Word and the reception of the Eucharist is a subtle but important example of the assertion of *Sacrosanctum Concilium* that Word and Sacrament are one act of worship (n. 56). Originally the text is from the Gospel miracle of the raising of the centurion's servant (Matt 8:5–11), which is proclaimed every year on Monday of the First Week of Advent. In its original setting, the text was an act of humility on the part of the one beseeching Christ's help, and it reiterated the man's confidence in Jesus' powerful words. When placed in our Advent readings, this Gospel text is another kind of powerful reminder, that especially in Advent we are to listen to and ponder the words of the Gospel as we await the Word of God to be born among us once again at the incarnation feast of Christmas. It is appropriate that our annual Advent journey begins with this reference to healing from the word of God— "only say the word and my soul shall be healed"—which healing is concretized and renewed throughout the whole liturgical year, for example, at Christmas.

The point made through references to scriptural texts used in the liturgy is that God's speaking continues and deepens every time we celebrate the liturgy and the scriptures are proclaimed. It is at God's gracious invitation that we come to the liturgy and it is from his word that we are fed and nourished spiritually. That the centurion's act of faith in Christ's word is part of the very liturgy of the Eucharist tells us of the import of hearing God's word and what it means to welcome God's speaking through the proclaimed scriptures at liturgy.

The very first words that St. Benedict uses to begin his Rule for monks are these: "Listen, my son, to your master's precepts and attend to them with the ear of your heart." The Latin term here, *ascolta*, is an imperative, which usage carries the sense of command—"Do it!" To reinforce that what he is talking about is not a mental exercise, Benedict goes on to invite the monks to "attend to them [your master's precepts] with the ear of your heart." What an interesting turn of phrase and juxtaposition of words—"the ear of our hearts." Yet how often does our liturgy also place in relationship things that normally do not fit together? The classic psalm verse often used in the Roman liturgy at communion is Psalm 34:8: "Taste and see how good the Lord is." What we taste is bread and wine become Christ's body and blood. What we are to "see" by tasting is something that physical senses or abilities cannot provide—namely, God's graciousness and mercy. Two physical capacities are juxtaposed—tasting and seeing—and the combination of the two means that what we taste and see at the Eucharist is far more than senses can give us. We taste and see sacramental signs of the fullest reality possible: the grace, mercy, and peace of Christ.

Something of the same thing is at stake in Benedict's *ear* and *heart*. Again we have two physical realities. The one is the organ through which we can hear; the other is the organ that pumps the principle of life—blood—throughout our bodies. But what is meant is far more than physical senses or actions. *Ear* signifies more than the sense of hearing. Benedict's challenge is whether we truly listen to what we hear, whether we choose to be attentive to what comes to us through our ears. This is strengthened by the reference to our heart, but not in the sense of a physical organ. For Benedict and for so many of us, *heart* means the center of our affections, the source of our self-giving in love, the most sensitive reality that humans experience—all summarized by the word *heart*. Small wonder, then, that our continual Lenten prayer is for "a heart, humbled and contrite" (Ps 51:19). That we repeatedly use Psalm 51 during Lent is significant. That we pray for a *humbled* heart means a heart that knows its need for God. Far from groveling before an angry God, we offer a true Lenten prayer that we knows our need for God and petition that God would reshape and remold us according to the divine image and likeness.

It is simply no wonder, then, that St. Benedict would choose to begin his Rule by referring to the challenge of taking what he says so seriously that it would mean allowing the words of his Rule to take deep root in the depths of our being. Again, *heart* here means "our inmost being," the very thing that shapes the way we experience and look at life. And all of this from the invitation to *listen*.

Improved Preaching

In his post-synodal exhortation *Sacramentum Caritatis*, Pope Benedict XVI states:

> Given the importance of the word of God, the quality of homilies needs to be improved. The homily is "part of the liturgical action" and is meant to foster a deeper understanding of the word of God, so that it can bear fruit in the lives of the faithful. Hence ordained ministers must "prepare the homily carefully, based on an adequate knowledge of Sacred Scripture." Generic and abstract homilies should be avoided. In particular, I ask these ministers to preach in such a way that the homily closely relates the proclamation of the word of God to the sacramental celebration and the life of the community, so that the word of God truly becomes the Church's vital nourishment and support. The catechetical and paraenetic aim of the homily should not be forgotten. During the course of the liturgical year it is appropriate to offer the faithful, prudently and on the basis of the three-year lectionary, "thematic" homilies treating the great themes of the Christian faith, on the basis of what has been authoritatively proposed by the Magisterium in the four "pillars" of the *Catechism of the Catholic Church* and the recent *Compendium*, namely: the profession of faith, the celebration of the Christian mystery, life in Christ and Christian prayer. (n. 46)[17]

In the context of John Paul II's and Benedict XVI's (repeated) calls for a new evangelization, preachers should see part of the fulfillment of their ministry to be "spokespersons" for correct Catholic teaching. This does not mean that the homily becomes the setting for catechetical instruction independent of or apart from the scriptures of the day. But it does mean that among the kinds of homilies that can be given, some with explicit catechetical and mystagogical content are possible, sometimes even necessary. In such cases, the mystagogic catecheses and catecheses from the patristic tradition can be very influential.

One potential contribution of classic mystagogical catecheses is to help preachers place appropriate emphasis on a catechetical approach to preaching that is doctrinally sound. This will require contemporary preachers to style themselves as interpreters of mystagogy for the contemporary Catholic Church and not simply as someone who repeats words and phrases from treatises from a former age. The meanings of words can and do change. The reality content of a word cannot be guaranteed by using that term in different contexts, especially if those contexts are from different historical periods. For example, describing the Eucharist with such terms as *figura* and *symbolon* was rich in theological insight and content in many patristic treatises. But the reality content of such words was less sure in the medieval period. By the time of the Council of Trent, the church found herself in a position of insisting that the Eucharist had to be described with additional terms in order to convey much of the same depth conveyed by *figure* and *type* in the earlier era. Thus, the opportunity, not to say requirement, for preachers in our day is to convey the theological insights from mystagogical catecheses in a contemporary language and idiom, reflecting the continuing revelation of God in and through Christ by means of the sacred liturgy.[18]

Despite the frequency of liturgical preaching having grown exponentially since the reformed rites from Vatican II, it can well be argued that we have yet to achieve an adequate theology of such preaching. Recourse to mystagogical catecheses would be a significant step in redirecting preaching to one of its first purposes—to explore and explain the sacred mysteries celebrated in the liturgy (more on this in chapter 9).

Practical Helps Toward More Effective Preaching

KNOW WHAT THE HOMILY IS NOT

The homily is not a summary or a retelling of the stories of the scriptures. Rather, the texts of the scriptures should be revered for what they are—a summary of the words and acts of God through Christ on our behalf. And it is through their proclamation that what they recount happens again and again in the liturgical assembly of believers.

The homily is not Bible study, even though study of the Bible is critical for appreciating how to interpret the scriptures for a particular community.

The homily is not moralizing about how these scriptures have to be lived, but an invitation, showing ways in which what is proclaimed may always be experienced as the good news of salvation and how it can be reflected in correct thought and conduct.

The homily is not about the details of what happened to Jesus, but in this act of proclaiming the Gospel in the liturgy, recounting the words and deeds of Jesus is an occurrence of salvation here and now.

MAKE THE HOMILY A BRIDGE

Because of its precise location in the flow of the eucharistic liturgy, the homily leads to the rest of the liturgical action. It can well be seen as something of a "bridge" between the proclamation of the scriptures and the rest of the eucharistic liturgy.[19] One way in which preachers can help assemblies appreciate the fact that what occurs in the Proclamation of the Word and at the altar table is one act of worship is to make specific reference to what will follow the homily in the Eucharist. This is also true for the celebration of other sacraments during the Eucharist, such as marriage and the anointing of the sick, and especially when (infant) baptisms take place at the Sunday Eucharist. Some explicit reference to our continuing from the word through to the rest of the eucharistic action can help avoid any possible separation within the Eucharist as well as underscore how the Proclamation of the Word is itself sacramental. Again we can apply the insight of St. Augustine that if a sacrament is a *visible word*, then the proclamation of the scriptures can be called an *audible symbol*.

USE LITURGICAL SOURCES

Especially during seasons of the church year and on feasts celebrated on Sundays, reflection on the prayers of the Sunday liturgy and the (mostly) patristic texts from the Liturgy of the Hours can provide a most helpful lens through which to read and appreciate the scriptures for that day. For example, the Collect prayer for the Christmas Day Mass offers the keen insight that what the liturgy at Christmas celebrates and enacts is the incarnation of the Word and humans once again being made sharers in divinity through him.[20] Similarly, references in the prayers of the Christmas liturgy to our "wait[ing] in hope for our redemption," to the fact that the Christmas vigil "marks the beginnings of our redemption," and to Christmas as a "most holy exchange" whereby we ask that "we may be found in the likeness of Christ, in whom our nature is joined to you"—all serve as important reminders that liturgical commemoration is about our being drawn into the very mystery of God's act of saving and redeeming us through Christ. The liturgy effects what it commemorates; in commemorating the mystery of Christ, which began at his incarnation, the liturgy uniquely makes us sharers in it.

In addition, selections from several patristic sermons on the incarnation (for example, by St. Leo the Great, St. Augustine, and St. Athanasius) are read in the Office of Readings in the Liturgy of the Hours during the Christmas season. Reflection on these rich sources can help to ground theologically our interpretation of the scriptures that are proclaimed on a given day.

The same is true for the Easter Triduum. On Holy Thursday night, after the eucharistic gifts are prepared, in the Prayer over the Gifts we pray the Lord to grant us

That we may participate worthily in these mysteries,
For whenever the memorial of this sacrifice is celebrated
The work of our redemption is accomplished.

On Easter Sunday itself at this same moment in the liturgy we pray:

> Exultant with paschal gladness, O Lord,
> We offer the sacrifice
> By which your Church
> Is wondrously reborn and nourished.

Such texts help shape the liturgical context in which we hear the scriptures proclaimed. So do the patristic sermons on Good Friday from St. John Chrysostom, and on Holy Saturday from an anonymous second-century Christian author. They cannot but help preachers appreciate how what is proclaimed occurs among us through what the sacred liturgy always enact—our participation in the paschal mystery of Christ.

TAP INTO CONTEMPORARY CULTURE AND CURRENT EVENTS

Like all peoples and communities, liturgical assemblies grow and develop. They are never stagnant. When preachers take deliberate steps to stay current with world and church events, and with contemporary culture, especially in terms of the arts, the language and idioms in their homilies can be more readily accessible and understandable. References to contemporary literature and art in homilies can go a long way toward inviting an immediate resonance with today's liturgical assemblies. Staying conversant about the state of the world helps preaching from becoming too parochial or provincial. A wise use of Internet communication can help put a worldwide lens on the news of the day and cannot help but be influential on the way a given set of scripture readings interfaces with the contemporary world.

DRAW EXAMPLES FROM PASTORAL CARE

Another obvious but often untapped aspect of the preachers' preparation is the pastoral care in which they are engaged on a daily basis. The liturgy and liturgical preaching should be understood to flow from and return to daily ministry. We do not live in "two different worlds" of liturgy and life but in one world in which the liturgy shapes and forms the rest of daily life. When preachers reflect on the kinds of things they are called upon to do in pastoral care, they cannot help but realize the interfacing of the perennial good news of the scriptures proclaimed at (Sunday) Eucharist with the challenges that their people face and the opportunities they encounter. When trying to apply the scriptures to help them become actualized in the lives of the Sunday assembly, a preacher's reflection on his own daily life in ministry can offer a wealth of real-life examples to comment on. In this way homilies are rooted in the real lives of real people—the very assembly one is preaching to.

OFFER THE SAINTS AS MODELS

Sunday is the primordial and foundational feast day for Christians. It is both the first day of the week and the eighth day—it is a celebration of creation, redemption, and the second coming. It is the enactment of the paschal mystery for the sake of the church's recreation in and through Christ. Like all liturgy, it is done in the name of and in the power of the Trinity. Sunday preempts celebrating the feast of saints, even those whose feasts occur on a Sunday.

However, the commemoration of saints and the sanctoral cycle in the liturgy are chief characteristics of Catholic life and worship. The saints who are commemorated in the liturgy are named (and many times acclaimed so) by the church as models and exemplars of sanctity, true witnesses to Christ who deserve emulation and imitation.

Given the current keen interest in spirituality, preachers can put forth some models of deep Christian spirituality from the saints who have gone before us and who have left us a legacy in their followers. For example, giving examples in homilies from the lives and writings from the religious orders and apostolic communities that are part of the fabric and vitality of the Catholic tradition can help underscore that true spirituality goes beyond the self and one's relationship to God to a wider experience of discovering God in daily life and serving God as one serves others.

156

When homilists refer to those saints who are acknowledged to have achieved heroic sanctity, to have served the church in particularly trying times, to have accomplished important benchmarks for our theological tradition, or to have given their lives as martyrs for the faith, they reflect the breadth of the Catholic tradition in their preaching. When they speak about the struggles that these saints experienced, they encourage contemporary Catholics to strive for similar holiness of life despite their (our) own difficulties and struggles.

USE DIRECT SPEECH AND AVOID THEOLOGICAL JARGON

Technically the word *homily* derives from the Greek *homilia*, which means a kind of address that is readily accessible and understandable. This definition reminds preachers that one of their main tasks is to make connections with and for the assemblies in which they preach. The clearer the explanations and the more concrete the examples given, the better—especially for contemporary congregations who are accustomed to sound bites and executive summaries. Direct speech can be of great value in the art of preaching.

Deacons, priests, and bishops have been trained theologically for their roles in the church. Therefore, they have grown accustomed to precise theological words and phrases that are not necessarily (immediately) understandable to the whole congregation. It is to everyone's advantage if these terms can be broken down and applied without "dumbing down" their content.

For example, a preacher who wants to address *ecclesiology* and *ecclesiological implications* of Catholic identity might well speak about ways of belonging in society, one's role as parishioner of this particular parish (or other liturgical congregation), how parishes together form a diocese, and how dioceses are related to each other worldwide to comprise the universal church. A preacher wishing to address issues about the *parousia* (especially in a season like Advent) might speak about Christ's second coming at the end of time to bring time to an end, and emphasize that one of the real challenges of focusing on the end of time is to live well in the present.

In discussing Christ's *paschal mystery*, a preacher might want to begin by speaking about the phenomenon of suffering, terminal illness, care giving, and death. The naming of these real-life experiences can invite appreciation of the way God chose to redeem us—through the dying and rising of his Son. Furthermore, a preacher who invites the assembly to name their limitations, trials, sufferings, and defeats at the Eucharist can also remind the assembly that the Eucharist joins our limitations to the humiliation, obedience, suffering, death, and resurrection of Christ through the very Eucharist we are celebrating.

Any homiletic rhetoric that sets up a possible dichotomy between the preacher and the congregation should be avoided. The use of the word *you* to address the congregation should be avoided in favor of an inviting rhetoric that almost always uses *you and I...we...our...and us.* It is not coincidental that almost all of the pronouns referring to human beings in the liturgy are plural. The same should be true for the homily.

WRITE THE TEXT

Preachers differ with regard to how they deliver a homily. Some use a word-for-word text; others do not. (The document *Preaching the Mystery of Faith* asserts that "normally the effective homilist will not be content to simply read a written text of his homily but will have so internalized what he wants to preach that the text or outline serves only as an aid to the direct proclamation of his message.")[21] But there is considerable agreement on the value of writing a text. Here the discipline of writing the text is almost as important as its contents. Preachers ought to know *what* they want to say and *how* they want to say it. They ought to know well their introduction, the flow of the contents, and the homily's conclusion. One of the most important aspects of homily *preparation* is deciding what not to say. Writing a text will trim unnecessary words and focus the message. One of the most important aspects of *delivering* the homily is knowing very clearly how to begin it and how to end it. Having a written text is of enormous assistance. (In addition, when people may challenge what one has said in a homily, it is helpful to have a written text to refer to for explanation, not to say one's defense.) What needs to be avoided in delivery is anything that could come across as stilted or wooden. The genre of a homily requires that it be accessible for the entire assembly. Rhetoric that is too heightened or aimed only to be read can be deadly. But rhetoric that is well crafted, incisive, and compelling can serve to invite attention and interest

DETERMINE THE PROPORTIONATE LENGTH

Trying to determine one hard-and-fast rule of thumb for the length of the homily is difficult. One needs to respect a variety of things, including the particular occasion, the cultural diversity of the group, and the community's customary expectations. But foremost is that the homily should not be so long as to minimize the particularly eucharistic aspects of what is celebrated in and through the Mass. Therefore, a better way to ask the question is this: What is the proportion between the two parts of the one act of worship—the Proclamation of the Word and the rest of the Eucharist?

If a homily is too long, the other parts of the Mass may end up being done in a summary manner that would diminish their importance. The repeated or almost exclusive use of Eucharistic Prayer II, for example, can diminish the assembly's appreciation of the Eucharistic Prayer as a proclamation of good news, albeit in a different manner from the Proclamation of the Word. A wise selection from the Sunday Prefaces and Eucharistic Prayers can help echo what was proclaimed in the Gospel for that Sunday and would also ensure that, over time, the assembly hears the breadth of what is contained in these prayers. Likewise, an abbreviated procession with the gifts diminishes the intrinsic connection between what the assembly brings as an offering, the offering of the Eucharist, and the transformation of the presented gifts of bread and wine into the body and blood of Christ. Theologically, the presentation of what results from "the work of human hands" fittingly becomes, through eucharistic consecration, "the work of our redemption."

The question of length also raises the question of respect for ethnic diversity and cultural assumptions. It is difficult, if not impossible, to describe the "average American parish" and thus to determine the best "average" length of the Sunday homily. Certain African American and Latino assemblies have grown accustomed to Sunday homilies that last more than what is often proposed as the eight-to-ten minute norm. Further, certain liturgical celebrations, such as ordinations or the installation of a new bishop, may well require a longer homily than "usual." In trying to deal with the catechetical challenges for adults in today's church, some parishes devote the homily at one of the Sunday Masses to a decidedly longer, more instructional homily. Such practices should obviously be respected, with the proviso that other aspects of the eucharistic liturgy are not eclipsed or diminished.

CHAPTER SEVEN

Liturgical Roles and Presiding at Liturgy

The Celebrant of the Liturgy

The 1971 document *Music in Catholic Worship* from the Committee on the Liturgy of the then National Conference of Catholic Bishops states: "No other single factor affects the liturgy as much as the attitude, style and bearing of the celebrant: his sincere faith and warmth as he welcomes the worshipping community, his human naturalness combined with dignity and seriousness as he breaks the Bread of Word and Eucharist" (n. 21). It then goes on to emphasize the importance of the celebrant's singing of the most important parts of the Mass.[1] In the more recent document *Sing to the Lord*,[2] the thought is repeated (n. 18), with the addition that "the priest must serve God and the people with dignity and humility, and by his bearing and by the way he says the divine words he must convey to the faithful the living presence of Christ."[3]

I have always judged that this statement is correct as far as it goes and is both an appropriate challenge and a support to priest-presiders. But I have also wondered whether it might militate against the clear (r)evolution in liturgical ministries in the reformed liturgy, namely, that it presumes there is no active involvement of a number of other ministers to help enact and accomplish it. My sense is that it places so much emphasis on the priest that it could be read as endorsing a post-Tridentine "attitude" in which there was, in the liturgy, a clear separation between the actions of the priest and the passivity of the congregation. While I was heartened to see that in the revision the text added some admonitions that challenge priest-presiders, I still think that the presider's role (bishop or priest) ought always be seen in relation to the plurality of ministries and ministers presumed in the reformed liturgy.

This is to say that the baptismal priesthood and the ministerial priesthood should be in evidence in every liturgy, and that the distinctions among liturgical roles go as far back in our tradition as the second century (and likely in practice before this) and are reflected in all of the reformed liturgies since Vatican II. The misunderstandings of the clear teaching of Vatican II's Constitution on the Church (*Lumen Gentium*), nn. 10 and 11, about the difference "in essence" between the ordained and the baptized was one reason why Pope John Paul II wrote *Dominicae Cenae* in 1980 and other subsequent "Holy Thursday Letters."[4]

Lumen Gentium stresses the fundamental equality of all the faithful, established as the new people of God through baptism. In the words of Avery Dulles: "This view serves as a corrective to a traditional understanding of the Church as a *societas inaequalium*."[5]

Allow me to offer here the operative image of three concentric circles. The largest is the priesthood of Christ, the second within it is the priesthood of the baptized, and the third at the center is the ministerial priesthood. For me, this image indicates the importance of Christ's high priesthood to ground the others, and indicates the others as related intrinsically to Christ and to each other. Baptism is the foundation and fundamental ecclesial identification sacrament. The charisms of all the baptized are charisms and gifts for the upbuilding of the church. Priests minister to and serve all the baptized, among whom are delegated and selected other ministers. Classic Catholic theology notes that the sacramental distinction between the ordained and the priesthood of all believers is deep and abiding in the person: a baptized Christian is not and cannot do things that the ordained bishop, priest, or deacon is called to be and to do.

But the laity are also to be involved in Christ's life and mission, as asserted in *Lumen Gentium*:

[Jesus Christ] associates [the laity] intimately with his life and mission and has also given them a share in his priestly office of offering spiritual worship [...] For all their works, if done in the Spirit, become spiritual sacrifices acceptable to God through Jesus Christ; their prayers and apostolic works, their married and family life, their daily work, their mental and physical recreation. (n. 34)

The *Code of Canon Law*, however, omits this specific foundation for the mission of the baptized (canon 225.2, for example, speaks about the lay mission to bring the spirit of the Gospel to temporal affairs, but does not refer to the common priesthood). Canon 216 states that all the *christifideles* participate in the church's mission, but it does not specify the origin of this participation in the *munus* of Jesus Christ, the priest.[6]

As a sacramental theologian, I find it theologically important that in the Rite of Presbyteral Ordination (translated as "ordination of a priest"), which was revised after Vatican II, the bishop consecrates the hands of the ordained with chrism and not with the oil of catechumens, as in the rite used after Trent.[7] The fact that chrism is used at baptism, chrismation/confirmation, and ordination is of import liturgically and theologically. Recall the prayer at the anointing with chrism at baptism: "The God of power and Father of our Lord Jesus Christ...now anoints you with the chrism of salvation, so that, united with his people, you may remain forever a member of Christ who is Priest, Prophet and King." Also recall that the bishop says the following when he anoints the palms of the hands of the new priests:

The Lord Jesus Christ,
whom the Father anointed with the Holy Spirit and power,
guard and preserve you
that you may sanctify the Christian people
and offer sacrifice to God.

It is at least ecclesiologically notable that this translation places sanctifying the church ("the Christian people") before offering

163

sacrifice to God. This clearly reflects the church's magisterial teaching on (ordained) ministry.[8]

The Theology of Liturgical Ministries

I noted above that the variety of roles intrinsic to the celebration of the liturgy goes as far back as the second century. In the *First Apology* of Justin Martyr, we read what is regarded as a classic and formative description:

And on the day called Sunday, all who live in cities or in the country gather together to one place, and the memoirs of the apostles or the writings of the prophets are read, as long as time permits; then, when the reader has ceased, the president verbally instructs, and exhorts to the imitation of these good things. Then we all rise together and pray, and, as we before said, when our prayer is ended, bread and wine and water are brought, and the president in like manner offers prayers and thanksgivings, according to his ability, and the people assent, saying Amen; and there is a distribution to each, and a participation of that over which thanks have been given, and to those who are absent a portion is sent by the deacons. And they who are well to do, and willing, give what each thinks fit; and what is collected is deposited with the president, who succours the orphans and widows and those who, through sickness or any other cause, are in want, and those who are in bonds and the strangers sojourning among us, and in a word takes care of all who are in need. But Sunday is the day on which we all hold our common assembly, because it is the first day on which God, having wrought a change in the darkness and matter, made the world; and Jesus Christ our Saviour on the same day rose from the dead. For He was crucified on the day before that of Saturn (Saturday); and on the day after that of Saturn, which is the day of the Sun, having appeared to His apostles and

164

disciples, He taught them these things, which we have submitted to you also for your consideration. (n. 67)[9]

There are countless commentaries on this text and on the profusion of post–Vatican II ecclesial and liturgical ministries. What follows are some observations of a pastoral liturgical nature on the enacted theology of liturgical ministries.

THE GATHERED ASSEMBLY

After Vatican II, given the attention that the liturgical community received in fostering active participation, especially in the first initiatives, there should be no surprise at the wealth and profusion of commentaries on the theology of the gathered assembly and its importance in enacting the liturgy. That there was over-reaching and blurring in some writing, including several pieces of then Cardinal Joseph Ratzinger, was the subject of critiques. Whether liturgical communities were too focused on themselves, whether they were not obviously attentive to God's initiative and sustaining presence, and whether they were as concerned for others as they should have been (as suggested in several places in the above quote from Justin) were certainly matters for reflection and, in some places, correction.

One of the reasons why the rhetoric of official liturgical documents added the term *gathered* to the word *assembly* is to sustain the theological reality that always and everywhere what communities do at the liturgy is to respond to God's initiative and abiding presence in the liturgy. At the same time, that the assembly "gathers" from various places to one place is a theological datum of the liturgy (again, going as far back as Justin). This is the ecclesial reality that is the liturgy. That liturgical communities are increasingly multicultural today is repeatedly asserted. That this challenges us all to be open to this variety is also clear. Liturgical communities that are too focused on themselves or their talents without the requisite communal self-transcendence presumed and fostered by the liturgy are a contradiction in terms.

The way that gathered assemblies comport themselves is also a point at issue. Any kind of presumed passivity that has lingered from the Tridentine liturgy should not be countenanced in the way the reformed liturgy is enacted. Additionally, a passivity that comes from a culture bred on television and computer watching can spill over into the liturgy when, in fact, we are all *actants*—we all participate—with the gathered assembly as the liturgy's foundation and context.

The manner and bearing of the entire gathered assembly matters a great deal because the liturgy is sacred and deserves all our engagement—mind, heart, and bodies. Recall how I earlier described (in chapter 4) those receiving holy communion: they process (rather than "just walk"), with recollected spirits (rather than greeting other people on the way), singing the song that accompanies this sacred action. The way we comport ourselves means that we show reverence for the species: by bowing, by receiving the species reverently, and saying "Amen" with all the faith and devotion that the acclamation deserves.

Moreover, individual members represent the entire assembly as they bring forward the gifts at the Presentation of the Gifts and the Preparation of the Altar. How they comport themselves is important. They should be fully aware of what they are doing and walk forward deliberately and reverently. At the same time, I do recall when I was in Africa when the entire gathered assembly participated in this act of offering, and not just of bread and wine. They all came forward with foodstuffs—vegetables, cheese, oil, fruit, and meat—and placed them before the altar, sometimes with the assistance of the priest-presider (a word also found in Justin). Given all of today's discussion about "liturgical dance" and the problems of drawing attention to oneself, it would be worthwhile for some to witness such an event; it was clear that these liturgical participants took their time, walked slowly and reverently (some to a two-step), and returned to their places as reverently.

As a final matter of comportment is when we dismiss children from the larger assembly for a Children's Liturgy of the Word. Here it is the adults' responsibility to invite the children to walk forward slowly to receive a blessing and then to move quietly to another location, following the Lectionary carried in procession. In my own pastoral experience, the return of the children to the larger assembly needs some attention, lest it seem happenstance and occur when the collection is being taken or, worse, when the Preface is being sung. Procession both out *and* back matters a great deal and can help underscore the importance of liturgical gestures and ritual for the children. When I was under the tutelage of Sofia Cavalletti[10] in Rome in the late 1970s, she insisted that we require children to act in such a way that they are being assimilated into the adult liturgical experience. She was very concerned that we not adapt or adjust the liturgy to a level that would not distinguish it from other events of daily life.[11]

Behavior matters. Bodies matter. The way we reflect in our bodies who we are—the baptized and ordained members of the body of Christ—matters a great deal. The bodiliness of worship is reflected in actions and in evident signs of reverence and decorum.

LECTORS

The fact that *Sacrosanctum Concilium* states that Christ "is present in His word, since it is He Himself who speaks when the holy scriptures are read in the Church" (n. 7) shows how far we have come since the polemics of the Reformation. The fact that Pope Benedict XVI called the Synod on the Word of God in the Life and Mission of the Church and issued the post-synodal exhortation *Verbum Domini* is another example of how much the ecumenical climate has changed and how together the liturgical churches who rely on a lectionary system are challenged and consoled by texts that are more or less the same day after day.

One would be hard-pressed to overestimate the changes in Roman Catholic attitudes toward the Bible—in personal prayer, in *lectio divina*, and in spirituality in general—that have resulted from the structure and contents of the revised set of scripture readings in the lectionaries for all the reformed liturgies. The fact that the scriptures are read in such abundance attests to the way the directives of *Sacrosanctum Concilium* have been followed and to the way the proclamation of the (assigned) scripture readings has been implemented.

The way the scriptures are proclaimed clearly matters a great deal. I am reminded here of two very memorable personal occasions when the way the lectors proclaimed the texts made all the difference in the text coming alive (literally) for me. The first was at the Easter Vigil in the Cathedral in Detroit, when the woman who proclaimed the text from Exodus 14 about the Red Sea made me feel as though I were indeed immersed in that mysterious act of salvation. I will never forget how she read the reiterated phase "water on the left and water on the right." I am also thinking of the woman who proclaimed the first reading at the Liturgy of the Lord's Passion on Good Friday (the Servant Song of Isaiah). Although this is a longer text than many, the way in which she proclaimed the text made me wait on every word. And when she read, "He was pierced for our transgressions, crushed for our iniquities" (Isa 53:5), I was invited into that same saving act then and there.

I regularly shy away from using the word *performance* to describe the way ministers function in the liturgy or the liturgy itself. I do that to avoid any notions of passivity on the part of the gathered assembly during the liturgy. Yet there is an important body of literature about the *performative* value of words and about the fact that in the liturgy words do something. Able and experienced lectors facilitate the performative aspect of what the liturgy is and does.

At the same time, we all have had experiences in the liturgy, not only when lectors were poorly prepared, but when the way they proclaimed the texts did damage to their meaning. And all that is said here about lectors can also be said about deacons (addressed more fully later). Liturgical performance matters. What also matters is the assembly's preparation to welcome the texts by meditative reading beforehand. The liturgy may be the "source and summit" of the church's life, but that apex needs a base, part of which is biblical literacy and preparation for the liturgy. Countless initiatives since Vatican II have marked efforts toward greater understanding of and comprehension of the Bible, especially as designed to be proclaimed in the liturgy and to be appropriated by all who celebrate.

ACOLYTES, ALTAR SERVERS, AND EUCHARISTIC MINISTERS

The former minor orders of porter, reader/lector, exorcist, and acolyte were revised by Pope Paul VI to install candidates for the diaconate and priesthood to the ministries of reader and acolyte.[12] The fact that these installations are limited to candidates for ordination means that, in theory, the role should only rarely be performed by the laity. In practice, the liturgical roles of reader and acolyte are carried out most often by laypeople who are not installed but whose ministry is nonetheless important for the carrying out of the liturgy. The vast majority of dioceses in the United States allow female as well as male altar servers; in some quarters where this is not allowed, it is a source of disappointment, not to say angry frustration. Given this state of affairs, there are at least two ways of interpreting this latter ministry: as one step in the process of leading one to sacred ordination, or as an exercise of the baptismal priesthood with both male and female servers.[13]

In the end, it is at least debatable whether the elimination of a rite of installation is a loss in the sense that it would support the theological and liturgical importance of proclaiming the word in the assembly and serving the holy sacrifice at the altar. My own sense is that if we do, in fact, have rites for commissioning eucharistic ministers and catechists, something is lost with no installation rites for readers and acolytes who are not ordination candidates.

A related issue concerns who serves when installed acolytes are present at the same liturgy as altar servers who are not installed. The official documents say that preference is always to be given to installed readers and acolytes. Nonetheless, it is the custom at St. Peter's in Rome for male and female readers who are not installed to proclaim the scriptures at papal Masses. This reflects the value of liturgical *custom*, which sometimes can trump what official documents say. This precedent leads me to suggest that there be no necessary preference given to installed acolytes over altar servers. And, in fact, especially in a parish or other pastoral liturgical setting, it would seem preferable to allow the altar servers to minister, which would reflect the variety of gifts in the liturgical community and the fact that the community is comprised of males and females.

While acolytes and altar servers have a myriad of tasks in the liturgy—carrying candles in procession, holding the book for the presider at the Collect and the Prayer after Communion, carrying the eucharistic vessels to the altar, and so forth, the ministry of the eucharistic minister is specific: to assist with the distribution of communion (in both forms) in the eucharistic liturgy and also to bring communion to the homebound or those in hospitals or nursing homes. This was attested to as early as Justin Martyr's writings in the second century to be a ministry of the deacon. The broadening of this ministry to baptized lay eucharistic ministers resulted from the post–Vatican II liturgical reforms. One can only applaud the expansion of this ministry and be amazed at how many people have benefitted from it and are able to receive communion regularly, despite their inability to participate in the celebration of the Eucharist.

CANTOR, SCHOLA, CHOIR, MUSICIANS

Notably in the reform of the liturgy the importance of those who lead the music has been enhanced, whether it be an individual cantor, a schola (a group), a choir (who sometimes leads and also complements the assembly's participation by singing specific parts of the liturgy), or those who play accompanying instruments. While more will be said about this ministry in the following chapter, the fact that these are true liturgical ministries—that the music in the liturgy as led by a variety of people has a *ministerial* function—should always be borne in mind. Their clear and obvious engagement in the enactment of the whole liturgy should be presumed, and the quality of their participation should be an example for the whole gathered assembly. The fact that they lead only specific parts of the liturgy does not ever mean that they do not participate in the whole of the liturgy in the manner designed for the whole gathered assembly.

DEACONS

The role of the deacon at the liturgy is clearly delineated in all the revised liturgical books. The story is told that in preparation for the visit of Pope John Paul II to Charleston, South

Carolina, where he presided at an ecumenical prayer service, the normal custom was followed by which a local planning committee met with some Vatican officials far in advance to discuss the plans for the liturgy. In reviewing the outline for the liturgy, one member of the local committee said that "after the pope reads the Gospel," he would deliver the homily. The chair of the Vatican team did not hesitate to say immediately that "the pope never reads the Gospel, the deacon does." Again, this practice has been documented as far back as Justin Martyr.

While the initial documents governing the liturgical reform of the Mass indicated that there was to be a book of readings and a separate book of the Gospels, the common practice in the United States was to have one book for the readings until the published revision of the *General Instruction of the Roman Missal* (GIRM) in 2003 and the publication of a General Instruction of the Gospel book. Part of the ministry of the deacon at Mass is to carry the *Book of the Gospels* in procession, to place it on the altar, to proclaim the Gospel itself, and "on occasion" to deliver the homily and announce the intentions in the Prayer of the Faithful. This indicates the importance given to his ministry. Then the deacon assists in collecting the gifts brought in procession, prepares the altar and gives the gifts to the priest, and assists at the altar through communion and the dismissal rites. In accord with rich liturgical tradition, he then can assist with taking communion to the sick and homebound.

That these liturgical functions until only recently were part of the priest's proper functions was the result of the demise of the diaconate in history, and eventually several liturgical ministries became limited to the priest and the altar server.

It is to be hoped that the variety and (with trust) the complementarity of the liturgical roles as envisioned in the reform are carried out with reverence and decorum and without any turf battles about who has the "right" to do what in the liturgy. It is regrettable that some lingering issues exist that might divide priests and deacons (among others). Not uncommonly, the tensions between priests and deacons concern the extent to which liturgical ministry is paralleled by pastoral charity and service outside of the liturgy. The role of the deacon can be said to be something of a bridge between altar and marketplace; it is not meant to be ministry only "inside the church building." That the deacon announces the intentions for the Prayer of the Faithful stems from the fact that he would know whom to pray for because of his ministry in homes, hospitals, prisons, nursing homes, and so forth. That he would assist at the collection of gifts at the Presentation of the Gifts reflects that it was he who would distribute the collected gifts to the poor. That some deacons today are assigned not to specific parishes but to a more general ministry of and from the bishop (such as prison or hospital ministry) reflects, in my opinion, a move from parish-based diaconal ministries, where there might be tensions between the ordained (priests and deacons) to situations where deacons can function to a large extent on their own (realizing that a priest must preside at the Eucharist if Mass is celebrated and must anoint the sick).

My own sense is that determining what the diaconate is and what deacons properly do is a work in progress. For some time I have thought that until and unless deacons had ministries for which they are specifically responsible and, therefore, are not regarded as the priest's substitute, the diaconate will not mature. For this to occur sacramentally would mean to shift the expectation that priests perform all infant baptisms and marriages. If deacons and their wives become responsible for preparation for these sacraments and celebrate them regularly outside of Mass, then these actions may lead to a more firm identity for the deacon. This shift would also require that communal celebrations of infant baptism take place regularly on the parish liturgical schedule with the same preparation and execution required for the Eucharist. Then these could be true communal liturgical celebrations. If deacons become the customary presiders at marriages, this would diminish the emphasis we have legitimately placed on the importance of celebrating the nuptial Mass, but given the number of interfaith weddings at which the reception of communion reflects separation, not *communion* in the sense of "common union," a wedding with the Liturgy of the Word leading to the marriage rite proper might be pastorally advisable. In addition, the fact that significant numbers of Catholics do not request a church wedding means that we have a serious pastoral problem. It might well be that deacons and their wives could be the "bridge" between what some young people perceive as church bureaucracy, with lots of paperwork and regulations to be followed, and careful and sensitive pastoral care in marriage preparation and celebration. Again, I believe the issue is to share liturgical and ecclesial ministries and at the same time to avoid turf battles.

PRESIDING BISHOPS AND PRIESTS

The very term *presider* can, at times, be off-putting. Its regular use in the revised liturgical documents is a clear attestation to its value, but not as a purely "functional" term. It means to suggest that the one who presides does not do everything and that several others are deputed to do so. In addition, in an American context, *preside* can carry associations with a democratically elected head of state. That is not the case with the one who presides at liturgy. He is ordained for this ministry. Another meaning of *preside* reflects the axiom in our earliest extant (patristic) liturgical and church documents that the one who presided at the liturgy did so because he was the one who presided over the church in leadership, pastoral care, and love.[14] Liturgical ministry was meant to reflect an ongoing relationship with the community one served in pastoral care and sometimes oversight (a term originally used to describe the bishop).

At the same time, we should not be anachronistic and neglect in any way the evolution of those in the mendicant tradition (Franciscans and Dominicans, for example), or in apostolic communities who serve in a variety of ministries, including the missions (such as the Jesuits), whose liturgical and ecclesial ministries are many and varied and are not tied to a diocese or parish (in other words, not geographically defined).

As a diocesan priest-professor, I have maintained close connections with the four parishes at which I have served as weekend presiding priest through my close to thirty years of service at the Catholic University of America. There is a world of difference for me to preside and preach on a regular basis at the same parish rather than be available on an "on call" basis to fill in at different parishes when needed. Eventually those you baptized graduate grammar and high school. Those to whom you gave first communion are high school altar servers and lectors. Those whose confirmation you concelebrated with the bishop return married and with children. Those whom you dismissed weekly as catechumens and candidates are initiated at the Easter Vigil, a liturgy you are privileged to concelebrate. And those whom you anointed with the oil of the sick have gone to God through funeral rites you were privileged to celebrate with grieving families whom you know and whose loss you share. This is part and parcel of a pastor's heart and ministerial experience. While it is not something I do full time, making the effort to be in close and regular contact with the parish makes all the difference for me as presider and homilist.

The variety of liturgical roles and the entire gathered assembly is to participate in a way that reflects reverence, attention, and awareness of others, not just awareness of the priest presiding. In the liturgy, the presider never uses the word *I* independently of the assembly. He always prays in the name of the church: *we...our...us.* Presiding is an ecclesial, not an individual act.

Ars Celebrandi

There has been a clear evolution from emphasizing rubrics (especially after Trent) to fostering *ars celebrandi* in describing the way the reformed liturgy should be conducted. The pithy phrase "say the black, do the red" flies in the face of countless instructions on the proper conduct of the liturgy as an art. Issues of presiding and the way ministers minister loom large here. These liturgical roles have great import for, not to say carry enormous power over (and not always for the good of) the assembly's participation. For example, the manner in which a leader of song directs the assembly makes a world of difference to the effect of the celebration: Is it "Speak, Lord, I love to listen to your voice"? Or is it "Speak, Lord, I love to listen to my voice"? Does a bishop's or priest's manner of presiding follow St. John the Baptist's statement, "I am not the Messiah"? Or does he preside in such an intrusive way as to convey the message, "Without me you can do nothing"?

I often argue that one of the goals of liturgy is communal self-transcendence. This is fostered by individual ministerial self-transcendence and engagement in one's role for the sake of the assembly, to engage them in the liturgy and to foster one's own communal participation in the liturgy. We should put enormous energy into the way we comport ourselves in liturgical roles. But that energy should always be directed toward the other—not the self—and aimed to assist one another to worship God and to be sanctified through the liturgy. To preside, preach, and minister at the liturgy is both an art and a craft. And dare I say more *art* than craft?

CHALLENGES TO PRESIDING: STRUCTURAL AND PASTORAL

The issue of frequency of the Eucharist on the priest's part is related to several factors, many of which are debatable. Among the concerns I will offer brief thoughts on three:

1. The role of the presiding priest in the post–Vatican II liturgy and the demands it makes upon him...

British historian Eamon Duffy observes that the present rite lacks the objectivity and structured form that would allow the priest-presider to be engaged in this unique act of prayer without being unnecessarily attentive to the need to choose from a number of options: for example, whether to commemorate the saint; which Penitential Rite, Preface, and Eucharistic Prayer to use; which songs to sing at the Entrance and the Communion Processions; what intercessions to make at the Prayer of the Faithful; whether to preach; and so on. Some parish priests say that while they can appreciate these concerns, they judge that the scripture readings offer them the material for their daily *lectio divina* and that the study of commentaries and praying over these texts is a great stimulus to their spiritual lives. For monks and mendicants, this issue is mitigated by daily eucharistic concele-bration of the conventual Mass.

2. The structure of the Order of Mass...

The fact that we have one Order of Mass in the revised Missal is a marked change from the previous Tridentine Missal with its three forms: Low Mass, High Mass, and Solemn High Mass. Now that we have one structure, the parish priest can choose from a number of options to simplify the celebration on weekdays. As early as the 1980s, Father Anscar Chupungco, former professor at Sant'Anselmo, argued for a much simpler form of the Order of Mass designed for daily use, called a "ferial Order of Mass."

3. The number of Masses in different locations...

It is common that the (parish) priest must celebrate Masses in more than one location: for example, the parish church, school, hospital, nursing home, or prison. This requires a certain flexibility and also necessitates that he travel to several sites. This is a variation on the issue (noted above) about the number of Masses some priests celebrate on a weekend. While the multiplicity of Masses attests to people's desire to celebrate and participate in the Mass, for the priest it can be an overload in terms of the burdens placed upon him by these multiple Masses.

The daily celebration of the Eucharist has traditionally been urged as a baseline of priestly formation and the priestly life. Indeed, it is the "source and summit" of the Christian, not to say the priestly, life. But a number of factors have influenced (parish) priests to devise strategies so that overload and "eucharistic burnout" do not occur. Conversations about this phenomenon at in-service days for clergy are always spirited, thoughtful, and respectful of the church's tradition and teaching.

THE REALITY OF PRESIDING

Sometimes even the priest presumes that presiding is about what we *do* and *say* and *how we act* at the liturgy. But more often than not, presiding starts long before the liturgy begins. The act of presiding begins when we choose the prayers, or even the Mass formula itself on weekdays of Ordinary Time, or the parts of the

176

Mass that require decisions, such as the Penitential Rite and the Dismissal Rites.

Sometimes the role of presiding starts in the sacristy before the liturgy, when we realize who has not shown up for required roles and try to see who can take their place and whether the job will be done decorously, hopefully with little or no reference to the fact that the ministers have changed.

No one can predict what will actually happen at the liturgy. It is the presider's role to be attentive, to facilitate the flow of the liturgy, not to get in the way, but not to let unnecessary mistakes happen. We celebrate the liturgy day in and day out. For most of the others in liturgical roles, it is an occasional ministry.

Within the one Order of Mass the presiding priest has several other variables to keep in mind. Do we dismiss the children for the Liturgy of the Word? Do we dismiss catechumens and candidates after the homily? Is there a second collection? When are the announcements to be given? Is the hospitality committee serving coffee after Mass? Is there a guest speaker before or after Mass? How many baptisms today? The list goes on and on. As a student of the liturgy, I can assure you that in all my study of the sacramentaries and rituals from the church's tradition, none of these questions is raised, much less answered!

There is an *asceticism* to presiding. One has to be very, very attentive to each and every thing that goes on before and during a liturgy. One of our responsibilities is to facilitate the action, not dominate it. I find a good role model for the presiding priest in the words of St. John the Baptist (which I mentioned previously), who says in John 1:20, "I am not the Messiah," and then two chapters later says, "He must increase; I must decrease" (John 3:30).

Sometimes after two, three, or more Sunday liturgies, a priest is worn out. I wonder sometimes if the Hippocratic oath does not apply to presiding: "Do no harm." To which I would add, "Don't get lost."

I suspect many people judge that, in the act of presiding, the priest feels close to God and experiences great spiritual consolation. Yes, we do, but it is sometimes because of and through the hard work of presiding. We know well that the times we take for personal, quiet prayer and for *lectio divina* can most often be the times when we "feel" closest to the divine, the Other. Liturgy is about the human and the divine intersecting; but sometimes in the liturgy the all-too-human is front and center and takes all our attention. That is as it should be, because our role is to facilitate other people's prayer and intimacy with God in Christ through the power of the Holy Spirit.

"Styles" of presiding are a major factor of post–Vatican II liturgy. Both excessive informality and excessive rubrical stiffness can be a diminishment if attention is drawn to the presider. In either direction, an overpersonalization of the liturgy can be narcissistic.

The eminent liturgical scholar Aidan Kavanagh, OSB, after commenting on the liturgy as a ritual to be followed and not something "to be tinkered with, " observed that we spend a lot of important energy in preparing and celebrating the liturgy, especially in determining who does and says what and where. We do a lot about the liturgy; but then, *presiding is an art and a craft*. It is meant to unleash moments of amazing and astounding grace and to be an event of salvation from what binds us and sanctification to bring us into deeper union with God; it is a privilege beyond words. But it is also work. And that work involves asceticism and humility. We are not the Messiah; we come with the entire gathered assembly to worship the living God and grow into holiness. Part of any real spirituality is being humble and honest before God and before one another.

Here is a final practical suggestion based on my experience of presiding. I strive never to be out of the role of presiding. There is an inherent logic in what the liturgy says and does. One part leads to the next and the next. In the Mass this means that the act of gathering leads to proclaiming the Word, to presenting the gifts, to praying the Eucharistic Prayer and the Consecration at the altar, to distributing communion, and to dismissing the *christifideles*. The only places at which I might "interrupt" the flow of the intrinsic logic of the liturgy might be between the Universal Prayer and the Collection of Gifts. The traditional time for pastoral announcements is after the Prayer after Communion, which is another time when I would say something not in the liturgical books. I am very careful to avoid the temptation to insert a comment (much less something humorous) about what is happening. The structure of the liturgy demands reverence. It requires the asceticism of not making it an occasion for offhand remarks. I also offer commentaries during the liturgy about what the liturgy is enacting. While the GIRM allows a (brief) introduction to the scripture readings and before the Eucharistic Prayer, I normally reserve that option for when I celebrate Mass with those who might be unfamiliar with the ritual (such as when a number of children participate, not all of whom are Catholic and, therefore, who are not accustomed to the rite and structure of the Mass).

For the priest, the act of presiding can and should be a moment of both humility and honesty. After all, it is about God, not about us who lead the church in the worship of God. It is an event of the in-breaking of God's unpredictable and yet compelling kingdom among us. Again, our motto should be that of St. John the Baptist: "I am not the Messiah" (John 1:20).

CHAPTER EIGHT

The Arts

Liturgy Is Art

One of the most celebrated theologians and published preachers of the post–Vatican II church in the United States was our former esteemed colleague Walter Burghart. His insightful and topical homilies were published in several volumes, but in 1987 he published an important methodological exposition about the homily entitled *Preaching: The Art and the Craft*.[1] Liturgy is an art and a craft. Perhaps in emphasizing what we (legitimately) have to do to prepare and celebrate the reformed liturgy well, we have overemphasized the "craft" part of the equation, with the result that the "art" side has been somewhat eclipsed. Don Saliers, the esteemed liturgical theologian at Emory University, has said repeatedly and well in many of his books and articles that "liturgy is art." It is as simple, and again, as complex, as that.

For me that is part of what is behind some of the more virulent attacks on the "new Mass" with their not-illegitimate call for less wordiness, less didacticism, less activity and for more silence, more emphasis on symbolic engagement, and more an atmosphere in which to absorb and appropriate what is being done in and through the liturgy. I am, therefore, not surprised that church architecture and music receive the lion's share of such criticism with frequently impassioned rhetoric. The positive here is that we care deeply about where and with what artifacts we worship, surrounded by buildings intended to invite us into the Otherness of God and the liturgical experience that (literally) incarnates this here and now through music—sung prayer—that makes a deep and lasting impression on our imaginations, minds, and hearts. Architecture and music engage us on levels far beyond the cognitive or the intellectual. They affect us on levels of heart and identity that cannot always be named or codified. If there was ever a work in progress regarding the continuing implementation of the reformed liturgy, it is in the area of the arts. Part of that work requires us to take into consideration the variety of cultures and cultural expressions that comprise Catholicism, in the past and today. In a sense, to study the evolution of the liturgical arts is to study the inculturation of the liturgy.[2]

It is abundantly clear that there is diversity in liturgical celebration because of music and musical styles for which people are trained and through which they tirelessly serve the church; this diversity stems also from the art and the architectural styles of our churches in which the liturgy is celebrated. There is indeed one Roman Missal, as there was one *Missale Romanum* after Trent. But there are and were different musical styles and musical selections, the singing and performing of which strike different chords and bring out different emphases. And there are and were different styles of art and architecture that influence how we experience the one Roman Rite.

I think here of the time several years ago when I was asked by our campus ministry office at CUA to help them evaluate the weekend student liturgies. Two of them were celebrated in the Crypt Church at the Basilica of the National Shrine of the Immaculate Conception, and two of them were celebrated at a student chapel at the edge of the campus. The Shrine is the largest Catholic Church in this part of Christendom, with mosaics on the ceilings, more than sixty side chapels, and a dominating mosaic of Christ the Pantocrator (which almost always gets mixed reviews but also always makes an impression on people). The student chapel can seat about two hundred and reminds me of a New England community church with clear glass-paned windows, individual wooden chairs, no columns, no pews, and no kneelers. The music for the Shrine Masses was and still is largely taken from the then prevailing *Worship III*, and the opening hymn that weekend was "Rejoice, the Lord is King." At the student chapel, the music was largely taken from *Gather*, and the opening song was "Gather Us In." "Rejoice, the Lord is King" is largely christological; it expresses a "high" Christology and focuses on God. "Gather Us In" is ecclesiological and focuses on who we are, here and now, who gather at the Lord's invitation. At each Mass, the scripture readings and the prayers were all the same. Each retained "the substantial unity of the Roman Rite." But each was a different experience. I can attest that it was the same with the Tridentine Mass. There were Masses with lovely, simple Gregorian chant music. There were some (admittedly few, in my recollection) brilliant performances of Haydn, Mozart, and other composers of classical music for the Mass. And there was the more frequent use of such sentimental hymns as "To Jesus' Heart All Burning,"[3] "Mother Dearest, Mother Fairest," "O Lord, I Am Not Worthy," sung as we processed to communion (if we "went to communion"), despite the fact that that exact phrase was already said by the server to the priest's invitation to communion.

The value of liturgical diversity should be recalled and supported. At the same time, there were and are liturgical principles according to which the Roman Rite was revised that should help guide our thinking and shape the decisions we make in planning liturgies. The assertions of *Sacrosanctum Concilium* in this area deserve to be recalled.[4] In addition, here in the United States, we draw insight about the American implementation of the Constitution on the Sacred Liturgy from the second generation of implementation documents, specifically *Sing to the Lord* and *Built of Living Stones*.[5]

Music

Sacrosanctum Concilium states that

> sacred music is to be considered the more holy in proportion as it is more closely connected with the liturgical action, whether it adds delight to prayer, fosters unity of minds, or confers greater solemnity upon the sacred rites. But the Church approves of all forms of true art having the needed qualities, and admits them into divine worship. (n. 112)

As early as 1994,[6] I argued that hymns should not be used at the celebration of the Eucharist and that antiphons and psalm verses are more suited to the structure and ethos of the Roman Catholic liturgy of the Eucharist. They are derived from the liturgy, not added onto it. To say that that insight was not universally acclaimed or welcomed or followed is an understatement.

In the intervening years, as a member of the American United Methodist–Roman Catholic ecumenical dialogue, I have grown in a deeper appreciation of the theology inherent in the hymns sung at the liturgies in other Christian churches, specifically of the Methodist, Episcopalian, Anglican, Presbyterian, and Lutheran traditions. At the same time, I have followed with enthusiasm the evolution in Roman Catholic circles toward more "ritual music" rather than the exclusive use of hymns at the Eucharist. In addition to the arguments I adduced in *Context and Text*, I will now offer two more in favor of antiphons and psalm verses.

First, antiphons and psalm verses are derived from the scriptures, if not from the texts of the psalms themselves, or are almost always composed in light of the scriptures to reflect the theology of the liturgical day or season being celebrated. Given that the psalms are used daily in the Hours, in the *Lectionary for Mass*, and in the antiphons, these texts deserve pride of place in our liturgical and personal prayer. Singing them at the Eucharist can foster that hoped-for deep internalization (not to say hoped-for memorization) of them. Second, antiphons and psalm verses more easily accompany processions and enable us to view what is occurring while we are singing the antiphon to accompany that action. I wonder whether our worship aids at this part of the Mass are not so filled with hymn texts that we find ourselves glued to them at the risk of not participating in the liturgical action by watching. This is to suggest that the number of psalm verses sung varies depending on the length of entrance and communion processions. For the entrance, such factors as the use of incense and the number of ministers processing would influence this decision.

In the summers during the early years of my seminary studies, I attended noon Mass daily at the Catholic Chapel at New

York University while working at the Sheed and Ward Publishing Company. It was then, in the mid 1960s, that I first discovered the value of singing antiphons and psalm verses. Before Mass the Center's secretary would rehearse us in a simple adaptation of plainchant for the day's chants. (Those were the English texts sung at the then Tridentine Mass, parts of which were celebrated in the vernacular.) Antiphons and psalm verses were the daily regime for song at the Eucharist when I was in St. Anselm Abbey, in Manchester, New Hampshire, between 1983 and 1985. My experience of the latter is what fostered my favoring this practice over against the use of hymns.

There is still a more subtle theological issue at work when the music at the liturgy repeats or reiterates the scripture readings of the day. The presumed rule of thumb when preparing music for the liturgy, especially the Eucharist, seems to be to start with the day's assigned scripture readings and then choose music that will echo them.[7] From one point of view, this is understandable, especially given the value placed on the "sermon hymn" in other Christian liturgical churches. On the other hand, an overreliance on singing hymns at Mass needs to be evaluated. Preference should be given to singing the texts of the Mass, including the antiphons; the kind of music used to sing them need not be Gregorian chant.

This precedent seems to have been part of the influence on Roman Catholic worship after Vatican II. The vernacular music repertoire being sung at "dialogue Masses" prior to Vatican II was limited, and the theological content and lyrics of many of the hymns were questionable; I can recall singing hymns at Mass with such titles as "An Army of Youth Flying the Standard of Truth" and "Bring Flowers of the Fairest." Yet, the fact that we sang them at Masses made them seem desirable, despite the fact that they were, in fact, add-ons to the liturgy, not part of the liturgy itself. The subsequent adoption of hymns from the hymnals of other Christian churches seemed to be a step at least toward less saccharine theology. "A Mighty Fortress Is Our God," "Praise to the Lord," and "Now Thank We All Our God" became staples at Catholic Masses. They were and are sung robustly.

The way the antiphons and psalm verses are envisioned to be

sung in the Roman Rite is illustrative. For example, on the Solemnity of the Epiphany, verses from Psalm 72 are assigned to accompany the Entrance Antiphon, which is taken from Malachi 3:1 and 1 Chronicles 29:12: "Behold the Lord, the Mighty One, has come; and kingship is in his grasp, and power and dominion." Verses of Psalm 72 comprise the whole Responsorial Psalm with the refrain "Lord, every nation on earth will adore you" (from v. 11). Verses from Psalm 72 (1, 11–12) accompany the Communion Antiphon, from the Gospel of the day, Matthew 2:2: "You have seen his star in the East, and have come with gifts to adore the Lord." Psalm 72:10–11 also may be sung at the Preparation of the Gifts. This means that Psalm 72 deserves careful reflection to see how it draws out themes that may be applied to the Epiphany. Clearly, the universality of the Christ event to all nations is underscored, particularly exemplified in the refrain to the Responsorial Psalm and verse 11. The biblical term and notion of "justice" is seen throughout the psalm, with particular reference to care for "the afflicted," "the lowly," and "the poor." References to God's endowing judgment on "the king" and "the king's son" are applicable to the birth of the Son of God in the flesh and manifested as such, especially on this day. References to "the kings of Tarshish" and "the kings of Arabia and Seba" bringing the son tribute have influenced the theological and liturgical imaginations of those who selected these texts for today.

An observation about two standard Epiphany hymns: "We Three Kings of Orient Are" and the Latin "Reges de Saba Venient, Alleluia" ("The kings of Saba come"). When the verses of these hymns are juxtaposed with the psalm, it is obvious that the hymns take us back to the event of the first Epiphany as recounted in the Gospel of Matthew. We are placed back in history with the not-so-subtle implication that our keeping of feasts and seasons is to draw us back into the past. In reality, however, the psalm, embedded with theology of the liturgical year, recalls the past from the perspective of today, *hodie*—"*this* day"—and what we celebrate here and now makes us yearn for its fulfillment in the kingdom to come. Further, the use of Psalm 72 offers a multitude of images with which our imaginations can be filled. They are not a chronological retelling of the Magi's visit but are rich in images of who we believe Christ to be as we use this psalm on this important Christian feast. "Sonship," "kingship," "justice," and care for the poor, the lowly, and the afflicted burst forth from this important psalm. Those images are not in evidence in "We Three Kings."

I think it would be informative (and likely illustrative) to review the repertoire for music sung at liturgies in the Christmas-Epiphany season. A steady diet of songs that make us yearn for the past may well emerge: 'Silent Night," "O Little Town of Bethlehem," "Once in Royal David's City," "It Came Upon a Midnight Clear," and "Away in a Manger" take us back in history. The use of the antiphons and psalm verses assigned for this season are more nuanced, theologically complex, and multivalent.

Despite this, I do acknowledge an opposing view about the use of antiphons and psalms, namely, that chant settings and adaptations of those settings are fine for monasteries and universities but will not "work" in parishes. Music is seen to be a place for robust and enthusiastic participation of the gathered assembly, and people resonate with such musical participation through enthusiastic singing of hymns. I would not for a moment want to argue for less robust participation and do fondly welcome when "O God Beyond All Praising" is the hymn sung at Morning Prayer.

Part of my reply to this opposing view is that the genre of *chant* need not be the only way antiphons and psalms are sung in the liturgy of the Eucharist. As a personal example, for years I have welcomed the singing of Richard Hillert's "This Is the Feast of Victory for Our God" as music to accompany the Entrance Procession at Masses during the Easter season.[8] And the recent publication of *Announcing the Feast* by Jason McFarland is a superb study of the ritual, musical, and liturgical complexity involved in determining adequate music for the Entrance Rite in the Roman liturgy.[9]

I am concerned, however, that in some places antiphons and psalm verses are being sung by scholas followed by a congregational hymn. For me, this is to shift what an antiphon ought to be—the gathered assembly's participation in its singing, not listening to others sing the antiphon and then falling back into themselves singing hymns.

That we have made enormous progress toward better music for the liturgy, textually and musically, is clear. The decision was taken by the American bishops in the late 1960s not to publish a national hymnal for the reformed liturgy. My own judgment was that such a publication might have given some stability and shape to what was sung and done in the implementation of the reformed liturgy, and this would have fostered a certain familiarity with the liturgy. That we are being asked now to evaluate what we sing liturgically for a proposed *Directory* is, I think, a good thing. In the discussions that have taken place already about this agenda item, the issue of inculturation and the legitimate adaptation of musical styles and approaches to music needs to be valued and respected. No one envisions a national hymnal at this point. What *is* a pressing agenda item, however, is evaluating what we sing and whether we should continue to sing it. If it took centuries for the *Liber Usualis* to be codified for use up until the reformed liturgy of Vatican II, I think it not improper to suggest that not everything we have sung at the liturgy after Vatican II deserves to be continued.

Among the issues regarding the words of the hymns, I believe that the following should be considered, based on the contents and structure of the Roman Rite.

PRONOUNS

As I have argued here and elsewhere, 99.9 percent of the pronouns used in Roman Catholic worship are plural (the clearest exceptions are "I believe" in the Creed and "I am not worthy" at communion). Does a steady diet of individual personal pronouns derogate from the explicit and necessary ecclesiology that supports our liturgy? I am well aware of some recent popular songbooks for the liturgy that contain "I" and "me" in abundance. They reflect a real desire for intimacy with the Lord (often called "Jesus"—more on that follows). But is this what the liturgy is meant to foster? Does this make the liturgy the only way we pray? Are not devotions and time spent for *lectio divina* opportunities for a more intimate kind of prayer experience? Among the theological issues here is the importance given to *mediation*, part of which is among and through the church. We come together as a church. Almost always "we" pray through Christ "our" Lord.

NAMES FOR GOD

That the Roman liturgy uses a variety of names to describe God and to address God is part of its genius. That we use the word *Lord* in *Kyrie, eleison* and in "Lord, hear our prayer" is theologically rich. That we pray "Christ, have mercy" is important christologically as well. That we end prayers during Mass with the doxologies is a reflection of trinitarian theology, Christology, and ecclesiology. Such a variety should find its way into what we sing at the liturgy. In that sense, then, is it appropriate to sing "Alleluia, Sing to Jesus" when liturgical prayers are addressed to the Father, through the Son, in the Holy Spirit? Is it appropriate to sing "I Heard the Voice of Jesus Say" when what follows is indeed a treasured part of the proclamation of the Gospel of Matthew: "Come to me all you who labor and find life burdensome"?

AVOIDING REPETITION

Another factor in evaluating the words to a hymn would be that it repeats something that the liturgy is already saying in another place, such as the Gospel of that day. I am thinking here of the inappropriateness of singing "O Lord, I Am Not Worthy" when we will have said that in unison as part of our responding to the presider's invitation to communion. The use of "Praise to the Lord, the Almighty, the King of Creation" has become a staple in vernacular English-speaking worship. Yet, the very genre and words of Eucharistic Prayer, called "the high point" of the whole eucharistic liturgy (see GIRM, n. 78), are of praise and thanksgiving derived from the Jewish *berakoth* tradition, through the Greek *eucharistein,* to the Latin *"gratias agamus, Domino Deo nostro."*

RESPECTING MULTIVALENCE

It goes without saying that the Psalter can assist not only in public and liturgical prayer but also in one's personal prayer. My own sense is that more use of the psalms sung at liturgy can help to restore the psalms as the "church's prayerbook." Psalm 34, the traditional communion psalm, with variations on its opening lines—"I will bless the Lord at all times"—is something that can be easily committed to memory, and in celebration it underscores a number of images that refer to the act of processing to communion. That it is sung traditionally at communion opens up possibilities for how we understand it as we process to receive the sacred species. "Taste and see the goodness of the Lord" is the Responsorial Psalm refrain for Sundays in Ordinary Time when we proclaim John 6 (the Bread of Life Discourse) over five successive Sundays during year B of the *Lectionary*. That this is also derived from Psalm 34 is notable. It would be very appropriate to use this phrase as a possible antiphon during communion.

The Lutheran church historian and theologian Dr. Martin Marty comments that one-third of the psalms are laments in which the author cries out, "Where is God? And, Has God forsaken us?"[10] While his wife battled cancer, he read through the psalms with her. She had to wake at midnight to take a medication to combat the nausea caused by the chemotherapy. It took a while for both of them to go back to sleep so he would read the psalms aloud. One night she caught him skipping Psalm 88. Some have called it the one psalm that seems to have no hope: it ends with the thought that "darkness is my only companion," or, in another translation, "darkness is my closest friend." "Why did you skip that psalm?" his wife demanded. Marty said he wasn't sure she could take Psalm 88 that night. "Go back. Read it," she said. "If you don't deal with the darkness, the others won't shine out."

The psalms are the Christian prayerbook, indeed.

Church Buildings

In my own graduate education and travels, I have been privileged to experience various kinds of church buildings and architecture, from the enormous variety of buildings in Europe in a number of church settings, such as cathedrals, parishes, campuses, and monasteries, to church buildings in parts of Africa,

India, Australia, and the suburbs of Hong Kong. All of these churches have made deep impressions on me, mostly positive, and all have educated me into the possibilities that occur when artistic genius and imaginations are unleashed for the glory of God and to house the church at worship.

Enormous energies and resources have been put into constructing new and renovating existing buildings for the reformed liturgy. In the process I hope we have learned from this experience. Just as one size does not fit all when it comes to church buildings in both our past and present experience, so the fifty years since Vatican II have given us a good bit of experience at shaping more adequate worship spaces.

Allow me to insert here a distinction between building churches for the liturgy and shrines for devotion. Sometimes we need to build one building for both. But the distinction is important to bear in mind, lest we confuse liturgical spaces with devotional spaces, and vice versa. Churches built after the Reformation that emphasize the tabernacle front and center for veneration may not be the best to imitate in the post–Vatican II era, where chapels for reservation are emphasized in liturgical documents, precisely in order to allow for silence and devotion to the Blessed Sacrament while the liturgy is celebrated in the liturgical space.[11] That there has been an evolution in official liturgical documents on this issue is clear. That local diocesan bishops have made more specific directives about the location of the tabernacle requires that diocesan norms be reviewed in this connection.

The Catholic Church's role as a patron of the arts in a number of eras reflects the importance that our faith tradition has given to the promotion of the arts and its substratum—the importance of beauty. That the church has not adopted any specific style of architecture as its own was a principle of the reform of the liturgy as enunciated in *Sacrosanctum Concilium*.[12] I have used as a rule of thumb that there is no "golden age" of church architecture, so that imitating the structure of a building from a former age in not necessarily desirable. I say this well aware that some find variations on the Romanesque style quite applicable for the reformed liturgy. I say this also aware that the adage "form follows function" that was popularized some decades ago misfired in the construction of several contemporary churches.

I am less inclined to adopt one period's architecture to imitate for our churches today or to suggest that there is one preferred location for ambo, chair, altar, schola, and so on. The principal liturgical reason is that churches built for a former age were built for a former liturgy. Churches that are built today are for the celebration of the reformed liturgy. That particular kinds of worshipping assemblies require particular kinds of church buildings has been clearly demonstrated by the juxtaposition of cathedrals, parish churches, monastic enclosures, hospital chapels, campus chapels, and so forth. The requirements of designing a monastic choir for the regular praying of the Liturgy of the Hours will not be the requirement for the other contexts just noted.

Critiques of the new buildings that the community is worshipping itself and that there is a lack of mystery or transcendence ("bare ruined choirs") can be met by careful planning, imagination, and artistic execution. These critiques, while sometimes highly emotional, should be listened to, given some buildings that have already been built. That the critiques (and these buildings) lead to the conclusion that we ought to imitate styles or structures from a predetermined past is not a solution that squares with the evolution of the Catholic tradition on church buildings, art, and architecture.

In addition, having served on the Sacred Arts Commission of the Archdiocese of Washington for close to two decades, I am more convinced than ever of the need to commission good art and to support artists. The instinct to retreat to "catalog art," to choose what is already designed, or to choose predetermined colors or scale without the rest of the space in mind is misguided. Sometimes this is done for the sake of saving money. Sometimes it is because of a lack of appreciation for our liturgical and cultural traditions. Stewardship must always mark who we are and what we do when expending parish or other community resources. But stewardship also means being true to our artistic patrimony and legacy. We should want to pass on to the next generation the best of what we can imagine, produce, and manufacture. We should not settle for imitations, for the ephemeral, for materials not of the highest quality, or for results not of the best human imagination and ingenuity. At the same time, in terms of stewardship, I think it ought to be said that church buildings, and the artifacts for them and the liturgy, should not be opulent. A wooden chair designed along a Quaker style can be as fitting for church buildings today as gilded, ornate thrones were in a former era.

I have assisted some parish communities in the initial stages of discussing whether and how to go about the task of church renovation and construction. In one case I was involved from initial discussions through the rite of the dedication of the church. My personal reflection was one of deep satisfaction. But it was satisfaction wrought through the hard work and deep commitment of the parish leadership.

Once we determined the kind of structure we wanted and interviewed architect firms, the pastor wisely insisted in the interviews on the requirement that members of the selected firm would participate in the liturgies of Palm Sunday and the Triduum. Having worked previously on a major renovation of an existing church in another parish, the pastor realized that unless the architects understood the liturgy of these most sacred days, they would not be able to envision the liturgical demands that would be made on the building.

And so the architects participated in, or at least witnessed, the inner dynamics of Holy Week: on Passion Sunday, the celebration of processing from one building (space) to another; on Holy Thursday, the washing of the feet, the collecting of gifts for the poor, and the procession that night for the transfer of the Eucharist; on Good Friday, the prostration of the ministers at the start of the liturgy, and the community's adoption, one by one, of a kneeling or other posture to venerate the cross; and at the Easter Vigil, gathering elsewhere to light the new fire, the procession into church, the procession to the baptismal font, the immersion or pouring of water for baptism of adults, the newly baptized changing clothes after water baptism in a nearby place, the procession to where chrismation takes place, the sprinkling of baptismal water on the entire gathered assembly, the procession with gifts for the Eucharist—and so on—all these are intrinsic to these liturgies and need to be appreciated and understood. My own experience of this was that once the architects and builders had experienced the Easter Triduum with all its variety, beauty, complexity, richness in symbol, and symbolic engagement, they were then able to build a church for the celebration of the liturgy.

A HOUSE FOR THE CHURCH

In the immediate postconciliar reform, the phrase a "house for the church" dominated much literature. Often it was contrasted with a church as a "house for God." "A house for the church" remains true as far as it goes, especially if we appreciate how the earliest Christian places for worship were to be contrasted with pagan temples or with houses where the gods lived. In what I have argued above about architects understanding Catholic worship spaces and churches, it is clear that this principle remains true. At the same time, this phrase should not mean to imply that trying to create transcendence and help the gathered assembly appreciate the total Otherness of God should be avoided in the process of achieving liturgical participation. Spaces that try to foster "immanence" *as opposed to* "transcendence" simply will misfire.

Here "a picture is worth a thousand words," and so I defer to the reader's Internet search for images to accompany the few comments that follow about three well-known cathedrals and one basilica, and the opportunities and challenges the three of them offer for the celebration of the reformed liturgy.

St. Patrick's Cathedral, New York City

Neo-Gothic by design, this magnificent structure was clearly designed for the Tridentine form of celebrating Mass. That many of the people at Mass sitting in the side pews could not see the altar required that television sets be anchored to the cathedral's soaring columns to televise the liturgy "live" for those in those pews.

Understandably, because of when it was built, this cathedral is not serviceable or practical for the celebration of adult initiation. When the Liturgy of the Hours is celebrated, it is according to the "cathedral" form of the Hours; therefore, the locating of the cantor in the sanctuary leading the gathered assembly works well.

The presence of two altars in the main sanctuary is a problem, given the church documents' requirement governing buildings that there be only one single altar in any church. That the altar symbolizes Christ and is the place in which the eucharistic sacrifice is offered is the theology undergirding this regulation.[13] The principle in the reform of the liturgy that we avoid unnecessary duplication is also operative here.

Cathedral of Our Lady of the Angels, Los Angeles

This cathedral, which was years in the making, and which contains a major columbarium, has been hailed as a major achievement in relation to the planning of places for pastoral care, education, and community assembly in the outdoor plaza. The active leadership and constant involvement of the then local ordinary bishop, Cardinal Roger Mahony, ensured the success of the project. That it was designed with the reformed liturgy in mind is a major factor in its viability as a liturgical space. The architects clearly envisioned the celebration of the revised rites for adult initiation, the Lenten Scrutinies, and the rites celebrated at the Easter Vigil.

Among its particular artifacts are tapestries depicting the communion of saints on the side walls of the main worship space. It was a brilliant idea to have these tapestries depict saints from the entire sweep of the church's history, up through contemporary notables, such as Mother Teresa and Pope John XXIII. In my opinion, the tapestries were masterfully executed.

Basilica of the National Shrine of the Immaculate Conception, Washington, DC

The liturgy and music subcommittee of the board of the Basilica of the National Shrine struggled mightily for eighteen months to evaluate its sanctuary space, which normally has two altars. The fact that one was movable was its own issue (altars should be permanent). But the other issue was that when we used the high main altar during the period of evaluation, it emerged clearly that the action at the altar was far removed from the gathered assembly, even those in the first pews. The decision was made to table the issue and allow both altars to stand. The altar in front of the sanctuary is used regularly in accordance with the instructions of the GIRM:

> The altar should be built apart from the wall, in such a way that it is possible to walk around it easily and that Mass can be celebrated at it facing the people, which is desirable wherever possible. The altar should, moreover, be so placed as to be truly the center toward which the attention of the whole congregation of the faithful naturally turns. The altar is usually fixed and is dedicated. (n. 299)

PRAYERS AND THE RITE FOR THE DEDICATION OF THE CHURCH

Many communities never experience the Rite for the Dedication of a Church and the Consecration of an Altar. And when they do, sometimes it comes and goes too quickly. When the church was dedicated for which I served as a theological consultant, the pastor decided that we would do a catechesis beforehand. I composed five inserts for the bulletins for the five weeks preceding the dedication. Because of its theological prominence, we spent two of the inserts "unpacking" the Prayer for the Consecration of an Altar. In the week before the dedication, the topic of the adult education talk was "Baptizing the Church," and we spoke of the parallels between the use of water and chrism at baptism and its use at the dedication of the church. My own sense is that this rite is among the finest of the liturgies reformed after Vatican II and that its contents can serve as an excellent mystagogy on what it means to dedicate "a house for the church."

A fitting close to this chapter is the text of the Preface for the Rite for the Dedication of a Church:

> For you have made the whole world a temple of your glory, that your name might everywhere be extolled,

yet you allow us to consecrate to you
apt places for the divine mysteries.
And so, we dedicate joyfully to your majesty
this house of prayer, built by human labor.
Here is foreshadowed the mystery of the true Temple,
here is prefigured the heavenly Jerusalem.
For you made the Body of your Son,
born of the tender Virgin,
the Temple consecrated to you,
in which the fullness of the Godhead might dwell.
You also established the Church as a holy city,
built upon the foundation of the Apostles,
with Christ himself as the chief cornerstone:
a city to be built of chosen stones,
given life by the Spirit and bonded by charity,
where for endless ages you will be all in all
and the light of Christ will shine undimmed forever.

CHAPTER NINE

Liturgical Education and Mystagogy

The Study of Liturgy

Before *Sacrosanctum Concilium* calls for the reform of the sacred liturgy (nn. 21–40), it carefully and fully addresses the need for the "promotion of liturgical instruction" (specifically in nn. 15–19). The constitution decrees that

> professors who are appointed to teach liturgy in seminaries, religious houses of study, and theological faculties must be properly trained for their work in institutes which specialize in this subject.
>
> The study of sacred liturgy is to be ranked among the compulsory and major courses in seminaries and religious houses of studies; in theological faculties it is to rank among the principal courses. It is to be taught under its theological, historical, spiritual, pastoral, and juridical aspects. Moreover, other professors, while striving to expound the mystery of Christ and the history of salvation from the angle proper to each of their own subjects, must nevertheless do so in a way which will clearly bring out the connection between their subjects and the liturgy, as also the unity which underlies all priestly training. This consideration is especially important for professors of dogmatic, spiritual, and pastoral theology and for those of holy scripture. (nn 15–16)

What We Have Done, What We Have Failed to Do

In my opinion, one of the most egregious deficiencies in implementing the Vatican II liturgical reform has been the neglect of these conciliar admonitions about liturgical education and formation. I can say with pride that the Catholic University of America has made great strides in ensuring that liturgy and sacraments are taught under their theological, historical, pastoral, and juridical aspects. That many other faculties of theology still have but one course in liturgy (which is largely the historical evolution of the Roman Rite) and that sacraments are taught under dogmatic theology is at least problematic, if not fundamentally flawed. This often means, for example, that the church's *lex orandi* of the liturgy (prayers and rites in the present and as studied historically) is ignored in delineating a theology of sacraments, and that the not-illegitimate, but often defensive and limited assertions by the magisterium about the sacraments are the only sources from which theology is drawn.[1]

My own sense is that much of the American implementation energies went into the practical, hands-on, "how to do it" work of reform. It did not go into the deeper, admittedly more challenging work of offering theological, historical, and pastoral insight about the liturgy in broad-based education programs,[2] not to mention the very structure of university and seminary curricula.

Delineating a proper method for liturgical studies after Vatican II is still a work in progress. Further, regarding the inherent interdisciplinarity of the study of liturgy and sacraments as alluded to in the *Sacrosanctum Concilium* quotation previously, one of my main concerns is the relative weight that should be given to each of these elements under which the constitution says the liturgy is to be studied—*theological, historical, spiritual, pastoral*, and *juridical*. My own sense is that, more often than not, many of us who teach liturgy have been characterized as (only) historians simply because of the way we examine liturgical rites and texts as they have evolved in history and as they reflect a certain "diversity in unity," given the various adaptations of the reformed rites for various religious communities within the church, like the Anglican Ordinariate or the Neocatechumenal Way. This is often reflected, even to this day, in theological faculties that think of liturgy as either the "how to" course or "what we did at the liturgy in history" course. Meanwhile, the discipline of sacramental theology is regarded as the theological science. If this perception continues unabated or unchecked, then we will have not fulfilled the challenge of the constitution, and we will have indeed failed our students.

Let me take each of these terms in order:

THEOLOGICAL

Liturgy is not primarily history. Liturgy is primarily *theology* in the strict and best sense: *an act of theology*—of coming to grips with what it means to enter into the Otherness of the infinite and transcendent God through the very human means of texts and rites, words and gestures, speech and symbolic action. The church's decisions about what words, rites, symbols, and gestures to use matter a great deal; after all, they comprise the church's rule of faith, its *lex orandi*. Clearly we have made strides in the last five decades in refining the method for liturgical study. The more theological it is and becomes, I argue, the better off we are in appreciating the liturgy in its uniqueness for the life of the church. Liturgy is that privileged moment when God acts to reveal the fullness of the divine life and invites us to take part in and live that divine life. The history of rites serves this enterprise. But it cannot replace the study of liturgy as the descent of God to us and our ascent—always through, with, and in Christ, in the power of the Holy Spirit, in the communion of the pilgrim church on earth.

That Catholic theological curricula in universities and seminaries are highly specialized and scientifically rigorous are very good things. Appropriate specialization and refinement of skills and research is important. But at the same time, I wonder whether too much specialization can cause what should be integrated to seem not to be. For example, what would it be like if we collapsed master's level courses in ecclesiology, Christian initiation, Eucharist, and ordained ministry, and taught them together for a sum of twelve credit hours (the way former deans compute things!)? What, after all, is St. Augustine's *Treatise against the Donatists* but a study in early church order ecclesiology, specifically, how episcopal collegiality functioned, as well as a study in baptism and its effects in the life of the church, specifically because of heresy and schism? Can we or should we teach Christian morality that is not centered in the celebration of our redemption in and through the liturgy? Can the scriptures really be understood apart from the liturgical context in which they are first experienced, the liturgy? Can the various aspects of systematic theology—creation, Christology, trinitarian, ecclesiology, soteriology, and so forth—ever be fully appreciated except in the living context where they are experienced—the liturgy—and all at the same time?

HISTORICAL

It is clear that the study of the historic sources of the liturgy helped to break the logjam before Vatican II about whether and how the liturgy could be reformed and its rites revised. A legitimate emphasis in liturgical study was placed on sources, Western and Eastern, precisely because of the breadth and depth of what that historical investigation revealed. It is not a surprise that many of the post–Vatican II liturgies were revised on the basis of "traditional" liturgies, often from the patristic era.

But then again, certainly in the past decade, across denominational lines, there has been some very important revisiting of the premises as the "liturgical churches" reflect on what occurred in the 1970s in revising our liturgies.[3] Clearly, decisions were made after Vatican II by the various *coetus* groups and consultors about how to revise the Roman liturgy. Lingering questions do remain, however, about who decided what and on what basis. These issues are still debated, precisely because historical data and evidence often lead in more than one direction and can yield more than one result. To examine the liturgy under its historical aspects is to offer vistas and approaches to the study and celebration of the liturgy whose variety, yet complementarity, can assist in an appreciation of the various dimensions of feasts and seasons that is not possible when studying one liturgical family only. For example, if one studies the evolution and present structure of the season of Advent in the Ambrosian liturgy with its six-week duration and the emphasis placed on the Blessed Virgin Mary toward its end, then one can appreciate the theological depth of the Roman Rite in which, starting with the thirty-third week of the year, eschatological themes dominate the readings and prayers in both the Eucharist and Hours. Similarly, the Marian emphasis in Milan is present in the scripture readings proclaimed in the Roman Rite on the Fourth Sunday of Advent. Also, a study of the evolution of the liturgy of Passion (Palm) Sunday in Gaul from the seventh century on with street processions on that day can be helpful alongside a study of the Roman Rite, which did not follow suit for four centuries, and then with a certain reluctance and mitigation. (This is why, in the reformed Roman Rite, the blessing of palms and procession takes place at the start of the liturgy, and once the Collect is prayed there is no other reference to the palm procession in the liturgy.)

SPIRITUAL

Related to this is my concern about how the study of liturgy is integral to and integrative of the Christian life. It is, I think, one thing to study the historical evolution of rites along with the theology of the present revised rites of the liturgy; it is another to allow this study to influence what we say and do during the liturgy and, in light of the liturgy, the way we view reality. In effect there is no such thing as "just" a liturgical change. Changes in the liturgy affect anthropology, theology (specifically about Christ and the Trinity), ecclesiology (who it is who participates, and when, and how), and spirituality—the living out of the Gospel values central to and celebrated in the liturgy. The "academic" study of liturgy should guide and direct how and why we do what we do in the enactment of the liturgy.

Definitions of spirituality abound today both in Catholicism and in the world at large. A great source of Catholic pride is the breadth of "spiritualities" that coexist and comprise the genius of Catholicism both in history and today—"spiritualities" in the sense of approaches to God, to prayer, and to the Christian life abound in Catholicism. One example of this is the proliferation of monastic, mendicant, and apostolic orders and communities, as well as the variety of ordained, religious, and lay associations in the church. I would also argue that a Catholic approach to spirituality itself stands as both an invitation and a challenge today to many who are "believers but not belongers," who are "religious but not church-goers," who are "spiritual but not followers of a creed." (More on this in chapter 10.)

PASTORAL

All liturgy is pastoral. But by *pastoral*, I do not mean a "how to" (rubrical) set of instructions. Pastoral concerns the implementation of the revised rites in the various contexts in which the liturgy is celebrated. The academic study of liturgy is meant to bear fruit in the way it is celebrated and appropriated pastorally. But I believe we need both—the academic and the practical—for the discipline and practice of pastoral liturgy. Otherwise what we learn from history or theory can be perceived to be unimportant "pastorally."

One of the most important lessons we can learn from the history of the liturgy is that "one size does not fit all." It was never thus in the history and evolution of the liturgy. For example, liturgical history reveals a variety of non-Roman Western liturgical rites, whose differences are largely based on cultural and geographical differences. Liturgical history reveals a variety of ways of celebrating the Liturgy of the Hours, with principal and obvious differences between and among monastic communities, religious communities, and what is often termed the "cathedral" or the "parish" tradition.[4] The same variety is seen in stational or cathedral liturgies presided over by the diocesan bishop and those presided over by the parish priest/presbyter. In fact, the city of Rome exemplified these differences because at the same time it had papal liturgies (stational and at the basilicas), liturgies in the papal household, and liturgies celebrated in the parishes of Rome. All were and are celebrated in the Roman Rite. Even after the promulgation of the 1570 Missal after Trent, any community or location that had its own usage of the Missal in place for two hundred years could continue that usage—for example, the Ambrosian, Dominican, and Carthusian liturgies.[5]

Pastoral does not mean the implementation of "the one Roman" liturgy for every and all pastoral contexts in the church today. Historical study reveals that it was never so in Catholicism. The spark of pastoral liturgy for me is where the historical, the theological, the spiritual, and the juridical intersect. That is pastoral liturgy. And all liturgy is pastoral.

At the same time, it must also be asserted that, in the implementation of the reformed post–Vatican II liturgy, certain liberties were sometimes taken with the rites that have fostered a certain "parochialism" whereby neighboring parishes celebrate the liturgy differently, most evidently in their choice of music, the presiding priest's style of celebrating, or the way the churches are arranged or even constructed. The criticism of the revised liturgy by some social anthropologists cautions us not to make too many (more?) changes too quickly in the liturgy. Curiously, what was legitimately prized as a source of stability and familiarity in Catholicism—the liturgy—has sometimes become a source of instability and lack of familiarity. I would argue that the "fault" lies less in *Sacrosanctum Concilium* and more with individual, local leadership about the liturgy.[6]

JURIDICAL

When *Sacrosanctum Concilium* was first promulgated, the previous *Code of Canon Law* was in force. Twenty years later, the revised *Code of Canon Law* was promulgated, which offers a very different source for study and reflection on liturgy and sacraments. The brief section in book 3 titled "The Ministry of the Divine Word" (canons 756–80), combined with the extraordinarily complete treatment titled "The Sanctifying Function of the Church" in book 4 (canons 849–1258), make for rich study and reflection on the sacred liturgy. That each section on individual sacraments (except for marriage) begins with a description of "the celebration of the sacrament" before treating "the minister of the sacrament" is just one indication of the broad ecclesiological and liturgical context and understanding that the new Code brings to its understanding of liturgy and sacraments. That the canons on marriage (1063–72) begin with a thorough description of "pastoral care and those things which must precede the celebration of Marriage" indicate the seriousness with which the church approaches the celebration of marriage. (These are enriched by the *Praenotanda* of the revised Rite of Marriage itself, published in Latin in 1990, which we still await in a revised English translation.)

My own sense is that the more our teaching about the canonical aspects of the sacraments can be figured into the regular courses on liturgy and sacraments (for example, the sacraments of initiation, the Eucharist, and so forth), the more adequate will be our implementation of the vision of *Sacrosanctum Concilium* in its description of the way the liturgy should be studied.[7]

ARTISTIC

While the arts are not mentioned specifically as part of liturgical studies, *Sacrosanctum Concilium* states:

> During their philosophical and theological studies, clerics are to be taught about the history and development of sacred art, and about the sound principles governing the production of its works. In consequence they will be able to appreciate and preserve the Church's venerable monuments, and be in a position to aid, by good advice, artists who are engaged in producing works of art. (n. 129)

Since I have already addressed this topic, I will simply reiterate that a major part of the Catholic imagination, the Catholic worldview, and "the Catholic thing" concerns art, the arts, and the church as fostering the creativity of artists. While obvious testaments to this come from the patrimony of twenty centuries of church life in the variety of its contexts and cultures, it is important to mention the Renaissance and subsequent eras and to point out that the arts have been emphasized by recent popes. Consider Pope Paul VI's concern for modern church art from all five of the world's continents and the art he had placed in the Vatican from contemporary sculptors and bronze workers, among others. Pope John Paul II fostered the arts in several writings, including his "Letter to Artists" of 1999.[8] In several of his writings, Pope

Benedict XVI placed considerable emphasis on the beauty of the liturgy and beauty in the liturgy.

I mentioned earlier that delineating the method for the study of liturgy and sacraments is a work in progress. Much work still needs to be done in this area to come near to what is envisioned in *Sacrosanctum Concilium* about method and the priority to be given to the liturgy in theological curricula. This is part of the "unfinished business" of the promulgation of the Constitution on the Sacred Liturgy.

Mystagogy

When designing this chapter, I debated whether to delve into the important field of liturgical catechesis. In the end, I chose not to because I want to defer to those many pastoral theologians who do this all the time and whose expertise is precisely in this area.

Instead I chose to offer a glimpse into a way to assist those engaged in the liturgy to realize ever more fully what it is we are engaged in through words, actions, and signs. In what follows, I am suggesting that this kind of commentary on the principal prayers of the liturgy—blessing and consecrations—could become important as those initiated and welcomed into the church through the RCIA might benefit from this kind of exercise.

As I noted previously, one of the most dramatic changes in the reformed liturgy of baptism after Vatican II has been the repeated use of the prayer for the blessing of water at every baptism. This ensures that the water is fresh in baptismal fonts or that the flowing water in some fonts is freshly blessed. (Formerly the water blessed at the Easter Vigil with chrism poured in was kept in a container in baptisteries.) The history and liturgical tradition behind this prayer is rich, making it a prime candidate to be restored to prominence in the reformed liturgy.[9] Like all of the church's *lex orandi*, however, this prayer is best understood as proclaimed in the assembly of the faithful and as accompanied by gestures that draw attention to particular parts of the prayer and then, through the gestures, to the water used in baptism. The fact that the prayer is filled with scriptural allusions is part of its genius and part of the genius of consecratory and blessing prayers in the liturgy. Each of these deserves reflection like that used in *lectio divina*. Taken together, these allusions one after another can be overwhelming. The fact that this prayer and the Eucharistic Prayers, among others, are repeated means that they can be heard and appropriated again and again.

Thus, one can reflect on one or another image and find a way to participate in a prayer that is admittedly an "embarrassment of riches." That one may not pay strict attention to each and every phrase of the prayer is fine; after all, these prayers recur again and again. Their depth and multivalence make them prime opportunities for returning to them repeatedly for insight and continual formation in the church's prayer. I often think and have stated previously that liturgical prayers "tether the imagination"; they do not control our minds or our appropriation of it. For example, possible avenues for reflection on the prayer are noted below, but given that it is so rich and condensed invites other ways of appropriating this scripturally and theologically rich text for one's own. Several of the prayer's biblical references are to the scripture readings at the preceding Liturgy of the Word. When these phrases function in a prayer, they serve to "echo" what was proclaimed and offer reminders of how what was proclaimed through the scriptures comes to bear in the liturgical action that follows them.

Here is the full text for the Blessing of Water for Baptism, interspersed with my comments:

> O God, who by invisible power
> accomplish[es] a wondrous effect
> through sacramental signs
> and who in many ways have prepared water, your creation,
> to show forth the grace of Baptism...

The use of terms such as *sacramental signs* and *your creation* reflect the sacramental principle. Blessing prayers are always about praising God for creation and redemption.

The blessing continues:

O God, whose Spirit
in the first moments of the world's creation
hovered over the waters
so that the very substance of water
would even then take to itself the power to sanctify...

This is an explicit reference to Genesis 1:2, accommodated to the trinitarian belief of our theological tradition. The fact that the Spirit moves over the water in Genesis is an important reminder of the action and life-giving attributes of God. In this second paragraph of the prayer as throughout, water is again mentioned directly. Here it is referred to as having the power to make holy. (Recall that the first reading at the Easter Vigil is Genesis 1:1—2:2.)

The prayer continues:

O God, who by the outpouring of the flood
foreshadowed regeneration,
so that from the mystery of one and the same element of
   water
would come an end to vice and a beginning of virtue...

The text continues to reflect the Book of Genesis, specifically chapters 6 to 9. These references deserve prayerful reflection as they deal with sin, alienation from God, the covenant relationship, all God's creatures being saved, and human reproduction. The prayer again explicitly refers to water. Here its death-dealing qualities are noted as well as its life-giving properties. The fact that water can destroy as well as sustain life is paramount here and offers insight into the struggle between life and death in all our lives. Putting an end to vice and living the virtuous life is always a struggle, if not an outright fight.

And further:

O God, who caused the children of Abraham
to pass dry-shod through the Red Sea

so that the chosen people,
set free from slavery to Pharaoh,
would prefigure the people of the baptized...

The reference here to Abraham and his progeny and, by extension, to us who now share in a covenant relationship is an important introduction in the prayer's movement from Genesis to Exodus. As in the preceding section, here too the possible destructive qualities of the Red Sea are turned on their side to refer to Israel's being sustained in life through this event of salvation accomplished in water. (The call of Abraham in Gen 2:1–22 is the Easter Vigil's second reading; Exod 14:15—15:1 is the third reading, accompanied by the canticle from Exod 15.)

Returning to the prayer:

O God, whose Son,
baptized by John in the waters of the Jordan,
was anointed with the Holy Spirit...

The above reference to filiation (son-/daughtership) is very important for underscoring the personal relationship enjoyed by the baptized with the three persons of the Trinity. The anointing of Jesus with the Holy Spirit in the Jordan stands as a moment of demarcation for his role as Messiah. The fact that these texts (Matt 3:13–17; Mark 1:7–11; Luke 3:15–16, 21–22) are read on the now restored Feast of the Baptism of the Lord is very significant.

The next part follows immediately as part of the same verse:

...and, as he hung upon the Cross,
gave forth water from his side along with blood...

These references to John 19:34 and 1 John 5 are very important because they have been used in a number of ways, especially by patristic authors, to describe the saving effects of Jesus' death and resurrection as commemorated in the sacraments. The classic reference is Augustine's comment that the church is born from the wounded side of Christ.

And then concluding that same verse:

...and after his resurrection, commanded his disciples:
"Go forth, teach all nations, baptizing them
In the name of the Father, and of the Son,
And of the Holy Spirit"...

This reference to the end of the Gospel of St. Matthew offers a number of interpretations, including that the baptized now share in the life of the Trinity and that all the baptized are to be evangelizers and are to go forth and witness in the world to the life-giving, saving mysteries of the ascended Christ, who intercedes for us at the Father's right hand, principally through the liturgy.

Look now, we pray, upon the face of your Church
And graciously unseal for her the fountain of baptism.

The recounting of significant moments of salvation history now turns to the experience of the same gracious intervention by the God of the covenant and to the three-personed God in whom we live and move. The reference to the "fountain" of baptism can serve as a reminder that baptism is often referred to as "the fountain of life."

May this water receive by the Holy Spirit
the grace of your Only Begotten Son,
so that human nature, created in your image,
and washed clean through the Sacrament of Baptism
from all the squalor of the life of old,
may be found worthy to rise to the life of newborn
    children
through water and the Holy Spirit.

The prayer again explicitly refers to water (twice) and to humans being created in God's image—both taken from Genesis (the Easter Vigil's first reading). The use of "only begotten Son" is important here when we pray that those to be baptized will be begotten by God and from above (recall the Nicodemus dialogue

209

in John 3). That within six lines the Holy Spirit is referred to twice is again significant of the Spirit's role in baptism and in sustaining the life of God given to those who are baptized in the communion of the church.

> May the power of the Holy Spirit,
> O Lord, we pray,
> come down through your Son
> into the fullness of this font...

Again the Holy Spirit is invoked in the classic way of liturgical prayers—from the Father through the Son. This trinitarian mediation is important as it underscores how, through the Trinity, we experience the presence and action of God in our lives. The reference to the word *font* for water baptism is important; it recalls that patristic authors have capitalized on this as both a "womb" and a "tomb." The multivalence of these words should not be lost here. It is a womb to give birth as does a mother's womb, and it also begets new members in the church. It is a tomb because it recalls the days Jesus spent in the tomb between his death and resurrection and is a tomb in which we are to place all that is death-dealing in our lives.

Continuing the same verse:

> ...so that all who have been buried with Christ
> by Baptism into death
> may rise again to life with you.

This explicit reference to Romans 6 reiterates a classic understanding of what baptism accomplishes (and recalls the first New Testament reading from the Easter Vigil). The use of the word *may* is interesting, again because of its possible multivalence. One meaning is that we ask that God accomplish this now, namely, that we have new life with Christ here and now. But when read against the actual text of Romans 6 there is an eschatological motif here, namely, "that we shall also live with him," not only here and now but in heaven forever. A play on the "already" and "not yet" of all Christian liturgy is operative here.

The blessing concludes:

Who lives and reigns with you in the unity of the Holy
  Spirit,
One God, for ever and ever.

The prayer's conclusion reiterates that it is through the power of the Holy Spirit that we can do anything liturgically. It is also a reiteration of the unity and diversity of the church as it is incorporated into the Trinity ("in the unity of...").

As I have noted previously, the American implementation of the RCIA has been a pastoral success story in that it has literally reshaped the season of Lent in terms of the Rite of Election, the Scrutinies, and the Celebration of the Sacraments of Initiation at the Easter Vigil. Yet, as I have also noted, there are problems with those so initiated remaining in the Catholic Church. The period of mystagogy has been cited as that part of the RCIA structure that needs firming up and lengthening. I think that part of the "unpacking" of the rites of initiation should also include a careful study of the parts of the Mass, the contents of those parts, and a similar "mystagogy" on all of the church's rites. This would allow for an ongoing, progressive assimilation into and experience of the liturgy as the center of the church's life. If we do not equip the newly initiated to appreciate this centrality of liturgy, why should we be surprised that the post–Easter Vigil falloff is so great?

But in the end, the study of liturgy is not about texts only. It is about a multifaceted and experiential phenomenon of assimilation into the Triune God through the specificity of Christ's paschal victory in the communion of the church through signs, senses, words, actions, music, silence, and so on. One of the purposes of re-envisaging the way liturgy is studied is to foster such assimilation and ongoing appropriation of these central mysteries. Liturgy is a learned set of behaviors. To enter into it as fully as possible means that we expend every energy and means to do so. In an age when educational institutions are retooling for the Internet, those involved with theological and liturgical curricula can benefit from the use of such technology.

In my own case, the international collaborative effort to produce the interactive DVD *Become One Body, One Spirit in Christ* on the occasion of the implementation of the revised and newly translated Roman Missal was an eye-opener and a very exciting project. Four foundational essays on theology, spirituality, history, and the *ars celebrandi*, plus an introduction to the new texts, were the basis for the filming of about forty people and hundreds of film clips of actual celebrations for the sake of elaborating and illustrating what the essays had to say. This was as close to an integrative, interactive way of going about the study of the liturgy as I have been involved in. That this DVD continues to be in demand and used beyond the implementation of the revised Missal attests to its staying power. I cannot help but think that it is a step toward the kind of education in and about the liturgy envisioned by *Sacrosanctum Concilium* and enabled by the technology available today. To unite the aims of the study of liturgy outlined by the constitution with expanding educational technology and resources will always be a work in progress, and to my mind an important work in progress indeed.

CHAPTER TEN

Devotions and Spirituality

Devotions: Among the More Complex Issues

Recent years have witnessed a marked resurgence of eucharistic adoration in (often called) "praise and worship" services, along with Benediction and the praying of the Rosary, especially among many younger Catholics. Anecdotal evidence points to dissatisfaction with the liturgical reform, specifically its perceived lack of transcendence or of formality, or to deficient celebrations of the liturgy and the loss of a sense of mystery, as the causes.[1] In my conversations with students, they express their desire for a structured prayer form that involves silence and quiet (necessitating turning off mobile phones and hand-held devices for an hour) and their eagerness to pray with songs and with texts that are particularly evocative and that resonate with their experience and their need for closeness with Jesus. That the lyrics of some of these songs deserve some critique, if not to say serious criticism, is obvious, at least to me. A similar resurgence of interest in "perpetual adoration of the Eucharist" in some parishes and nocturnal adoration in others reflects the same felt needs among the general Catholic population. But I also think that it reflects the innate desire of many today to say and do things that are obviously and externally "Catholic." Practices that were part of the Catholic repertoire of liturgy, devotions, and prayer before the Council but that initially waned in the wake of the postconciliar reforms are now on the rise. Recent pontiffs have lamented the almost complete absence of eucharistic adoration and Benediction, as witnessed by Pope John Paul II's encyclical *Ecclesia de Eucharistia* (n. 10) and Pope Benedict XVI's comments in the post-

213

synodal exhortation *Sacramentum Caritatis* (nn. 66–69). Diocesan bishops, too, have encouraged eucharistic devotions outside of Mass to pray for a variety of needs, including vocations to the priesthood, the diaconate, and the consecrated life.

At the risk of oversimplification, I wish to offer two examples of the way in which the liturgy and devotions existed in the church, not always in harmony but in a way that satisfied the prayer needs of the faithful.[2] Historians of the liturgy argue carefully and well that the patristic era was largely characterized by an integration among the celebration of the liturgy, the development of Catholic teaching and theology, the mutual enrichment and functioning of church ministries, and the living of the spiritual life among the baptized, especially those initiated as adults. They argue, further, however, that this presumed integration gradually came not to include all the faithful and that personal devotions eventually developed as something of a substitute for the liturgy, although the latter was still prized as the center of the church's prayer life. These devotions made the life of Christ tangible and real for the people. The evolution of the Rosary, in which one hundred fifty Hail Marys took the place of the one hundred fifty psalms prayed in the Liturgy of the Hours (by those whose education made it possible for them to do so) gave to many of the laity a means to pray that mirrored the official liturgy of the church.[3]

Regarding the celebration of the Eucharist, the focus on the showing of the consecrated bread and wine during the Eucharistic Prayer and the rise of street processions, Benediction, and adoration of the Eucharist outside of Mass were all related to the fact that, in many parts of the then Christian world, active participation in the Mass was minimal, and these devotions evolved so that the lay faithful could at least experience seeing the consecrated species, even if they were unable to receive it sacramentally or participate verbally in the prayers and responses of the Mass.[4]

That there was a very clear delineation between what comprised the liturgy—the church's official prayer—and what comprised devotions in church life before Vatican II is a fact of church teaching. But it was also a fact that those distinctions were not always understood and that a certain respectful coexistence existed between them, while at the same time Sunday Mass, which is at the heart of the church's liturgy, was (and is) a weekly requirement for Catholics.

My own experience of "growing up Catholic" in Mount Vernon, New York, in the 1950s included a raft of religious experiences and expressions that were, in fact, a mixture of liturgy and devotions. That we participated in Sunday Mass with hand Missals in order to follow what the priest was doing in the sanctuary, usually sang four hymns, and always received communion weekly was a given. Those of us who attended our (now closed) Catholic parochial school were required to attend Mass daily, this time with a larger hand Missal, but we only received communion on the first Fridays of the month. We did not receive communion daily. We watched from our pews as some adults who were at Mass did receive communion (from hosts in the tabernacle). Again, as students at the parochial school, we attended the Stations of the Cross every Friday during Lent, saying the devotional prayers written by St. Alphonsus Ligouri, and singing the stanzas of *Stabat Mater*, one after the other after each station. During May, the Stations were replaced by devotions to the Blessed Virgin Mary, with the annual crowning of a special additional statue of Mary carried in procession to the parish church. A girl from the eighth grade assisted the pastor, carrying a crown for Mary made of fresh flowers.

In elementary school, every day of class began with the praying of the Morning Offering in unison. The class day ended with similar prayers. As an altar boy (as we were called in those days), I took my turn serving at the Benediction that accompanied the weekly novenas to the Miraculous Medal (on Mondays) and to the Sacred Heart (on Fridays), who was patron of the parish church. In the contiguous parish (now closed), the preponderance of Italians and Italian Americans meant that devotions to St. Anthony of Padua (on Thursdays) were also conducted. We knew most of the devotional prayers by heart; they were always the same and easily committed to memory.

In our Catholic high school, each class period was begun with a prayer, and during homeroom we recited the Rosary in common (with some of the Marist brothers leading it in a more rapid fashion than others). We knew the three sets of the mysteries of the

Rosary by heart (at that time the Luminous Mysteries had not yet been added), as well as the Apostles' Creed to begin the Rosary and the Hail, Holy Queen to end it. My experience of the diocesan church was not attending a liturgy in St. Patrick's Cathedral in Manhattan, but being brought as a family by my father to Yankee Stadium for "the living rosary." This meant that the entire ball field was taken over by hundreds of mostly recent first communicants in their first communion finery, who encircled the field to form, in fact, a rosary comprised of children: ten in a circle making up each bead and others forming the crucifix. With all fifteen mysteries, this totaled sixteen hundred children. The center of the rosary was second base, over which had been constructed an altar where Cardinal Archbishop Francis Spellman would lead the closing Benediction. We were unaware that this repertoire of acts of piety, liturgy, and devotion were a mixture of the church's (official) liturgy and a number of private devotions said in common. Similarly, we did not know that we grew up in what might be called "ethnic parishes" with the Irish, Italians, and Germans populating different parishes despite geographical proximity. It was while watching the movie *Doubt*, whose cast was headed by the incomparable Meryl Streep and Philip Seymour Hoffman, that I realized I had grown up in a typical American parish in New York. The liturgies depicted at the beginning and end of the film were familiar. It was heartening to see the regimen of our liturgical participation and devotional praying reflected in the film.

At the same time, no one led us to distinguish "official liturgy" from devotions; it was all of a piece. Attendance and participation were required. We thought nothing about it; this was "ethnic" American Catholicism of suburban New York at its best, brought about through the sacrifices of second-generation parents of Irish descent (on my father's side) and German descent (on my mother's side).

In high school, I experienced a slow evolution toward a more liturgically grounded prayer life as we were instructed in religion classes, always taught by the Marist brothers. We participated more fully in the monthly First Friday Masses through some familiar and some new "hymns," as well as by reciting prayers in common, this time from an abbreviated form of the breviary. Members of the sodality movement also attended Mass every Friday morning in the brothers' chapel, and because we had received communion at that Mass, we were allowed to eat breakfast in the school cafeteria since we had fasted from food and drink since the night before.

When I entered the seminary, we came under the influence of several faculty members who were keen to share their knowledge of official liturgical documents, including Pius XII's *Mediator Dei* and *Mystici Corporis*. The faculty also led us in participating in the Mass and in Morning and Evening Prayer from the Divine Office in English by singing, speaking, and silence. I was in the seminary when the initial reforms of the liturgy were being implemented. The seminary professor of liturgy and sacred scripture gave us the theological background and liturgical principles that helped us understand the changes in the liturgy we experienced in the chapel. The (admittedly intimidating) professor of sacred music trained us in Gregorian chant and in English versions of the chant that he himself composed.

We began to read the writings of mostly European pioneers in the Liturgical Movement and to form an understanding of what comprised the liturgy and why we should value it over and above devotions. That daily spiritual reading in the seminary included the liturgical commentaries by Pius Parsch[5] and Aemiliana Lohr[6] was *de rigueur*, at least for some of us. However, there were others whose liturgical instincts were decidedly not in sync with the growing Liturgical Movement. Not surprisingly, this was reflected in the kind of surplices we seminarians wore over our cassocks at Mass. Those who were influenced by the writings from the Liturgical Movement often had longer white surplices in whole cloth with no ornamentation, sometimes with a round collar. The theology here was that this matched as much as possible the white garment worn by the newly baptized after their immersion in water, which became the precedent for the liturgical vesture common to all ministers, the alb.[7] Other seminarians of a more "traditional" bent would wear shorter surplices with lace ornamentation. Even then, I realize, we made statements about the kind of liturgy and liturgical "style"[8] we preferred by the kind of vesture we chose to wear or not wear. A certain minimalism in the style of the chasuble (also often called a "fiddleback") with affixed images started to be replaced by longer and fuller styles with no images attached but by some more liturgically oriented signs (such as a cross) in colors different from the vesture itself. The quality of the (natural) fabric was important, as was the fact that the alb underneath was plain white and the chasuble over it was ample. The revival of "conical vestments" with layers of material to be negotiated on one's arms was not uncommon. What came to be called the "noble simplicity" of the Roman Rite as described in *Sacrosanctum Concilium* was certainly reflected in a move toward simpler vesture.

I am well aware that these experiences come from a particular time and place and that others may well have very different experiences of the relationship between official liturgy and devotions. But what I have come to understand in my academic study of liturgy and devotions and in my reflection on my own experience of them means that, as in much of this book, I have more questions than answers and that the issues at hand are more nuanced and complex than I had once imagined. While on the one hand the church's official liturgy was clearly defined in ecclesiastical books, the fact remained that in practice there was a confluence of devotions and liturgy.

Teachings of the Second Vatican Council

Given the growing influence of the liturgical pioneers and the work on the preparatory commission on the topic of the sacred liturgy,[9] and that at times these popular devotions came to substitute for the church's official liturgy (as in, for example, street processions on Good Friday instead of the liturgical Celebration of the Lord's Passion), it should come as no surprise that the Constitution on the Sacred Liturgy invited a critique of popular devotions to be done in accord with the liturgy. The text states:

Popular devotions of the Christian people are to be highly commended, provided they accord with the laws and norms of the Church, above all when they are ordered by the Apostolic See.

218

Devotions proper to individual Churches also have a special dignity if they are undertaken by mandate of the bishops according to customs or books lawfully approved.

But these devotions should be so drawn up that they harmonize with the liturgical seasons, accord with the sacred liturgy, are in some fashion derived from it, and lead the people to it, since, in fact, the liturgy by its very nature far surpasses any of them. (n. 13)

That the Congregation for Divine Worship sees this challenge as still a work in progress is reflected in the 2001 publication of the important and thorough document *Directory on Popular Piety and the Liturgy.*[10]

Given these admonitions from the highest ecclesiastical authority, I am concerned to see the republishing of "tried and true" staples of personal devotion and piety from the 1940s and 1950s, such as *My Daily Bread* and manuals of devotional prayers from the same period. If, in fact, devotions are to "harmonize with the liturgical seasons, accord with the sacred liturgy, are in some fashion derived from it, and lead the people to it," then I think we have our work cut out for us. Devotions must rely on the liturgy itself, especially on the principles that undergirded the reform of the liturgy and the theology derived from the reformed liturgy (*lex orandi, lex credendi*) as the indispensable center of our prayer lives since, as the constitution points out, "the liturgy by its very nature far surpasses any of [these practices]."

I would wish for devotions to be evaluated in light of the following things that are intrinsic to liturgy. At the same time, I also want to suggest that there can be something very tangible, tactile, and expressive in devotions that sometimes is not found in the celebration of the reformed liturgy. Thus I would argue that the proposed harmonization of devotions with the liturgy be based on the following seven elements:[11]

1. That they proclaim or at least express fidelity to the word of God...

My concern here is that the emphasis on the Proclamation of the Word of God in all the revised liturgical rites be a part of at least most devotions as well. That the Catholic Church has moved from a post-Tridentine framing of the issue about the word of God versus sacraments to the liturgical principle that the one necessarily involves the other would be helpful to sustain in devotions. It is important for devotions about the Eucharist to be derived from the celebration of the Mass, a principle found repeatedly in postconciliar documents.[12] And even more specifically, I think that preconciliar devotional books about the Mass should be evaluated so that they reflect the revised Order of Mass, the revised *Lectionary for Mass*, and the prayers of the revised Roman Missal.

2. That they reflect paschal mystery theology…

In effect, all liturgy is paschal. It is always about our appropriation of and incorporation into the paschal mystery of Christ, which becomes truly the mystery of our faith. Here I want to suggest that devotions that emphasize only the passion and brutal death of Jesus on the cross (such as in Mel Gibson's film *The Passion of the Christ*) should be evaluated in light of what surrounds the passion and death. This is to say that Christ's life of obedience, leading to his acceptance of death on the cross, as well as his glorious resurrection and ascension into heaven should be seen as part and parcel of the paschal mystery. Here the texts of the memorial section of the Eucharistic Prayers can be very helpful, enlightening, and spiritually enriching.

3. That participants pray in Christ and through the Trinity…

I am concerned that sometimes rather generic terms for God are used and that the name Jesus is invoked in devotional prayers without the requisite and complementary terms used for the exalted Lord in the liturgy: *Lord…Christ…Lamb of God…*and so forth.

The Catholic Church has spent considerable energy theologically and liturgically in ensuring that we pray in the name of the three-personed God—Father, Son, and Holy Spirit—as exemplified at the end of the Eucharistic Prayer, at the end of most blessing prayers of the liturgy, and in the Doxology at the end of each psalm in the Liturgy of the Hours.

4. *That the church offers thanks and praise...*

That devotions reflect deeply held personal intentions and needs is clear in many of their prayers. But the Judeo-Christian tradition, reflected in the psalms and in many liturgical prayers, is to name and "bless" God in praise and thanks by delineating such motives as creation, redemption, liberation, and forgiveness. The structure of almost all of the blessing prayers added to our liturgy after Vatican II contains a generous recounting of the events of saving history that, when retold, are themselves experienced anew and form a paradigm on which basis we then pray for our communal and personal needs. All prayer is always ecclesial. We are always a part of the church even when alone, and we always pray with and for the universal and local church.

5. *That praise and thanksgiving lead to prayers of petition and intercession...*

The pattern of liturgical prayer is that after recounting motives from saving history we then move, on that basis, to ask God for what we need. The logic inherent here is, unfortunately, not always reflected in devotional prayers. That devotions express felt needs with which we can identify is a great advantage. But devotional payers do not always express requisite praise and thanks, and this can diminish the balance that is struck in the liturgy between praise, thanks, personal need, and the needs of others. Again, it is an issue of ecclesial consciousness even when we pray for deeply held and urgently felt personal needs.

6. *That intercessory prayer is a statement of eschatology (the not-yet-ness of Christian life)...*

All liturgical prayer is decidedly prayer "in between" the death, resurrection, and ascension of Christ and his second coming at the end of time to bring time to an end. It is always a prayer that says, whether explicitly or not, "thy kingdom come." The very fact that we pray for what we judge we need, what we do not have, and what only God can grant us is a statement of eschatology, the not-yet-ness of the Christian life.

7. That intercessory prayer is a statement of, and a commitment to, the concerns of all here on earth...

Devotional prayers often refer to the individual without the ecclesial context inherent in all prayer. I can remember the words of what was regarded as "the" novena prayer in the Miraculous Medal Novena and the pause during which we spoke our individual needs to God in silence. Then the priest would lead us back to saying the rest of the prayer: "Thou knowest, O Mary, how often our souls have been the sanctuaries of your Son, who hates iniquity...." (At the same time this novena is notable for its invocation of the Holy Spirit at the beginning and for addressing "O Lord Jesus Christ..." specifically.) In addition to personal and communal needs, the ecological consciousness of our day might well lead us to add a prayer for all the good things on this earth, that they be shared and not overused by some peoples at the expense of others.

In his book *Prayers of the Faithful*, James P. McCain noted that a liturgically, largely eucharistically inspired devotional life was fostered in the laity in the early years of the twentieth century through the writings of the Liturgical Movement.[13] But it still seems to me that we have yet to accomplish a fuller realization of the expectation and challenge of *Sacrosanctum Concilium* in ensuring that devotions be harmonized with the theology of the liturgy.

The Tangible as "Really Real"

Allow me to raise an issue that, in my opinion, underlies a number of issues suggested here about devotions, namely, that what we often define or presume as real is what is physical only, tangible, or literal. In fact, what is "really real" in the liturgy is what is on the level of signs and symbols. The classic adage that sacraments "cause by signifying" (*significando causant*) means that what we experience through our senses matters a great deal and impacts on how we experience (not "just" think about) salvation and our continual sanctification. That is why the liturgical pioneers emphasized the artifacts of the liturgy—altar, ambo, font, chair, and so forth—as opposed to statues and art works that depict the past only. There is, after all, a world of difference in the celebration of the Eucharist on Holy Thursday night conducted at the altar, the ambo, and chair on the one hand and setting up a Passover table in the sanctuary as a help to understanding on the other. The latter diminishes the multivalence of the former. The perception that what is real is literal, physical, or tangible hints at notions of spirituality and prayer as inspired by the liturgy and leads us from and back to the liturgy. It also affects the appreciation of the Catholic principle of sacramentality as expressed in and through the liturgy. If what is tangible and physically expressed is what is "real," then a logical result is emphasis on statues, the Stations of the Cross, eucharistic miracles, and surprising physical healings. If what is "really real" is the sacramental and liturgical, then devotions that harmonize with the liturgy can be avenues through which we experience and appropriate the liturgy.

At the same time, I wonder whether there are some issues about the way the reformed liturgy is celebrated that do come to bear on this issue, specifically the terseness of some liturgical prayers and, paradoxically, the wordiness of many celebrations. Even though the liturgy is experienced and is an action meant to involve both our senses and our bodies, my own impression is that assemblies are in fact still passive before what occurs at the altar; that the way the gestures, signs, and symbols of the liturgy are enacted are in fact still minimal; and that the bodies and hearts (as well as minds) of gathered assemblies are in fact still not engaged. This can be at least a partial cause of the revival of devotional prayers and the revering of such "sacred" objects as statues, rosaries, and holy cards.

One of the initially highly acclaimed possibilities in the reform of the liturgy put forth in *Sacrosanctum Concilium* was the ongoing reform and renewal often summarized by the term *inculturation* (nn. 37–40). Important initiatives in this area were supported and enshrined in the works of the Benedictine scholar Anscar Chupungco.[14] Often, cited examples of contemporary liturgical inculturation include the translation of the Latin liturgy into vernaculars and the ongoing task of building church buildings adequate to the task of facilitating the celebration of the reformed liturgy. On the one hand, Fr. Chupungco envisioned a yet more fundamental adjustment of the reformed Roman Rite; on the other, under the pontificates of Pope John Paul II and Benedict XVI, a limit was imposed on the scope of liturgical inculturation. Two examples are the *"Fourth Instruction" on the Proper Implementation of the Liturgy* (*Varietates Legitimae*)[15] and, to some extent, the *"Fifth Instruction"* (*Liturgiam Authenticam*).[16] The former clearly influenced the formulation of chapter 9 of the GIRM, which treats inculturation.

In all likelihood, the issuance of these official documents to guide ongoing initiatives was motivated by the fact that some efforts undertaken under the guise of "inculturation" were judged to be immature in their conception and execution. My own sense, however, is that the authors of *Sacrosanctum Concilium* did not perceive that the "substantial unity of the Roman Rite" required lockstep implementation and that even in the Roman liturgy, absolute uniformity was not necessary. That the implementation of the Roman liturgy may be perceived to be cerebral and laconic (the texts are not highly expressive, given that they derive from Roman texts marked by succinctness) may well be because the inculturation that occurred, given the expansive role of devotions in Catholic faith life up to Vatican II, was not fostered after the reform. More specifically, I wonder whether the tenor of the post–Vatican II instructions and the GIRM may have discouraged initiatives about the use of gesture, symbol, and the body itself in the liturgy that could have been undertaken as legitimate liturgical inculturation. Specifically, bodily participation, as well as participation of mind and heart, could have received more emphasis. It seems to me that the usual celebration of the liturgy before Vatican II carried with it more sense of the bodiliness of worship, as well as the incarnational and sacramental principles, than does the usual celebration of the reformed liturgy. One might criticize the rubrical precision demanded of the Tridentine Mass; nevertheless, its bowings, genuflections, kneeling, singing, standing, and processing were all proscribed as part and parcel of the liturgy. In the reformed liturgy, many of these things became optional. The liturgy did not require such bodily engagement, and this may have left fertile field for the notion that the liturgy is about minds and hearts but not bodies and thus diminished the tangibility intrinsic to worship.

Spirituality

At the beginning of this book, I offered a working definition of *liturgy*. Now I would like to offer another working definition as part of framing my discussion of an appropriate spirituality for those engaged in the church's pastoral ministry and especially in liturgical leadership:

Working Definition of *Spirituality*

Spirituality is a way of thinking and acting shaped primarily by the church's corporate experience of God, who is immanent and transcendent, revealed yet remaining hidden, a Triune God who invites us into deep and abiding relationship with Father, Son, and Holy Spirit, and through them with the whole church and the wider world. Spirituality enables church members to maintain values that ensure our communal experience of the faith in a world that prizes the "self" and to uphold countercultural positions with confidence that may challenge the status quo in the face of contrary cultural pressures because of the power of God's enlivening Spirit within and among us. Spirituality guides a person's understanding of the world and provides a basis for discipline in one's life.

What underlies this definition is a Catholic worldview and a Catholic way of looking at and reflecting on the spiritual life. "Spirituality" is more than one's prayer or participation in the liturgy or one's devotional practices; it is a worldview that determines how we look at life and live the life of God.

A crucial factor in articulating this kind of deliberately *apostolic, relational,* and *liturgical spirituality* is to understand that what makes liturgy so important is that it is the church's privileged *experience* of and *participation* in the very being of God, with and among the community gathered by God to share in the very life of God in order that we might live the life of God in the world. Liturgy does not describe or define these relationships.

225

Liturgy is the privileged and unique forum in which these relationships are set in proper order and are experienced.

The following relationships are intrinsic to the life and ministry of pastoral ministers as they undergird an apostolic, relational spirituality. I will refer to the way the liturgy names and presumes these relationships in order to emphasize how they are understood and experienced in and through the celebration of the liturgy.

GOD

The first relationship, and the one that underlies all others, is with God—Father, Son, and Holy Spirit. The Judeo-Christian God of the scriptures and the God of our Catholic tradition is a God who invites us as a people into a relationship that is deep, abiding, sustaining, and nurturing.

Even as we acknowledge God's utter transcendence, texts, such as those contained in Sunday Preface VI, remind us that we believe and abide in a relational God:

> For in you we live and move and have our being.
> And while in this body
> we not only experience the daily effects of your care
> but even now possess the pledge of eternal life.

This is a dynamic, biblical, and liturgical way of expressing the conventional Catholic assertion that we are "temples of the Holy Spirit."

After this primary and foundational relationship with God, the following relationships are to be seen in relation to one another and to God as their absolute foundation. In effect, they might be imaged as circles within the widest circle, which is God and our relatedness to God in the church.

CHURCH LEADERS, THE CHURCH UNIVERSAL, AND THE LOCAL CHURCH

One who is ordained is privileged to give voice at the liturgy, specifically in the Eucharistic Prayer, to our relatedness to, and prayer with and for, church leaders. The naming of the pope and bishop in every Eucharistic Prayer is a statement of Catholic ecclesiology. No individual act of liturgy is ever "just" of this community gathered here and now; it is always of the universal church even as it is an act of this particular gathered assembly. Priests are ordained by the bishop for the service of the church, even as a variety of priests are ordained for and with their particular religious communities, institutes, societies, and dioceses. The naming of the pope and local bishop serves as a continual reminder for all pastoral ministers and for the entire gathered assembly of the wider church lens, which is always a part of Catholicism. It is also an invitation to continue to pray for and with them in their essential ministries for the church. From a slightly different point of view, this helps prevent any given liturgical context from being too focused on itself, which is often termed *congregationalism* and is not a natively Catholic way of looking at church-belonging or liturgical participation.

PRIEST-PRESBYTERS

Priests are ordained into the "order of presbyters"; they are not ordained in isolation or as individuals. One of the key elements of the theology of orders expressed in the documents of Vatican II and in the title of the revised ordination rites is that all ordinations are to the "order of bishops," to the "order of presbyters," or to the "order of deacons." The clear shift in the language of Vatican II to describe what we have come to call "priestly" ordination as ordination to the *presbyterate* is a major theological statement that needs to be reflected on and underscored as we describe the "the priestly life" and "priestly spirituality."[17] Again, this points to the relational character of one's priestly ordination: the priest is ordained into a preexisting body of fellow presbyter-priests. For many priests, this is their "first line" of support and challenge. Some priests live in stable religious houses and thus experience presbyteral relatedness on a day-to-day basis. Among other implications of this collegial understanding of the presbyterate is the opportunity to view the priestly character not as something that one receives for oneself but, rather, something that binds us together with other presbyters. Such an approach reflective of the

227

Vatican II emphasis on ecclesiology and collegiality would be a development from what has legitimately been argued to be a comparatively individualist understanding of the priestly character expressed at the Council of Trent.[18]

OTHER PASTORAL MINISTERS

In addition to the collaboration of ordained permanent deacons in pastoral ministry today, the phenomenon of lay ecclesial ministers, whose formation and education are carefully articulated in *Coworkers in the Vineyard*,[19] is a fact of vibrant American Catholic pastoral life. These ministers may include a pastoral associate, faith formation director, school principal and teachers, liturgical ministry director, youth ministers, social justice coordinators, campus ministers, hospital chaplains, and others. All those engaged in pastoral ministry know and rely on the fact that they are truly coworkers. Regular meetings during which different pastoral staff members share information and projects and at which they debate future plans in their ministries are staples of parish life today. Priests know only too well that the names listed on the front cover of the parish bulletin and the homepage of the parish's Web site are the people without whom the parish could not function. It is often said that the vitality of the life of the Catholic Church in America is due to the myriad ministries and high level of functioning of the parish. This presumes a high degree of cooperation among those on the parish staff, all of whom are related to one another and to the priest.

LAY VOLUNTEERS

Parishes presume on the personal gifts and the usually freely given talents of a variety of parishioners. The range is enormous and includes RCIA team members, liturgical ministers, choir members, extraordinary ministers of communion to the sick and homebound, catechists, food pantry and soup kitchen volunteers, and others. Lay "involvement" is almost a redundant term. It is the range of lay volunteers that enables the parish to function and to have the variety of ministries it is engaged in. This is "people to people" ministry. While priests have certain gifts and talents, they do not possess all the gifts and talents on which the parish relies. It takes the full complement of laypeople to make it "work."

PARISHIONERS AND THOSE WE SERVE

The ongoing day-to-day ministry of the pastoral minister is predicated on relationships with those whom he or she serves. That the demands of the apostolate are at the heart of a pastoral minister's life is reflected in this text from the Office of Readings on the Feast of St. Vincent de Paul (September 27). While it is addressed to priests, the kind of ministry it emphasizes should be a model for all pastoral ministers:

> Do not become upset or feel guilty because you interrupted your prayer to serve the poor. God is not neglected if you leave him for such service. One of God's works is merely interrupted so that another can be carried out. So when you leave prayer to serve some poor person, remember that this very service is performed for God. Charity is certainly greater than any rule. Moreover all rules must lead to charity.[20]

Spirituality derived from and sustained by the liturgy is not "getting away from it all"; it is putting those relationships into proper order and growing in holiness in the midst of those relationships. One central way that God does that for us again and again is in and through the liturgy.

One Example: Liturgy and Justice

The Catholic Church's social justice teaching has been called our best-kept secret.[21] It was, however, hardly a secret to the pioneers of the Liturgical Movement. It is not a coincidence that Pope Leo XIII's encyclical *Rerum Novarum* of 1890 coincided with the beginnings of the Liturgical Movement in Europe. This document is a watershed in terms of laying out Catholic principles of engagement in and of the world, with the "common good" and "subsidiarity" as its hallmarks. Those same hallmarks also reflect some of the pastoral inspiration that guided pioneers in the emerging Liturgical Movement. Thanks to the inspiration, teaching, and liturgical celebration of Father John Ryan, priest-professor at the Catholic University of America from 1915 to 1939, the burgeoning Catholic social teaching was a particular feature of the Liturgical Movement. His second major text, *Distributive Justice: The Right and Wrong of Our Present Distribution of Wealth*,[22] is as timely today as the day it was written. Concern for just wages and just working conditions were the concern of leaders in both social justice and liturgical arenas. They would have welcomed the U.S. bishops' pastoral on the economy *Economic Justice for All* (1986), as well as Pope John Paul II's encyclical letter *Centesimus Annus* (1991) and the *Compendium of the Social Doctrine of the Church* (2004). That the liturgy celebrated the advent of the Just One whose reign extended to all creation was a tenet of both the social justice activists and the proponents of the Liturgical Movement.

It has been asserted more than once that, in the American implementation of the reform, the liturgy and the justice agendas have gone in different directions. Publications by such important authors as Mark Searle, Bryan Hehir, and Anne Koester[23] were intended to help heal this breach. Clearly, they were valiant attempts.

That justice and liturgy have even been at any kind of odds is curious since the liturgy always celebrates and realizes the Just One in our midst. Despite politicizing rhetoric about power roles and hierarchy over laity, the liturgy is, in fact, a leveler. It is where society's status structures are overturned—poor and rich, weak and strong, male and female, slave and free—and all are one in the God we worship. Through him who was rich and became poor, we who are poor can be rich in him. One of the tasks is to see beyond what are seeming power structures in enacting the liturgy to the level of where the power of the liturgy functions for all of us who are really powerless. It is also the locus where God's justice reigns and from where our lives should be transformed to live according to his justice.

Walter Burghardt, SJ, often lamented that in the former English translation of the Preface Dialogue we did not say, "It is right and just," but, "It is right to give him thanks and praise."

This was the single instance, he pointed out, when the Roman Mass referred to "justice." Burghardt would be pleased that the revised text now says, "It is right and just."

In the end, however, the liturgy does not celebrate and enact the *concept* of justice; rather, the liturgy itself is an *experience* of the Just One. In Advent, we plead that the heavens rain down the Just One and that the heavens are rent open. A power is at work here that cannot be domesticated or tamed; it is a power from God alone that can shake us to our foundations, level us, and make us whole. Each year in the Lenten liturgy we are reminded to look beyond external observances to the real works of conversion: fasting, prayer, and almsgiving—all in secret, all for the right reasons. And on the very day when the church does impose ashes on us (paradoxically!), in the Office of Readings we listen to the words of Isaiah 58 that the real fasting God wishes is to release those who suffer injustice, to share our bread with the hungry, and to live in accordance with God's will.

The Assembly: Gathered and Sent

While a chief characteristic of all liturgy is that it is the self-expression of the community of the church, this sense of belonging has been legitimately critiqued when it has seemed self-generated or only an expression of oneself in community. For me, the words of the Third Eucharistic Prayer offer an assurance and a challenge: "You have gathered here before you..." We who gather do so at the Lord's gracious invitation, not out of our own self-will. We say, "Take and eat, for this is my body," in order to "become one body, one spirit in Christ." We are made members of one another in this worldwide Catholic Church through the waters of baptism and the invocation of the three persons in the Triune God—Father, Son, and Holy Spirit—at every liturgy we celebrate. Certainly *communio* has become an important watchword for how we should understand a number of things in the life of the church, including church-belonging itself.[24] At baptism, we are drawn into the communion of persons that is the Trinity, and we are members of one another in and through the Trinity. The three-personed God calls us into that divine indwelling, sustains us in the set of relationships that is the church, and "again and again" calls us to worship in and through the liturgy. Whatever can be said about coming together in the Lord's name for liturgy, it is always something we do because God calls us to do it. It is not self-generated and certainly not self-sustained; it is done at the invitation and sustaining action of the Trinity among us.

The other side of the inner dynamic of the liturgy is that we are then sent forth from it to live in accord with the life map that the liturgy sets out for us. This increased sense of mission was on the minds of the bishops assembled for the Synod on the Eucharist in 2005. They asked in their final propositions that mission be an important emphasis of the post-synodal exhortation. And indeed that is the case in the document itself and in the addition of two new dismissal texts to the Mass by Pope Benedict XVI. The Latin *Ite missa est* with which the Mass concluded does contain elements of sending forth to live what we celebrate. The word *missa* here contains the connotation of *mission*. But the additional texts from the pope are more explicit:

Go and announce the Gospel of the Lord.
Go in peace, glorifying the Lord by your life.

The inner dynamic of any liturgy is that we come together as the gathered assembly and are sent forth from the gathered assembly to be leaven in the world of the Gospel we have heard and the paschal mystery we have participated in. As the pilgrim church on earth, we know well that without what the liturgy celebrates we cannot have any life, and that this real life comes from God and the Gospel alone. Liturgy is always the worship of the pilgrim church on earth—barnacles on this bark of Peter and all—until we are called to the "supper of the Lamb" (Rev 19:7) when sacraments will cease and we will have no more need of them. Until then we have desperate need for them and for one another. This side of the veil it is always *the church's worship*.

CONCLUSION

The Integrity of Worship

As I conclude what I have intended to be a modest "discussion starter" about the implementation of the liturgical reforms from Vatican II, I want to recall the title of the Introduction—"Asking the Important Questions." Certainly, as I have written these pages, reflected on them, and edited and rewritten them, many more questions have occurred to me than when I had started to write. In light of the insight of the novelist I cited at the beginning, that is just as well. In fact, it is probably a sign of both wisdom (knowing what I do not know) and of humility to acknowledge what I need to learn and to continue to learn from others. In the end, it is important to know what you do not know, not to fake it, and to make the educational enterprise a lifetime of learning—especially from one's students. (I often say that my responsibility as a doctoral mentor is to guide a student into knowing far more about a subject that I ever could and to allow him or her to become a world's expert.)

I want to close with four insights taken from others that have shaped me in various ways.

Liturgy Does Us

One of my first teachers in the summer master's degree program in liturgical studies at Notre Dame was Aidan Kavanagh, OSB. His lectures were always well attended. He was noted for a particular kind of rhetoric that most of us enjoyed and some of us eventually emulated. His turn of phrase often made the difference between gleaning information from this master teacher and really

233

assimilating and appropriating what he had to say simply because of the way he said it.

One day in class, commenting on current and future efforts to implement the reformed liturgy, he said that we spend an enormous amount of time and energy implementing the liturgy and that what we do is very important. But then he looked over his horned-rimmed glasses and added, "Liturgy is about what we do. But really, what is far more true is that liturgy does us." This insight has stayed with me for all these years. And it makes me very conscious of respecting, valuing, and in fact revering the reformed liturgy. While I have made a number of observations throughout this book, indicated some areas for improvement, and suggested how some things could be done differently, in the end, I want to say that there is an integrity to worship from which we can and should learn and that we should assimilate.

One year before *Sacrosanctum Concilium* was promulgated at Vatican II, the poet e. e. cummings wrote, "be of love (a little) / more careful / than of everything [else]." I suggest that we should "be of liturgy a little more careful than of everything else" in church life. It is where it all comes together: revelation, theology, prayer, ritual, artistry, and much more besides. Be very careful of it because it is about nothing less than the renewal of the church.

We need to be very careful about what we do in the liturgy because, in the end, it is the liturgy that *does us*.

Something More

One of the earlier paragraphs of *Sacrosanctum Concilium* states: "Pastors of souls must therefore realize that, when the liturgy is celebrated, something more is required than the mere observation of the laws governing valid and licit celebration; it is their duty also to ensure that the faithful take part fully aware of what they are doing, actively engaged in the rite, and enriched by its effects" (n. 11).

This book is intended to contribute to the ongoing assessment of the reformed liturgy. Therefore, I have deliberately offered food for thought that might (or might not) lead to adjustments in the way the liturgy is celebrated. Throughout, I have also wanted to emphasize the intrinsic theological and spiritual dimensions of the liturgy. For me the issue is not integrating the sacred with the secular—which the liturgy itself does and is—but it is realizing and appropriating how the divine is experienced in the human and how broken humanity is healed by broken bread and by wine poured out. It seems to me that the phrase *something more* should always be before us as we plan, participate in, and minister to the sacred liturgy.

In the end, our liturgical examination of conscience should include the Gospel of Matthew 25: Where did we feed, clothe, and visit Christ in the hungry around us, the naked around us, and the imprisoned among us? I always found it compelling when over the front doors of many medieval cathedrals, the last judgment would be in the tympanum above with figures of the saved on the right and the damned on the left—and sometimes they were the same personages! For me it was a reminder that what we do in those buildings should lead us to more committed lives outside the building.

One Life Is Not Enough

In the mid-1970s, when I was a graduate student at Sant' Anselmo in Rome, I used several guidebooks to help me get to know the city and to share with friends who visited Rome. One of my favorites was very thorough and comprehensive. But what struck me and my friends about the guidebook was its first sentence: "For Rome, one life is not enough." I took that phrase to heart and, every Saturday for the first eighteen months I lived in Rome, I read different guidebooks about parts of St. Peter's Basilica. Then every Saturday afternoon I walked to the basilica, walked around it, and thought about what I had read and what I was witnessing. After about an hour and a half, I walked down the steps of the basilica and walked home, relishing what I had seen. And I knew that there was so much more to see and experience in that basilica and in a city I came to love.

235

I want to suggest that for liturgy, one talk is not enough, nor is one course, one book, one experience of the liturgical year, one two-year period to hear the daily scripture readings at Mass, one three-year period to hear the Sunday scripture readings, several years to experience the Liturgy of the Hours, or, indeed, decades to experience all the sacraments from baptism to last anointing. The liturgy is simply too rich, too profound, too multidimensional, too multivalent, too all-encompassing of so many things, persons (human and divine), words, images, gestures, artifacts, art, signs, and symbols. Indeed, for the liturgy, "one life is not enough."

Liturgy Is Who We Are

I noted in the Introduction that I am originally from New York but that I live and work in Washington, DC. Given my love for Manhattan, I do get back to "the city" now and then to visit family and friends, and, yes, to do some shopping(!). Buying something "wholesale" in New York is nothing more or less than the enduring indoor sport. Two years ago, I returned to New York just after Easter and Passover and visited a man who by now is a friend, a Jewish rabbi, John Banda, whose office is on the tenth floor of a building on 47th Street and Fifth Avenue. Despite the tony address, the office is vintage 1950s and is not just "low tech," it is "no tech." As usual, we sat down and spent some time catching up on news about family and friends. He beamed as he said that all of his children and grandchildren, including two from Israel, had come home to Brooklyn for Passover. On the day I visited him in his office, his grandson was bound for JFK airport to take a flight back to Israel for his last semester of graduate school. I replied that it must have been extraordinary to have been with the whole family for the High Holy Days. He peered over his (not half) glasses, smiled broadly, shrugged his shoulders, and said, "But that's who we are."

Two years later, I returned to New York City to visit. One of my stops was at the office of my rabbi friend. The elevator was in no better repair. The furniture was exactly the same as I remem-

236

bered it. The fluorescent light over the desk was eighteen inches wide and, despite his attempts to adjust it, always seemed slightly in the way. Mr. Banda asked about family and mutual friends. Regarding his own family, he said that on the following Wednesday, "We are going to make a wedding." He explained that this meant that his grandson, his daughter's son, was going to marry. I then told him that this past spring I used his story about Passover from my visit two years ago in my Holy Thursday homily. I reiterated how impressed I was with his insight—"That's who we are"—which I made the centerpiece of the homily. For the first time I can remember, Mr. Banda said nothing in reply. He looked over his glasses with misty eyes and he had a very slight smile on his face. He said nothing. Then again, what else is there to say than "that's who we are"?

Notes

Introduction

1. Chaim Potok, *In the Beginning* (New York: Ballantine Books, 1982), 295–96.

2. See, among others, *Young Adult Catholics* (Notre Dame, IN: University of Notre Dame Press, 2001), which contains summaries of surveys taken of a variety of young Catholics up to the age of thirty. Their reactions to liturgy were negative when the preaching and music were judged deficient and when there was not a sense of belonging.

3. See my own *101 Questions & Answers on the Mass* (New York / Mahwah, NJ: Paulist Press, 2012), xvii–xx.

4. See http://www.vatican.va/archive/hist_councils/ii_vatican _council/documents/vat-ii_const_19631204_sacrosanctum-con cilium_en.html. See this same source for all other citations from the Constitution on the Sacred Liturgy.

5. See *101 Questions & Answers on the Mass*, questions 22, 23, 60, and 98.

6. For a more complete digest and commentary on these two documents, see my own *Serving the Body of Christ: The Magisterium on the Eucharist and Holy Orders* (New York / Mahwah, NJ: Paulist Press, 2013).

7. See Patrick Regan, *From Advent to Pentecost: Comparing the Seasons in the Ordinary and Extraordinary Form of the Roman Rite* (Collegeville, MN: Liturgical Press, 2012).

8. See Robert Taft, *The Liturgy of the Hours in East and West: The Origins of the Divine Office and Its Meaning for Today* (Collegeville, MN: Liturgical Press, 1986), 345.

9. The only exception is chapter 5, "Liturgical Translations," because of the present interest in this topic. I judged that sketching *how* we got to the place where the revision of the translation of the Roman Missal came from was particularly topical and important.

Chapter 1

1. See Paul McPartlan, *The Eucharist Makes the Church: Henri de Lubac and John Zizioulas in Dialogue* (London: T & T Clark, 1993), and his *Sacrament of Salvation: An Introduction to Eucharistic Ecclesiology* (London: T & T Clark, 1995). The precise text from *Ecclesia de Eucharistia* states:

> If, as I have said, the Eucharist builds the Church and the Church makes the Eucharist, it follows that there is a profound relationship between the two, so much so that we can apply to the Eucharistic mystery the very words with which, in the Nicene-Constantinopolitan Creed, we profess the Church to be 'one, holy, catholic and apostolic.' The Eucharist too is one and catholic. It is also holy, indeed, the Most Holy Sacrament. But it is above all its apostolicity that we must now consider. (n. 26)

The full encyclical can be found at http://www.vatican.va/holy_father/john_paul_ii/encyclicals/documents/hf_jp-ii_enc_20030417_eccl-de-euch_en.html.

2. Cardinal Joseph Ratzinger, *Principles of Catholic Theology* (San Francisco: Ignatius Press, 1987), 53. This translation is amended by Paul McPartlan in his *Sacrament of Salvation*, xiv, fn. 3, who indicates that the last phrase was left out in the Ignatius Press translation of *Theologische Prinzipienlehre* (Munich: Erich Wewel, 1982), 55.

3. Robert Putnam, *American Grace: How Religion Divides and Unites Us* (New York: Simon and Schuster, 2010).

4. See Hans Urs von Balthasar, "The Mass as Sacrifice," in *Explorations in Theology*, vol. 3, *Creator Spirit* (San Francisco: Ignatius Press, 1993), 185–243.

5. See the Catholic Bishops' Conferences of England & Wales, Ireland, and Scotland, *One Bread, One Body: A Teaching Document on the Eucharist in the Life of the Church and the Establishment of General Norms for Sacramental Sharing* (Dublin: Veritas, 1998).

6. From the USCCB, "Guidelines for the Reception of Communion," available at http://old.usccb.org/liturgy/current/inter com.shtml:

For Catholics

As Catholics, we fully participate in the celebration of the Eucharist when we receive Holy Communion. We are encouraged to receive Communion devoutly and frequently. In order to be properly disposed to receive Communion, participants should not be conscious of grave sin and normally should have fasted for one hour. A person who is conscious of grave sin is not to receive the Body and Blood of the Lord without prior sacramental confession except for a grave reason where there is no opportunity for confession. In this case, the person is to be mindful of the obligation to make an act of perfect contrition, including the intention of confessing as soon as possible (canon 916). A frequent reception of the Sacrament of Penance is encouraged for all.

For our fellow Christians

We welcome our fellow Christians to this celebration of the Eucharist as our brothers and sisters. We pray that our common baptism and the action of the Holy Spirit in this Eucharist will draw us closer to one another and begin to dispel the sad divisions which separate us. We pray that these will lessen and finally disappear, in keeping with Christ's prayer for us "that they may all be one" (Jn 17:21).

Because Catholics believe that the celebration of the Eucharist is a sign of the reality of the oneness of faith, life, and worship, members of those churches with whom we are not yet fully united are ordinarily not admitted to Holy Communion. Eucharistic sharing in exceptional circumstances by other Christians requires permission according to the directives of the diocesan bishop and the provisions of canon law (canon 844 § 4). Members of the Orthodox Churches, the Assyrian Church of the East, and the Polish National Catholic Church are urged to respect the discipline of their own Churches. According to Roman Catholic discipline, the Code of Canon Law does not object to the reception of communion by Christians of these Churches (canon 844 § 3).

For those not receiving Holy Communion
All who are not receiving Holy Communion are encouraged to express in their hearts a prayerful desire for unity with the Lord Jesus and with one another.

For non-Christians
We also welcome to this celebration those who do not share our faith in Jesus Christ. While we cannot admit them to Holy Communion, we ask them to offer their prayers for the peace and the unity of the human family.

7. While sometimes on opposite sides of issues, including the scope of the reforming of the rites, the accounts of Annibale Bugnini in *The Reform of the Liturgy 1948–75*, trans. Matthew O'Connell (Collegeville, MN: Liturgical Press, 1990) and the accounts of Ferdinando Antonelli as presented in Nicola Giampetro's *The Development of the Liturgical Reform: As Seen by Cardinal Ferdinando Antonelli from 1948 to 1970* (Fort Collins, CO: Roman Catholic Books, 2009) are in remarkable agreement.

8. See, among others, the important essays in Mark Searle, ed., *Liturgy and Social Justice* (Collegeville, MN: Liturgical Press, 1980), especially the article by Brian Hehir.

Chapter 2

1. For these sixteen instances of the word *participation*, see *Sacrosanctum Concilium*, within numbers 14, 19, 27, 30, 41, 50,

113, 114, 121, and 124, and in the title preceding n. 14. The full text is available at http://www.vatican.va/archive/hist_councils /ii_vatican_council/documents/vat-ii_const_19631204_sacrosanc tum-concilium_en.html.

2. John Cardinal McCloskey, *Golden Key to Heaven: A Collection of Devout Prayers and Approved Devotions for Use Among the Faithful* (New York / Cincinnati / St. Louis: Benziger Brothers, 1884).

3. Rev. Joseph Stedman, *My Sunday Missal, Explained by Father Stedman* (New York: Catholic Book Publishing Co., 1958).

4. See Fr. Thierry Maertens, OSB, *Saint Andrew Bible Missal* (Bruges: Biblica, 1962, orig. 1960), with an Introduction by Richard Cardinal Cushing that begins with the words "The liturgical movement instituted by Pope Pius X has achieved much," (vii).

5. See the erudite treatment of its origins in Bryan D. Spinks, *The Sanctus in the Eucharistic Prayer* (New York: Cambridge University Press, 1991).

6. Tertullian, *On the Resurrection* 8.3, PL 2.806.

7. See *Sacrosanctum Concilium* online at http://www.vati can.va/archive/hist_councils/ii_vatican_council/documents/vat-ii_ const_19631204_sacrosanctum-concilium_en.html.

8. See *Lumen Gentium* online at http://www.vatican.va /archive/hist_councils/ii_vatican_council/documents/vat-ii_ const_19641121_lumen-gentium_en.html.

9. Among other sources, see the recent doctoral dissertation from CUA by Gabriel Pivarnik, now published as *Toward a Trinitarian Theology of Liturgical Participation* (Collegeville, MN: Liturgical Press, 2013).

10. Among others, see *Actuosa Participatio: Conoscere, comprendere, e vivere la Liturgia. Studi in onore del Prof. Domenico Sartore*, ed. Agostino Montan and Manlio Sodi (Citta del Vaticano: Libreria Editrice Vaticana, 2002).

11. Ibid. Also, see, among others, Frederick R. McManus, "Pastoral Ecumenism: The Common Lectionary," in *The Eucharist: Toward the Third Millennium* (Chicago: Liturgy Training Publications, 1997), 103–18.

12. William Hill, OP, *The Three-Personed God: The Trinity as a Mystery of Salvation* (Washington, DC: Catholic University of America Press, 1982).

13. See the magisterial study by John Baldovin, *The Urban Character of Christian Worship: The Origins, Development, and Meaning of Stational Liturgy* (Rome: Pontifical Institute Press, 1987).

14. See my own "Which Liturgy Is the Church's Liturgy?" *Origins* 38, no. 37 (February 26, 2009): 581–89.

15. Among others, see my own "On Critiquing Liturgical Critics," *Worship* (January 2000): 1–19.

16. Among others, see John Baldovin, *Reforming the Liturgy: A Response to the Critics* (Collegeville, MN: Liturgical Press, 2009).

17. *Missale Romanum* can be found online at http://www.vatican.va/holy_father/paul_vi/apost_constitutions/documents/hf_p-vi_apc_19690403_missale-romanum_en.html. It is short and is not broken down into numbers; the text quoted is the fourth paragraph.

18. See *Sacrosanctum Concilium* online at http://www.vatican.va/archive/hist_councils/ii_vatican_council/documents/vat-ii_const_19631204_sacrosanctum-concilium_en.html.

19. Ibid.

Chapter 3

1. St. Leo the Great, Sermon 74.2, quoted in the *Catechism of the Catholic Church*, n. 1115; all of number 1115 is available online at http://www.vatican.va/archive/ccc_css/archive/catechism/p2s1c1a2.htm.

2. For a detailed commentary on each of the Triduum liturgies, see my own *Easter: A Guide to the Eucharist and Hours* (Collegeville, MN: Liturgical Press, 1991), 13–102.

3. Among others, see Susan Roll, *Toward the Origins of Christmas, Liturgia Condenda 5* (Kampen, Netherlands: Kok Pharos, 1995), and my own "The Mystery of the Incarnation:

Advent-Christmas-Epiphany," *Assembly* 17, no. 1 (January 2011): 2–10.

4. See, among others, T. A. Schnitker and W. A. Slaby, eds., *Concordantia Verbalia Missalis Romani* (Munster: Aschendorf, 1983), 1138–46.

5. Among many others, see Marianne Micks, *The Future Present: The Phenomenon of Christian Worship* (New York: Seabury, 1970).

6. Geoffrey Wainwright, *Eucharist and Eschatology* (London: Epworth Press, 1971).

7. The absence from the Roman Canon of the Mass of explicit reference to the Lord's second coming has been judged to be a deficiency. The text says:

Therefore, O Lord,
as we celebrate the memorial of the blessed Passion,
the Resurrection from the dead,
and the glorious Ascension into heaven
of Christ, your Son, our Lord....

8. Chapters 1 to 4 of the *Rite for the Anointing and Pastoral Care of the Sick* are about visiting the sick and bringing them communion, which can be done by priests, deacons, and eucharistic ministers.

Chapter 4

1. In my opinion, among the most interesting and cogent of these critiques is David Torevell, *Losing the Sacred: Ritual, Modernity, and Liturgical Reform* (London: T & T Clark, 2001). Among the least successful critiques is Denis Couran, *The History and Future of the Roman Liturgy*, trans. Michael Miller (San Francisco: Ignatius Press, 2005).

2. See my own "Sacramentality: The Fundamental Language for Liturgy and Sacraments," in *Per Ritus et Preces: Sacramentalità della Liturgia*, ed. Pietro Angelo Muroni (Rome: Studia Anselmiana 150; *Analecta Liturgica* 28, 2010), 131–60. Also, among others, see "The Sacramentality of Creation and the Role

of Creation in Liturgy and Sacraments," in *Preserving the Creation: Environmental Theology and Ethics*, ed. Kevin W. Irwin and Edmund J. Pellegrino (Washington, DC: Georgetown University Press, 1994), 67–111; "Sacramentality and the Theology of Creation: A Recovered Paradigm for Sacramental Theology," *Louvain Studies* 23 (1998): 159–79; "Discovering the Sacramentality of Sacraments," *Questions Liturgiques* 81 (2000): 171–83; "The Sacramental World—The Primary Language for Sacraments," *Worship* 76 (May 2002): 197–211; "Cosmic Mass," in *Models of the Eucharist* (New York / Mahwah, NJ: Paulist Press, 2005), 39–66.

3. Augustine, *City of God* 10.5, PL 41.282. Aquinas, *Summa*, III, qq. 60ff.

4. See the classic study by John F. Gallagher, *Significando Causant: A Study of Sacramental Efficiency* (Fribourg: The University Press, 1965).

5. See Cipriano Vagaggini, *The Flesh Is the Instrument of Salvation: A Theology of the Human Body* (Staten Island, NY: Alba House, 1969), from *Caro Salutis est Cardo—Corporeta, Eucristia e Liturgia* (Rome: Desclee, 1966). The title of Vagaggini's book is taken from a famous quotation from Tertullian's treatise *On the Resurrection* 8.3, PL 2.806.

6. See *In Johannem* 80.3, PL 35.1840; *City of God* 10.5, PL 41.282; and *Epistle* 138.7, PL 33.527.

7. The hymn contains such familiar phrases as "strengthened for our task on earth...may we with fruitful deeds...serve others' needs," and so on.

8. See especially my own "The Sacramental World—The Primary Language for Sacraments," *Worship* 76 (May 2002): 197–211.

9. See Michael J. Woods, *Cultivating Soil and Soul: Twentieth-Century Catholic Agrarians Embrace the Liturgical Movement* (Collegeville, MN: Liturgical Press / Pueblo Books, 2010). This is a revised version of the author's doctoral dissertation defended at the Catholic University of America.

10. See Frank Senn, "Liturgical Reconnaissance 2000," *Liturgy: Journal of the Liturgical Conference: What's New About the Past?* 16 (Summer 2000): 4–5, where he states:

The essays in this issue of *Liturgy* do not add up to a program or even a direction for further liturgical revision. They do sound a note of self-criticism within the liturgical establishment that brought us our present liturgical orders and rites. We sometimes acted too precipitously on too little information or on insufficient information. Churches that use the historic liturgy certainly have to pay attention to history. But it is inadequate to pay attention only for the purpose of replicating ancient orders and retrieving ancient texts in contemporary patterns and books of worship. Those ancient orders and texts were used in a social context just as our orders and texts are—the context of an assembly that was as much enmeshed in the culture of which they were a part as we are enmeshed in our own contemporary cultures. If we use an ancient text or follow an ancient pattern today it should not be just because it expresses a worldview that we share with those who have gone before us in the faith or that we are in the process of recovering.

11. See my own "Cosmic Mass," in *Models of the Eucharist* (New York / Mahwah, NJ: Paulist Press, 2005), 39–62.

12. The letter can be found at http://www.vatican.va/holy_father/john_paul_ii/letters/documents/hf_jp-ii_let_23041999_artists_en.html.

13. See my own "God's Icon: Creation, Sacramentality and the Liturgy," in *Environmental Justice and Climate Change: Assessing Pope Benedict XVI's Ecological Vision for the Catholic Church in the United States.* In Press.

14. Something of a classic in this regard is the brief treatment by Hans Urs von Balthasar, *Cosmic Worship* (San Francisco: Ignatius Press, 2003, reprinted). Another way of coming to this is from some critiques of the celebration of the reformed Catholic liturgy, one of which runs through *The Spirit of the Liturgy* by the then Cardinal Ratzinger (*Einführung in den Geist der Liturgie*), trans. John Saward (San Francisco: Ignatius Press, 2000).

15. See Philip J. Murnion, "A Sacramental Church in the Modern World," *Origins* 14 (June 21, 1984): 81–90. Important insights about the anthropological foundation for liturgy and sacrament are in Carol Rochetta, *Sacramentaria fondamentele: Dal 'mysterion' al 'sacramentum'* (Bologna: Edizioni Dehoniane, 1989), 1–91.

16. I recently noticed the sign outside of a Methodist church in southern Maryland in mid-December "advertising" their Christmas services. The first was listed as "Candlelight Service 5 P.M. (forty-five minutes long)."

17. Tertullian, *On the Resurrection* 8.3, PL 2.806.

18. See http://www.usccb.org/prayer-and-worship/the-mass/ order-of-mass/liturgy-of-the-eucharist/guidelines-for-the-recep tion-of-communion.cfm.

19. See the statement of the bishops of New Zealand at http://cathnews.co.nz/wp-content/uploads/2012/04/Ipads-at-Mass.pdf, and also John Foster, "The Use of Electronic Devices by Liturgical Ministers at the Celebration of the Eucharist," in *Questions Liturgiques* 92 (2011): 93–111. As of this writing, the International Commission on English in the Liturgy is drafting guidelines for the use of electronic forms of liturgical texts as a service to their member countries. At present, the USCCB Committee on Divine Worship has not taken a position on their use.

Chapter 5

1. See my own "Which Liturgy Is the Church's Liturgy?" *Origins* 38 (February 26, 2009): 581–9.

2. See http://www.vatican.va/archive/hist_councils/ii_vati can_council/documents/vat-ii_const_19631204_sacrosanctum-concilium_en.html.

3. Annibale Bugnini, *The Reform of the Liturgy (1948–1975)*, trans. Matthew O'Connell (Collegeville, MN: Liturgical Press, 1990), 393–487.

4. See Piero Marini, *A Challenging Reform: Realizing the Vision of the Liturgical Renewal*, trans. and ed. Mark Francis,

John Page, and Keith Pecklers (Collegeville, MN: Liturgical Press, 2007), 121–27.

5. See www.vatican.va/holy_father_xvi/speeches/2005/dec ember/documents. He referred in this speech to the addresses of Pope John XXIII inaugurating the Council on October 11, 1962, and of Pope Paul VI at the conclusion of the Council on December 7, 1965, about the danger of what he called "the hermeneutic of discontinuity."

6. For one example concerning the *Ordo Missae*, see Alfredo Cardinal Ottaviani, Antonio Cardinal Bacci, and a Group of Roman Theologians, *The Ottaviani Intervention: Short Critical Study of the New Order of Mass*, trans. Anthony Cekada (Rockford, IL: TAN Books and Publishers, 1992).

7. See Bugnini, *The Reform of the Liturgy*, 284–95.

8. See my "Overview of GIRM," *Liturgical Ministry* 12 (Summer 2003): 121–32.

9. Paul VI, apostolic constitution, translation in *The Sacramentary* (New York: Catholic Book Publishing Co., 1985), 9.

10. See Frederick R. McManus, "Pastoral Ecumenism: The Common Lectionary," in *The Eucharist: Toward the Third Millennium* (Chicago: Liturgy Training Publications, 1997), 103–18.

11. Ibid., 10.

12. The official title is "The Instruction of Liturgical Texts for Celebrations with a Congregation," *Notitiae* 5 (1969): 3–12, French translation; original published in six languages. For an English translation, see *Documents on the Liturgy 1963–1979: Conciliar, Curial, and Papal Texts* (Collegeville, MN: Liturgical Press, 1982), n. 130, 284–90.

13. This work was spearheaded by Abbot Andrea Mariano Magrassi, OSB, deceased archbishop of Bari-Bitonto. See *Nuovo Messale Quotidiano* (Casale Mofferratto: Marietti, 1984).

14. That I was in sympathy with the latter observations is clear in my own *Context and Text: Method in Liturgical Theology* (Collegeville, MN: Liturgical Press / Pueblo Books, 1994), 198–201.

15. See *Second Progress Report on the Revision of the Roman Missal* (Washington: ICEL, 1990), 12.

16. These are listed in Bugnini's *The Reform of the Liturgy* in the footnotes to each section of the text.

17. Placide Bruylants, *Les oraisons du Misel Romain. Texte et Histoire* (Louvain: Abbaye du Mont Cesar, 1952).

18. Antoine Dumas, "Les Sources du nouveau Missel Romain (I–VI)," *Notitiae* 7 (1971): 37–42, 74–77, 94–95, 134–36, 276–79, 409–10; "Les Prefaces du nouveau Missel," *Ephemerides Liturgicae* 85 (1971): 16–28; and "Pour mieux comprendre les textes liturgiques du Missel Romain," *Notitiae* 6 (1970): 194–213.

19. See, for example, Lauren Pristas, "Theological Principles That Guided the Redaction of the Roman Missal (1970)," *The Thomist* 67 (2003): 157–95; "The Orations of the Vatican II Missal: Policies for Revision," *Communio* 30 (Winter 2003): 621–53; and "The Collects at Sunday Mass: An Examination of the Revisions of Vatican II," *Nova et Vetera* 3 (Winter 2005): 5–38.

20. See the insightful study by Patrick Regan, "Paschal Vigil: Passion and Passage," *Worship* 79 (March 2005): 98–130. Also see Christene Mohrmann, "Pascha, Passio, Transitus," *Etudes sur le latin des chretiens*, vol. 1 (Roma: Edizioni di storia e litteratura, 1961), 222.

21. Benedict XVI, "Litterae Apostolicae Summorum Pontificum motu proprio datae," *AAS* 99 (2007): 777–97.

22. See http://press.catholica.va/news_services/bulletin/news /27407.php?index=27407.

23. See the document from the Congregation for Divine Worship, *Quattuor Abhinc Annos,* October 3, 1984, and the apostolic letter of John Paul II, *Ecclesia Dei,* July 2, 1988.

24. See Patrick Regan, *Advent to Pentecost: Comparing the Seasons in the Ordinary and Extraodinary Forms of the Roman Rite* (Collegeville: The Liturgical Press, 2012). A taste of this comparison is found in the USCCB Committee on Divine Worship's *Newsletter* 43 (June–July 2007), 23–28. The chart on page 27 is especially instructive.

25. Ibid., 20–22. The very fact that the pope issued such a letter is a signal to some that he was aware that the decision to issue *Summorum Pontificum* would be controversial, not to say

contested. I myself find the letter weak in cogency and in precision of language.

26. Ibid., 21.

27. I also wonder whether picking and choosing would lead to the very thing that the pope noted earlier in this same letter when, referring to the perceived value of the Tridentine Mass compared to some decidedly troublesome examples of the implementation of the new Missal, he said that the request for a limited use of the Tridentine Mass

> occurred above all because in many places celebrations were not faithful to the prescriptions of the new Missal, but the latter actually was understood as authorizing or even requiring creativity, which frequently led to deformations of the liturgy which were hard to bear. I am speaking from experience, since I too lived through that period with all its hopes and its confusion. And I have seen how arbitrary deformations of the liturgy caused deep pain to individuals totally rooted in the faith of the Church.

28. See Claudio Crescimanno, *La Riforma della Riforma liturgica: Ipotesi per us "nuovo" rito della messa sulle traccce del pensiero di Joseph Ratzinger* (Verona: Fede a Cultura, 2009), and Mauro Gagliardi, *Liturgia fonte di vita: Prospettive teologiche* (Verona: Fede a Cultura, 2009).

29. See the *Jesuit Sacramentary* (St. Louis: Institute of Jesuit Sources, 2001), and the *Jesuit Lectionary* (St. Louis: Institute of Jesuit Sources, 2002).

30. See *Statuta* (Rome: Neocatechumenal Center, 2008), especially chapter 3, pp. 34–39.

31. Among others, see Gerald Moore, *Vatican II and the Collects for Ordinary Time: A Study in the Roman Missal (1975)* (San Francisco / London / Bethesda, MD: International Scholars Publications, 1998), 252–76, for a discussion of the Collect assigned for the Fifteenth Sunday in Ordinary Time.

32. *The Sacramentary*, 304.

33. One of the best is the succinct and clear summary of the events, persons, and documents from the sixteenth century

through 2007 by Russell Hardiman, "Classified Timelines of Vernacular Liturgy: Responsibility Timelines and Vernacular Liturgy," *Pastoral Liturgy* 38:1 (2007), reprinted from Research Online@ND.

34. See *Thirty-Five Years of the BCL Newsletter 1965–2000* (Washington, DC: United States Conference of Catholic Bishops, 2004), 588.

35. There were a number of significant changes between the first and second editions of the rite. For a succinct summary and a list of other bibliographical references to other authors, see my "Justification and Ordained Ministry," in *Giustificazione, Chiese, Sacramenti, Prospettive dopo la Dichiarazione cattolico-luterana*, ed., Ermanno Genere and Andrea Grillo (Rome: Studia Anselmiana, 2003), 129–62. Despite the title of the article and of the volume, the article offers a liturgical theology of the rites of ordination by way of comparing the ordination rites in use after Trent with those newly composed after Vatican II.

36. See *Rites of Ordination of a Bishop, of Priests, and of Deacons: Second Typical Edition* (Washington, DC: United States Conference of Catholic Bishops, 2003). Among the many issues involved here was how to translate the Latin term *presbyterorum*, the literal meaning of which is "of presbyters," to distinguish this order from the order of bishops and the order of deacons. In the end, the translation throughout the rites is "of priests," despite the fact that from the earliest data we have about ordination and certainly through the patristic era is the fact that both "bishops" and "presbyters" were referred to as "priests," largely because of their role at the eucharistic sacrifice.

37. For a very brief overview of the background, see NCCB's Committee on the Liturgy's *Newsletter* 31 (April 1995): 1437–38.

38. In 1967, the ICEL bishops drew up three principles that would guide its later work:

- The best existing versions, both critical and literary, should be consulted.
- Greater freedom should be allowed in translating the psalms than most of the books of the Bible because they are poetry and must be such in English and because

they are meant for the frequent and inspiring use of the people, choirs, and cantors in the liturgy.

• Rhythm suited to the English language should be used in the translation. (See n. 37 above.)

39. *Psalms for Morning and Evening Prayer* (Chicago: Liturgy Training Publications, 1995). The added note on the title page reads: "The Four-Week Cycle of Psalms and Canticles Arranged for Morning and Evening Prayer and Including Psalms for Midday and Night Prayer in a Study Translation Prepared by the International Commission on English in the Liturgy."

40. The balance of the cover page states: "Intended primarily for communal song and recitation. This translation is offered for study and for comment by the International Commission on English in the Liturgy."

41. Taken from "On File," www.originsonline.com, *Origins* 29:44 (1998): 1.

42. See the Foreword by Francis Cardinal George to the Benedictine Monks of Conception Abbey in their *Revised Grail Psalms: A Liturgical Psalter* (Chicago: GIA, 2010), xiii–xiv.

43. From ICEL's original *Psalms for Morning and Evening Prayer*, 118.

44. From *Revised Grail Psalms*, 13.

45. *Liturgiam Authenticam* (On the Use of Vernacular Languages in the Publication of the Books of the Roman Liturgy), http://www.vatican.va/roman_curia/congregations/ccdds/docu ments/rc_con_ccdds_doc_20010507_liturgiam-authenticam _en.html.

46. *Ratio Translationis for the English Language* (Vatican City: Sacred Congregation for Divine Worship, 2007).

47. The literature critiquing this document is vast. Among others, see Peter Jeffrey, *Translating Tradition: A Chant Historian Reads* Liturgiam Authenticam (Collegeville, MN: Liturgical Press, 2005); also the series of essays in *The Voice of the Church: A Forum on Liturgical Translations*, ed. Dennis McManus (Washington: USCCB Publications, 2001).

48. A number of bishop members have recently been changed, with the present American bishop representative to the

Episcopal Committee of ICEL, Bishop Arthur Serratelli, now named as a member of *Vox Clara*.

49. Dame Maria Boulding, *The Coming of God* (Collegeville, MN: Liturgical Press, 1982).

Chapter 6

1. These include "The Word" in *Context and Text: Method in Liturgical Theology* (Collegeville, MN: Liturgical Press, 1995), esp. 90–99; and chapter 2 of *Models of the Eucharist* (New York / Mahwah, NJ: Paulist Press, 2005).

2. See Benedict XVI, *Jesus of Nazareth: Holy Week. From the Entrance into Jerusalem to the Resurrection* (San Francisco: Ignatius Press, 2011).

3. See *General Instruction of the Roman Missal* (hereafter GIRM), in the *Lectionary for Mass,* second edition, n. 93.

4. For example, in the first weeks of Ordinary Time, the first reading is either from 1 Samuel or the Letter to the Hebrews, followed by a continuous reading from the Gospel of Mark.

5. *Preaching the Mystery of Faith: The Sunday Homily.* This USCCB document was approved November 2012, and appeared in *Origins* 42 (November 29, 2012): "We are well aware in survey after survey over the past years the people of God have called for more powerful and inspiring preaching. A steady diet of tepid or poorly prepared homilies is often cited as a cause for discouragement on the part of the laity and even leading some to turn away from the church" (p. 406).

6. See http://www.vatican.va/archive/hist_councils/ii_vatican _council/documents/vat-ii_decree_19651207_presbyterorum-ordi nis_en.html.

7. In doing so, I stand with a number of comparatively recent documents from the USCCB and from Rome, including *Fulfilled in Your Hearing* (USCCB Committee on Priestly Life, 1982); Pope Benedict XVI's *Sacramentum Caritatis* (2007), at http://www.vatican.va/holy_father/benedict_xvi/apost_exhorta tions/documents/hf_ben-xvi_exh_20070222_sacramentum-cari tatis_it.html, and his *Verbum Domini* (2010), at http://www.vati

can.va/holy_father/benedict_xvi/apost_exhortations/documents/h
f_ben-xvi_exh_20100930_verbum-domini_it.html; and the recent
USCCB document *Preaching the Mystery of Faith* (see n. 5 above).

8. Because *Sacrosanctum Concilium* states that "the two
parts which, in a certain sense, go to make up the Mass, namely,
the liturgy of the word and the eucharistic liturgy, are so closely
connected with each other that they form but one single act of
worship" (n. 56), might this not signal the complementarity, or at
least the intrinsic connection between, word and sacrament?

9. *Preaching the Mystery of Faith*, 410.

10. It states:

> The increasing presence of international priests in the
> pastoral life of the United States is a great blessing but
> also requires sustained efforts at cultural and linguistic
> adaptation, particularly in relationship to effective
> preaching. Dioceses and religious communities need to
> offer these brother priests opportunities for intense lan-
> guage preparation and help in understanding the varied
> social and pastoral contexts of Catholics in this coun-
> try. (Ibid., 420)

11. Ibid., 419.

12. "*Ecclesia in Europa*: Post-Synodal Apostolic Exhorta-
tion on Jesus Christ Alive in His Church, The Source of Hope for
Europe," *AAS* 95 (2003): 649–719; English trans., *Origins* 33
(July 31, 2003): 149–76, at 161; italics in the original.

13. *Young Adult Catholics* (Notre Dame, IN: University of
Notre Dame Press, 2001), 160–62.

14. James D. Davidson, *Catholicism in Motion: The Church
in American Society* (Liguori, MO: Liguori/Triumph, 2005), 68.

15. James D. Davidson et al., *The Search for Common
Ground* (Huntington, IN: Our Sunday Visitor, 1997), 217–18.

16. More precisely, it is proclaimed both on Wednesday of
the first week of the year, Year II, and on the Second Sunday of
Ordinary Time, Year B.

17. See http://www.vatican.va/holy_father/benedict_xvi/apost
_exhortations/documents/hf_ben-xvi_exh_20070222_sacramentum
-caritatis_en.html.

18. It should be noted, however, that Pope Benedict XVI uses the term *figura* in the post-synodal exhortation *Sacramentum Caritatis*, n. 11. See http://www.vatican.va/holy_father/benedict _xvi/apost_exhortations/documents/hf_ben-xvi_exh_20070222 _sacramentum-caritatis_en.html.

19. See *Preaching the Mystery of Faith*, 412, which states: "One might even say that the homilist connects the two parts of the Eucharistic liturgy as he looks back to the Scripture readings and looks forward to the sacrificial meal. This is why it is preferable that the celebrant of the Eucharistic liturgy also be the homilist." The document then references GIRM, 66. Post–Vatican II liturgical documents have regularly asserted that deacons can preach "on occasion." In some communities, deacons have come to preach more regularly because international priests who staff the parishes can experience significant linguistic challenges in composing an acceptable homily in English and making themselves understood. Again, see GIRM, n. 66, with this documentation in the footnote: Cf. *Codex Iuris Canonici*, can. 767 §1; Pontifical Commission for the Authentic Interpretation of the *Code of Canon Law*, response to *dubium* regarding can. 767 §1: *AAS* 79 (1987): 1249; Interdicasterial Instruction on certain questions regarding the collaboration of the non-ordained faithful in the sacred ministry of priests, *Ecclesiae de Mysterio*, August 15, 1997, art. 3: *AAS* 89 (1997): 864.

20. See chapter 3, p. XXX for the text of this prayer.

21. *Preaching the Mystery of Faith*, 422.

Chapter 7

1. See http://home.catholicweb.com/npmdayton/files/MUS ICinCATHOLICWORSHIP.pdf.

2. This time, the document was approved by the entire body of U.S. bishops in the USCCB, and not just the Committee on Liturgy.

3. See http://www.npmrc.org/documents/SingToTheLord .pdf. At this point the document quotes the GIRM, nn. 33 and 93.

4. See *Letters to My Brother Priests* (Chicago: Midwest Theological Forum, 1994). That *Dominicae Cenae* invited some debate and critique from sacramental theologians (largely for presupposing and arguing from a medieval mentality about liturgy and the sacraments as opposed to the largely patristically inspired liturgical reforms) is reflected in works such as Edward J. Kilmartin's *Church, Eucharist, and Priesthood: A Theological Commentary on "The Mystery and Worship of the Most Holy Eucharist"* (New York / Mahwah, NJ: Paulist Press, 1981).

5. Avery Dulles, *The Priestly Life* (New York / Mahwah, NJ: Paulist Press, 1997), 11.

6. See Robert Kaslyn, *"Communion with the Church"* and the *Code of Canon Law: An Analysis of the Foundation and Implications of the Canonical Obligation to Maintain Communion with the Catholic Church* (Lewiston, NY: Mellen Press, 1994).

7. The history of what oil was used for ordinations and when it was used is a complex historical study of liturgy (particularly in Carolingian sources). See Gerard Ellard, *Ordination Anointings in the Western Church Before 1000 A.D.* (Cambridge, MA: The Medieval Academy of America, 1970). For the pre–Vatican II rite see, among others, *The Rite of Ordination According to the Roman Pontifical* (New York: The Cathedral Library Association, 1924), 64.

8. For more on this distinction and on the magisterium on ordained priesthood, see my own *Serving the Body of Christ: The Magisterium on Eucharist and Ordained Priesthood* (New York / Mahwah, NJ: Paulist Press, 2013).

9. The full text of Justin Martyr's *First Apology* is at http://www.newadvent.org/fathers/0126.htm.

10. Sofia Cavalletti is the author of the recently translated and increasingly influential *Catechesis of the Good Shepherd* (Chicago: Liturgy Training Publications, 2007).

11. In this connection I have also been influenced by the writings of Marva J. Dawn: *Reaching Out without Dumbing Down, A Theology of Worship for This Urgent Time* (Milwaukee: Eerdmans, 1995), and *A Royal "Waste" of Time: The Splendor of Worshiping God and Being Church for the World* (Milwaukee: Eerdmans, 1999).

12. See *Ministeria Quaedam* (1972).

13. Whether or not Pope Paul VI intended the rite of installation for females and was persuaded against it is at least debated, with some "in the know" at the time indicating that such was his intent.

14. See Hervé Marie Legrand, "The Presidency of the Eucharist according to the Ancient Tradition," in *Living Bread, Saving Cup*, ed. Kevin Seasoltz (Collegeville, MN: Liturgical Press, 1987), 196–210.

Chapter 8

1. Walter Burghardt, *Preaching: The Art and the Craft* (New York / Mahwah, NJ: Paulist Press, 1987).

2. See my *Context and Text: Method in Liturgical Theology* (Collegeville, MN: Liturgical Press / Pueblo Books, 1994), chapter 6, "The Arts," 219–61.

3. If you "Google" "To Jesus' Heart All Burning," in 0.14 seconds you get 35,300 hits, the first one of which is a sung YouTube rendition.

4. *Sacrosanctum Concilium*, chapter 6, n. 112, and chapter 7.

5. This is not to suggest that their predecessors, *Music in Catholic Worship*, *Liturgical Music Today*, and *Environment and Art in Catholic Worship*, are of no value. But my judgment is that, thanks to the experience of implementing the reformed liturgy, these texts have been improved upon with time. For example, the approval of *Sing to the Lord* was preceded by particularly wide consultation.

6. *Context and Text*, 242–48.

7. See Paul Turner's "Introduction," in Jason McFarland's *Announcing the Feast* (Collegeville, MN: Liturgical Press, 2011).

8. A performance of the song may be seen at http://www. youtube.com/results?search_query=This+is+the+feast+of+victory+for+our+God&oq=This+is+the+feast+of+victory+for+our+God&gs_l=youtube-reduced.3..0l3.10845.19064.0.19394.40.13.0.27.27.0.80.799.13.13.0...0.0...1ac.1.0xXMnltbfAo.

9. Jason McFarland, *Announcing the Feast: The Entrance Song in the Mass of the Roman Rite* (Collegeville, MN: Liturgical Press / Pueblo Books, 2012).

10. Martin Marty, *A Cry of Absence: Reflections for the Winter of the Heart* (San Francisco: Harper, 1983; revised edition 1993; Grand Rapids, MI: Wm. B. Eerdmans, 1997).

11. The exact quotation from the GIRM is:

The Place for the Reservation of the Most Holy Eucharist

In accordance with the structure of each church and legitimate local customs, the Most Blessed Sacrament should be reserved in a tabernacle in a part of the church that is truly noble, prominent, readily visible, beautifully decorated, and suitable for prayer.

The one tabernacle should be immovable, be made of solid and inviolable material that is not transparent, and be locked in such a way that the danger of profanation is prevented to the greatest extent possible. Moreover, it is appropriate that, before it is put into liturgical use, it be blessed according to the rite described in the Roman Ritual.

It is more in keeping with the meaning of the sign that the tabernacle in which the Most Holy Eucharist is reserved not be on an altar on which Mass is celebrated. Consequently, it is preferable that the tabernacle be located, according to the judgment of the diocesan Bishop:

   a. Either in the sanctuary, apart from the altar of celebration, in a form and place more appropriate, not excluding on an old altar no longer used for celebration;
   b. Or even in some chapel suitable for the faithful's private adoration and prayer and which is organically connected to the church and readily visible to the Christian faithful.

In accordance with traditional custom, near the tabernacle a special lamp, fueled by oil or wax, should be kept alight to indicate and honor the presence of Christ. (314–16)

That local diocesan bishops have made more specific directives about the location of the tabernacle requires that one review diocesan norms in this connection.

12. *Sacrosanctum Concilium* states:

The Church has not adopted any particular style of art as her very own; she has admitted styles from every period according to the natural talents and circumstances of peoples, and the needs of the various rites. Thus, in the course of the centuries, she has brought into being a treasury of art which must be very carefully preserved. The art of our own days, coming from every race and region, shall also be given free scope in the Church, provided that it adorns the sacred buildings and holy rites with due reverence and honor; thereby it is enabled to contribute its own voice to that wonderful chorus of praise in honor of the Catholic faith sung by great men in times gone by. (n. 123)

13. The GIRM puts it thus: "It is appropriate to have a fixed altar in every church, since it more clearly and permanently signifies Christ Jesus, the living stone (1 Pt 2:4; cf. Eph 2:20). In other places set aside for sacred celebrations, the altar may be movable" (n. 298). An altar is called "fixed" if it is attached to the floor so as not to be removable; otherwise it is called "movable."

Chapter 9

1. I am thinking here of the STB curriculum of the Gregorian and Angelicum universities in Rome as prime examples. With regard to more popular catechesis and religious education in general, we look to the liturgical movement's pioneers and

see, for example, the important work of Virgil Michel in this country collaborating with the Sisters of St. Dominic, Grand Rapids, Michigan, in authoring the Christ-Life series of grammar and high school religion textbooks.

2. Regrettably, one of the great divorces in much post–Vatican II religious education has been the split between liturgy and catechesis. I judge that the same call for an integral theological curriculum centered on the liturgy can and should be used to evaluate catechetical programs. Despite what I might regard as flaws in some of the efforts to use a Lectionary-based catechesis—especially in RCIA programs—nonetheless, there is a genius in the instinct to view the ordered proclamation of the scriptures at the Sunday liturgy as the heart and center of the Catholic faith, as well as a genius in the way we participate in the sacred mysteries of the liturgy, understood as our privileged experience of redemption and sanctification.

3. See Frank Senn, "Liturgical Reconnaissance 2000," *Liturgy. Journal of the Liturgical Conference. What's New About the Past?* 16, no. 1 (Summer, 2000): 4–5.

4. At the risk of oversimplification, I need to note the important work being done today by Robert Taft and W. Jardine Grisbrooke about nuancing these distinctions popularized by Juan Mateos.

5. See my own "Which Liturgy Is the Church's Liturgy?" *Origins* 38 (February 26, 2009): 581–89.

6. Paragraphs 37 to 40 of *Sacrosanctum Concilium* are legitimately cited as inviting the accommodation of the liturgy to a variety of pastoral settings, even to the point of a "more radical adaptation of the liturgy...." Yet these paragraphs continually refer to the "competent ecclesiastical authorities" and to "the Apostolic See." Hence, there are built-in "check and balances" in the ongoing implementation of the reformed liturgy.

7. At the same time, I also judge that courses about the theology, celebration, and canonical aspects of marriage cannot be so easily combined, especially given the very serious issues of marriage preparation, its indissolubility, divorce, remarriage, and the annulment process.

8. Available at http://www.vatican.va/holy_father/john_paul_ii/letters/documents/hf_jp-ii_let_23041999_artists_en.html.

9. See the important commentary by Dominic Serra, "The Blessing of Baptismal Water at the Paschal Vigil in the Post Vatican II Rite," *Ecclesia Orans* 7 (1990): 343–68.

Chapter 10

1. See, among others, David Torreveld, *Losing the Sacred: Ritual, Modernity, and Liturgical Reform* (London: T & T Clark, 2001). As I noted above, I am in sympathy with some of the assertions and critiques of the implementation of the reformed liturgy argued here, but I am not convinced of the author's overall thesis or of some of the historical arguments he uses to argue the thesis.

2. This is a complex and fascinating study that in recent years has understandably drawn the attention of a number of specialists, especially in church history and religious studies.

3. Among others, see the important work by Josef Jungmann, *Christian Prayer Through the Centuries*, trans. Christopher Irvine and John Coyne (New York / Mahwah, NJ: Paulist Press, 2008).

4. Among others, see Nathan Mitchell, *Cult and Controversy: The Worship of the Eucharist Outside of Mass* (Collegeville, MN: Liturgical Press / Pueblo Books, 1982).

5. Pius Parsch, *The Church's Year of Grace*, 5 vols., trans. William Heidt (Collegeville, MN: Liturgical Press, 1957).

6. Aemiliana Lohr, *The Mass through the Year*, vol. 1, *Advent to Palm Sunday*; vol. 2, *Holy Week to the Last Sunday after Pentecost*, trans. I. T. Hale, Foreword Damasus Winzen, OSB (New York: Newman Press, 1958). A one-volume edition titled *The Year of Our Lord* has the addition of ember days, Advent, Lent, Easter week, the vigils of Christmas, and Epiphany.

7. See the GIRM, n. 199c.

8. *Style* is, admittedly, a charged word open to being misinterpreted as "showmanship" and appearing to place the emphasis on an individual in such a way that the liturgy is "entertaining."

9. See the debates summarized in Reiner Kaczynski, "Toward the Reform of the Liturgy," in *A History of Vatican II*, vol. 3, *The Mature Council*, ed. Giuseppe Alberigo, English ed. Joseph A. Komonchak (Leuven: Peeters / Maryknoll, NY: Orbis, 2000), 192–255.

10. Congregation for Divine Worship, December 2001; see http://www.vatican.va/roman_curia/congregations/ccdds/docu ments/rc_con_ccdds_doc_20020513_vers-direttorio_en.html.

11. See my reflections in "Evaluating *Sacrosanctum Concilium*: Context, Text, and Unfinished Business," *Chicago Studies* 49, no. 2 (2010): 124–48; and in "Implementing *Sacrosanctum Concilium*: Undertaken and Unfinished," *Chicago Studies* 49, no. 2 (2010): 149–72.

12. See the important document from the Congregation for Divine Worship, *Directory on Popular Piety and the Litugy*, at http://www.vatican.va/roman_curia/congregations/ccdds/docu ments/rc_con_ccdds_doc_20020513_vers-direttorio_en.html.

13. James P. McCain, *Prayers of the Faithful: The Shifting Spiritual Life of American Catholics* (Cambridge, MA: Harvard University Press, 2010), 58–69. McCain's findings about how the faith was passed on in many communities without the presence of a priest or the regular celebration of the Eucharist are pertinent and compelling.

14. Among Anscar Chupungco's books are *Cultural Adaptation of the Liturgy* (Eugene, OR: Wipf & Stock, 2006), *Liturgical Inculturation* (Collegeville, MN: Liturgical Press / Pueblo Books, 1992), and *Liturgies of the Future* (Eugene, OR: Wipf & Stock, 2006).

15. See http://www.fdlc.org/liturgy_resources/Liturgy_Doc uments_files/LITURGYVeritatesLegitimae.htm.

16. See http://www.vatican.va/roman_curia/congregations/ ccdds/documents/rc_con_ccdds_doc_20010507_liturgiam-au thenticam_en.html.

17. Among others, see the excellent study by Paul Josef Cordes, *Sendung zum Dienst: Exegetische-historische und sys-tematische Studien zum Konsilsdekret "Vom Dienst und Leben der Priester"* (Frankfurt am Main: Josef Knecht, 1972).

18. Among others, see Alexander Ganoczy, "Splendors and Miseries of the Tridentine Doctrine of Ministries," in *Office and Ministry in the Church*, ed. Roland Murphy and Bas van Iersel (*Concilium* 80; New York: Herder and Herder, 1972), 75–86; and Hervé-Marie Legrand, "The Indelible Character and the Theology of Ministry," also in *Office and Ministry in the Church*, 54–62.

19. See www.usccb.org/laity/laymin/co-workers.

20. *The Liturgy of the Hours*, vol. 4 (New York: Catholic Book Publishing Co., 1975), 1425.

21. See *Catholic Social Teaching: Our Best Kept Secret*, ed. James Hug, Peter Henriot, and Edward Deberri (Washington, DC: Center for Concern, 1987).

22. See John Augustine Ryan, *Distributive Justice: The Right and Wrong of Our Present Distribution of Wealth* (New York: Macmillan, 1916).

23. Mark Searle, ed., *Liturgy and Social Justice* (Collegeville, MN: Liturgical Press, 1980); Dianne Bergant and Edward Grosz, eds., *Liturgy and Social Justice* (Collegeville, MN: Liturgical Press, 1989); Anne Koester, ed., *Liturgy and Justice: To Worship God in Spirit and Truth* (Notre Dame, IN: University of Notre Dame Press, 2001).

24. At the same time, I think it important to offer the caution that *communio* is not a univocal term and has been used for a variety of purposes since the Council, including how to interpret the Council itself.